Locating Race

I0895612

SUNY series, Explorations in Postcolonial Citizenship

Emmanuel C. Eze, editor

Locating Race

Global Sites of Post-Colonial Citizenship

Malini Johar Schueller

SUNY PRESS

Published by State University of New York Press, Albany

© 2009 State University of New York

All rights reserved

Printed in the United States of America

No part of this book may be used or reproduced in any manner whatsoever without written permission. No part of this book may be stored in a retrieval system or transmitted in any form or by any means including electronic, electrostatic, magnetic tape, mechanical, photocopying, recording, or otherwise without the prior permission in writing of the publisher.

For information, contact State University of New York Press, Albany, NY
www.sunypress.edu

Production by Ryan Morris
Marketing by Michael Campochiaro

Library of Congress Cataloging-in-Publication Data

Schueller, Malini Johar, 1957–
Locating race : global sites of post-colonial citizenship / Malini Johar Schueller.
p. cm. — (SUNY series, explorations in postcolonial studies)
Includes bibliographical references and index.
ISBN 978-0-7914-7681-9 (hardcover : alk. paper)
ISBN 978-0-7914-7682-6 (pbk. : alk. paper)
1. American literature—Asian American authors—History and criticism. 2. Race in literature. 3. Imperialism in literature. 4. Globalization in literature. 5. Postcolonialism in literature. 6. Postcolonialism—United States. 7. Race—Philosophy. 8. Globalization—Philosophy. 9. United States—Race relations. I. Title.
PS153.A84S36 2009
810.9'895—dc22

2008005662

10 9 8 7 6 5 4 3 2 1

Contents

Illustrations

Acknowledgments

Writing a book is an intellectual journey that is always, to an extent, collaborative and one of the pleasures of completing a book is being able to acknowledge one's interlocutors. My greatest debts are to Michael Omi and Howard Winant for their pivotal work, *Racial Formation in the United States*, Edward Said for his persistent focus on imperialism, and to the particularist analyses of subaltern studies scholars. I would not have been able to formulate my arguments without the invigorating conversations and critiques of numerous colleagues and scholars. Ashley Dawson and Lee Quinby have served as sounding boards for many ideas in this book. Special thanks to Lee Quinby for the many theory discussions we've had, for helping me structure the book at its inception, for offering useful critiques of the introduction and the chapter on feminist theory, and for brainstorming with me on the title. I am grateful to Ashley Dawson for reading the introduction, pointing me to many sources, and for our collaboration on *Exceptional State* which helped me sharpen my ideas in this book. My collaboration with Edward Watts on *Messy Beginnings* was enormously useful in helping me think about race and postcoloniality and this project.

Many other colleagues have helped me rethink and refine my ideas. I would like to thank Leslie Bow, Marsha Bryant, Pamela Gilbert, David Leverenz, Paul Lyons, Bill Mullen, and Amy Ongiri for reading and commenting on different chapters and the book proposal. While writing this book, I've participated in lively reading groups with different colleagues, and the ideas generated during those discussions have been invaluable in thinking about this book. I would like to thank Apollo Amoko, Pamela Gilbert, Leah Rosenberg, and Matthew Watson for the enjoyable discussions we've had. This book has also benefitted from the debates of my graduate students in my classes on Postcolonial Theory and American Studies and Nineteenth Century Racial Formations. No small thanks to

John Leavey, then department chair, who helped negotiate part of the leave that made it possible for me to complete the book. Finally, I owe a special gratitude to Larin McLaughlin for taking on this project and moving it efficiently along to publication.

My children Divik, Maya, and Neena make my work enjoyable more than they realize. Without their hugs, laughter, and yes, arguments, life would be dull. I am proud of all of them and thrive in the love and affection they surround me with. Writing would be no fun without them periodically bursting through my study door. I cannot begin to thank my husband, John, for his patience, love, and understanding. He's never been too busy to solve my computer problems or listen to my distress stories along the way. Even though they live halfway around the world, my mother, Usha Johar, and my sister, Kavita Nayar, have been wonderfully supportive.

A version of chapter two was published in *Cultural Critique* 55 (2003) 35–62; parts of chapter three appeared in *Signs* 31 i (2005), 63–92; and a version of chapter five was published in *Asian North American Subjectivities: Beyond the Hyphen*, eds. Eleanor Ty and Donald C. Goellnicht (Bloomington: Indiana University Press, 2004), pp. 170–85.

CHAPTER ONE

Theorizing Race, Postcoloniality, and Globalization

In late August 2005, hurricane Katrina, a category-four storm, hit the predominantly African American city of New Orleans, flooding the homes of the city's residents, killing hundreds, and destroying water and power supplies. In the aftermath of the storm, with no emergency relief in sight, poor people wandered the streets in search of food, and over twenty thousand sought refuge in the New Orleans Superdome. Within days of Katrina's landfall, the hurricane had foregrounded the systemic racism at the heart of the country. Eerily recalling post-Reconstruction representations of dangerous and degenerate African Americans threatening the social order—popularly commemorated in works like D. W. Griffiths' *Birth of a Nation*—media reports inundated television and newspapers with coverage of African American looters engaged in a wild orgy of stealing, shooting, and raping. Rapper Kanye West's comments at a benefit concert four days after the tragedy, captured what was glaringly evident to most Americans: "You see a black family, it says, 'They're looting.' You see a white family, it says, 'They're looking for food.'"[1] Nevertheless, unverified (and later discredited) stories about the rampant violence and disorder at the Superdome continued to be churned for days; predictably, gun sales in the nearby whiter city of Baton Rouge skyrocketed, as citizens strove to "protect" themselves from an influx of undesirable African Americans from New Orleans.

An event like Katrina questions the rhetoric of globalization theories with their emphasis on hybridity, fluidity, migration, postnationalism, and transnationalism and seems to demand, instead, the engaged particularity of critical race studies. But if globalization theories, most of which see the local and race as atavisms, fail to provide an analytic for reading Katrina, this does not mean that Katrina's racial politics are limited to the workings of the nation-state alone. Simultaneous with representations of African American degradation were scores of references to Katrina as similar to the third world; fighting in Iraq and battling in Katrina seemed eerily alike as Katrina was declared a "war zone";[2] most ominously, Louisiana Governor Kathleen Blanco pegged New Orleans as enemy territory, a city needing colonial occupation, when she said, "These troops are fresh back from Iraq, well trained, experienced, battle-tested and under my orders to restore order in the streets."[3] In Blanco's vision, citizens in need became irascible law-and-order problems, just like unruly denizens of a colony. Such hostile representations of New Orleans demonstrate not postnationalism because the nation-state was (and is) alive and well, if only as a disciplinary force rather than for public good; neither do they illustrate simply transnational linkages of corporate power. Rather, they attest to a violent synergy of imperialism and racism as New Orleans, the colony within, is literally subdued by armies controlling the reaches of empire in occupied Iraq, a suggestion decisively made by Spike Lee when he posed before a ravaged New Orleans house tagged "Baghdad" during the shooting of *When the Levees Broke* (2006).[4] The symbiosis of structural racism and imperialism in the responses to Katrina point, in part, to the object of this book: practically, to link the project of race with that of anti-imperial resistance and, theoretically, to suggests tactical ways in which postcolonial theory and critical race studies can come together.

The chapters in this book demonstrate how race is both the site of particular, located oppression and of postcolonial resistance; understanding race demands specific historical knowledge at the same time as opposition to systemic racism produces powerful forms of local, translocal, and transnational resistance. The theoretical premise underlying the analysis of race is that of particularism, a position in philosophy that contends that almost every moral reason is capable of being reversed by changes in context.[5] Thus, the larger concepts at play in thinking race—oppression, resistance, Othering, color, rights—need to be constantly rethought, redefined, indeed reformulated, through different contexts. This does not mean that analysis becomes simply descriptive, but rather that, in order precisely to be theoretical, analysis must incorporate a reflection of its own immediate conditions, the singular forces that shape it in a particular context.[6] I therefore use the terms "local" and "locatedness" in two ways: first, as synonyms for context in relation to race because systemic racism is necessarily tied to the juridical apparatuses of the nation-state that legislate *de jure* and affect *de facto* racism for particular raced groups; racial categories do not travel similarly across or even within nations, and might, as in the case of Hawai'ians and Puerto Ricans, also be affected by the specificities of place;

second, to emphasize that raced resistances, tied to particular national or even regional communities, can often be the sites of progressive and radical resistances within the nation and to alliances beyond. My approach thus differs sharply from those like Paul Gilroy who, despite acknowledging some racial hierarchies, see racial politics as inherently limiting;[7] it is in solidarity with arguments like those of Nikhil Pal Singh who see a liberatory potential in black nationalism.[8] I argue that globalization, in its economic, political, and cultural manifestations, is a *different continuation* of an established, raced U.S. imperialism; this raced, imperial culture requires micrological analysis as well as a larger analytics of center and periphery. The book begins with a critique of globalism-inspired forms of analyses as inadequate in dealing with U.S. narratives of race and gender; it then moves to a reading of narratives of globalization as narratives of imperialism; finally it analyzes possibilities for what I call Post-Colonial citizenship, a form of activist citizenship, which, as I will explain later, is grounded in antiracist and local activism in the United States and is vitally connected to transnational anti-imperial struggles. The trajectory of the book is thus from negative hermeneutics to affirmative exegesis, deconstructive critique to constructive possibilities, theory to practice. The book also demonstrates the urgent need for local knowledge dealing with how subalterns (in this case racial minorities) are historically, nationally, and regionally constructed in order to resist the power relations established by the nation-state as well as neocolonial and imperial systems that intersect with the nation-state.

The theoretical impetus of the book—to bring postcolonial theory and critical race studies together—might well appear contradictory, particularly because postcolonial theory in its universalist and globalist guises simply absorbs the specific functioning of racism into a narrative of diaspora and migration. Yet there is no reason for these two forms of oppositional knowledge to be so positioned. Indeed, as the work of subaltern studies scholars reminds us, postcolonial analyses at the local level, for instance, the insight that modernity in Bengal did not, unlike Europe, result in the repudiation of parental authority, can challenge or provincialize the putative universality of (European) modernity.[9] And critical race studies itself, as evidenced by Howard Winant's *The World Is a Ghetto*, might be witnessing a global turn. Moreover, the disproportionate military recruiting of racial minorities in the service of imperialism, in Iraq and elsewhere, attests to the continuing unholy alliance of imperialism abroad and racism at home.

There is also a political urgency motivating this book. As I will discuss later, much theory in the last fifteen years, ominously paralleling the dictates of neoliberal global capitalism, has reflected the concerns of Western metropoles. In the spirit of contesting knowledge production as an accessory of Western capitalist hegemony, I suggest that the certainties of globalization theories need to be rigorously critiqued. Particularly since the end of the cold war, globalization, initiated by European and largely U.S. interests, has been taken as an explanatory model for postulating a world culture, and has replaced models of systemic inequality such as first world and third, North and South. Even critics of such global models insist on the obsolescence of national and local perspectives. Not only is such a postulation "Americocentric" because it ignores the violent conflicts over nationhood worldwide that have marked the last decade, as well as the gross disparities between North and South, but it is also dangerous in its disavowal of racial hierarchies within the nation. In order to argue for the centrality of racism and imperialism, and the importance of resistance to these, I use what I call "resistance postcolonialism," as well as critical race studies, in reading narratives of U.S. culture. Most importantly, I also demonstrate how located, raced resistances simultaneously invoke and generate transnational forms of opposition and thus create possibilities for an anti-imperial, "Post-Colonial citizenship" in the belly of the beast, as it were.

I use the term "Post-Colonial citizenship" because its very contradictions open up spaces for activism in ways that purely national conceptions of citizenship or postcolonial solidarities do not. Citizenship has been the cornerstone of liberal democracies, which putatively turn subjects into citizens, empowering them through equality to be sources of political authority rather than simply the objects of political power.[10] Although Marx rightly critiqued liberal democracy for protecting capitalist relations of exploitation through citizenship by which people become "imaginary member[s] of an imaginary sovereignty," and although citizenship can be viewed as an invidious membership category designed to demarcate insiders from outsiders, the ideas of citizenship I am invoking are meant neither to bolster capitalism nor to designate aliens.[11] Rather, through citizenship I intend to invoke both the rhetoric of rights and of activism. Liberal political theory follows a rights-based model (liberal democracy as the universal promise of civil, political and social rights) of contract derived from Hobbes and Locke, continuing in the works of T. H. Marshall and John Rawls.[12] The civic republican model of citizenship as political activity, emphasizing participation and obligation, has been the object of scholars like David Scobey who have called for a revitalization of citizenship.[13] Because race has historically fractured the practice of citizenship in the United States, turning minorities into second-class citizens, I believe it is crucial to hold on to the idea of rights-based citizenship in order to articulate what Iris Young calls "special rights" (differentiated citizenship) necessary to undermine oppression and disadvantage.[14] The civic republican model is useful for racially oppressed groups but with a difference because the conditions that create a lack of civic participation for them cannot demand universal but rather differentiated obligation.

Although citizenship has historically been based on the nation-state, citizenship theory in recent years has dealt with various forms of citizenship beyond the nation. Different kinds of rights are given to people residing within a territory of which they are not citizens;[15] the EU stands as a repudiation of the link between citizen and nation; debates about transnationlism bring forth the question of universal rights apart from the nation-state;[16] humanism begs the question of cosmopolitan citizenship;[17] and migrations create notions such as diasporic citizenship.[18] The concept of Post-Colonial citizenship participates in the move beyond the nation, but not to the denial of it, and it suggests a specific kind of citizenship beyond the nation. Instead of a cosmopolitan citizenship based on a universal idea of the human as adumbrated by Nussbaum, it shares with Andrew Dobson an emphasis on asymmetries of effects and therefore obligations which he characterizes as definitive of "post-cosmopolitan" citizenship.[19] Post-Colonial citizenship names the asymmetries and uneven structures engendered by imperialism and seeks to articulate alternatives to empire.

In order to retain a politicized sense of differentiated citizenship that can address the intersection of national racial and imperial structures by participating in anti-imperial solidarities seen beyond the nation, I propose the idea of Post-Colonial citizenship. This citizenship speaks to the imaginative possibilities of an activist racial politics at once grounded in the nation and looking beyond it, but a nation the very idea of which is reconfigured through antiracist and anti-imperialist struggles.[20] My use of capitalization for both "post" and "colonial" indicates the fact that the post for many subaltern groups can only be imagined because colonialism is a living reality for indigenous populations and that the internal colonialism of minorities in the United States is alive and well. On the other hand, I retain the use of the term "postcolonial" because of its radical potential and emancipatory possibilities as a theoretical and political position. As Robert Young argues, postcolonialism "combines the epistemological cultural innovations of the postcolonial moment with a political critique of the conditions of postcoloniality."[21] "It attacks the status quo of hegemonic economic imperialism and the history of colonialism and imperialism, but also signals an activist engagement with positive political positions and new forms of political identity."[22] Postcolonial citizenship thus names the affective solidarities forged between racial minorities in the United States and people who have overthrown political, if not economic and cultural, domination; it also challenges the definitional boundaries of liberal citizenship.

In this chapter, I offer a critique of globalization theories and demonstrate the centrality of imperialism to U.S. culture, and the usefulness, therefore, of a certain kind of postcolonial theory that I call "resistance postcolonialism"; I then suggest how a dialectic between the particularism of critical race studies and the terms of postcolonial theory—decolonization, Orientalism,[23] chronopolitics,[24] for instance—can be productive in understanding minority experiences in the United States. Finally, I briefly consider the intersection between theories of globalization and the transnational turn in American studies.

THE PITFALLS OF GLOBALIZATION AS EPISTEMOLOGY

Ever since the mid-1980s, and increasingly since the collapse of the communist bloc in 1990, globalization has been accepted as an explanatory mode for understanding not simply economic, but also political and cultural realities. The broad strokes of the argument are that although transnational trade and capitalist structures have long linked the world together, the increased mobility of the means of production, the emphasis on information technology, as well as the growth of multinational corporations, have brought about a new era in which nation-states no longer control economies and are therefore weak as political agents. (These arguments are made with an almost religious sense of inevitability that belies the new nationalisms of the twenty-first century and its heightened levels of nationalist violence.)[25] Furthermore, the qualitative changes in the speed of communications through computer and cable technologies and the rapid movement of images across the globe have created fundamentally new conditions for a democratic, global culture; cultures are neither isolated nor imposed on one another. Most theorists of globalization accept that globalization is a historical turning point that has displaced outdated models of center and periphery, of domination and subjection—in other words, the key terms of anticolonial and antiracist thinking that still remain central to questions of social justice.

While launching the journal *Public Culture* in 1988, for instance, the editors explicitly positioned themselves as critics of outmoded forms of analysis such as neocolonialism or third worldism. Global cultural flows, they argued, "raise the theoretical problem of conceptualizing modernity as a multi-directional, open-ended process, in which the Euro-American experience is significant, but neither singular nor always the exemplary center."[26] These ideas were further developed by Arjun Appadurai in his well-cited 1990 essay, "Disjuncture and Difference in the Global Cultural Economy," in which he postulated a decentered global cultural economy, operating through complex disjunctures between economy, culture, and politics; the major features of this economy are deterritorialization and massive immigration to Western metropoles.[27] Media, migration, the pleasures of cosmopolitanism and a modernity at large constitute features of this new globalized world, one that, in contrast to the vertebrate structure of the nation-state, is cellular.[28]

A less sanguine, though in some ways similar view of the globalized world was offered by Manuel Castells in his three volumes, *The Information Age*, published between 1996 and 2000. Although Castells characterizes the contemporary world as an "Athenian democracy" in which the affluent elite have access to tools of information while most of the world, like the masses in Greece, are switched off,[29] he, like Appadurai, continues to characterize the information world as decentered. Taking a Foucault-like approach to authority, he argues that power in the information age is "no longer concentrated in institutions (the state), organizations (capitalist firms), or symbolic controllers (corporate media, churches). It is diffused in global networks of wealth, power, information, and images, which circulate and transmute in a system of variable geometry and dematerialized geography. . . . The sites of this power are people's minds."[30]

This emphasis on the decentered, globalized world was continued in Michael Hardt and Antonio Negri's highly influential and controversial book, *Empire* (2000), and later in *Multitude* (2004), which focuses on global and expansive networks of resistance. Hardt and Negri argue that we live in a postmodern age of "empire," which, although it converges around and derives its energy around the United States, is not localizable.[31] As opposed to the age of imperialism, which was modernist and functioned through ideas of center and margin, inside and outside, empire has no outside.[32] Like Appadurai and Castells, the authors of *Empire* focus on the migrations from South to North as the loci for change and characterize empire as preeminently about information.[33] Although Hardt and Negri state that their relationship to empire is analogous to that of Marx to capitalism—that is, a system that must be overthrown, but one that through its very structure breeds change and resistance[34]—they also emphasize the noncoercive, fluid nature of empire; empire, they argue, is participatory and called into being.[35]

More recently, Anthony Appiah, focusing on the cultural aspects of globalization, posits "cosmopolitanism" as an enlightened perspective on the contemporary world. Working through problematic and simplistic binaries of authenticity/purity versus the reality of cultural contamination, Appiah declares the idea of cultural imperialism as the outdated province of cultural preservationists. "No army, no threat of sanctions, no political saber rattling," he argues, "imposes Hollywood on the French."[36]

A universality of values, rather than different conceptions of good, guides even the most contentious of issues, including abortion.[37] One need hardly point out that such liberal conceptions of universalism suppress socioeconomic oppressions even more than notions of hybrid or radical cosmopolitanisms.[38]

Of course, the works of these four scholars by no means exhaust cultural analyses of globalization. I use them simply to illustrate some common features of, and problems attendant on, the wholesale acceptance of globalization theories. First, some of the premises of globalization theories are clearly Eurocentric. The prominence given to technologies of information, the cyberculture of virtuality, and the fast movement of hyperreal images assumes a networked or at least techno-linked world in which virtuality predominates. However, the laboring and nonlaboring lives of the majority of the world do not, in fact, revolve around virtuality. Despite the supposed ubiquity of television for instance, its impact in a country like India is severely limited where only 44 percent of rural families, and 56 percent nationwide, have access to electricity.[39] Indeed, given the extreme disparities in technologies of cultural mobility, it seems irresponsible to eliminate vocabularies of unevenness.

Second, along with stressing the mobility of culture, proponents of globalization also map the world through the mobility of populations, particularly the movement of people from South to North. Whether conceptualized as Hardt and Negri's multitude against empire, Appadurai's mass migration of workers, or Anthony Appiah's cosmopolitanism as perspective based on the ability to travel,[40] transiency is central to all these formulations. Of course one cannot deny the movement of labor from South to North, particularly since the major decolonizations of the 1950s and 1960s. However, to focus solely on migrancy to the North as perspective is not only to privilege it as vantage point but also to marginalize the majority of the world's labor that is not migrant. Interestingly, in the most recent comprehensive analysis of the world's workers done by the World Bank, *World Development Report 1995, Workers in an Integrating World*, only 2 percent of people in low and middle income countries like Mexico do not live in the country of their origin. Between two to three million migrants leave developing countries each year, only half of whom go to industrial countries. As the report adds, "Migration among industrial countries has actually declined since 1970 from 2.5 migrants per thousand inhabitants to about 1 per thousand in 1990."[41] The very acceptance of migrancy as a central perspective thus illustrates Harvey's contention about the triumph of the ideology of globalizing neoliberalism.

Third, because globalization theories have stressed the decentered flow of capital and cultural goods, as well as migrancy, they have tended to dismiss any local movements as reactionary. Thus, Castells sees forms of resistance identities created through local communities as defensive and retrenched. Localists, he argues, affirm the transcendent values of god, nation, family, and community. "Thus, against the informationalization of culture, bodies are informationalized. That is, individuals bear their gods in their heart. They do not reason, they believe."[42] Castells distinguishes these local forms of resistance from proactive social movements like feminism and environmentalism. Hardt and Negri similarly see local resistances as entirely reactive, given to romanticization and primordialism and ineffective because they obfuscate the real potentialities for liberation within empire that comes only from the global multitude.[43] However, the rejection of the local, both as a site of resistance and of knowledge, can only be made if one accepts the logic of globalization as inevitability. As David Harvey soberly writes, "The more the left adopted this discourse as a description of the state of the world (even if it was a state to be criticized and rebelled against), the more it circumscribed its own political possibilities. That so many of us took the concept on board so uncritically in the 1980s and 1990s, allowing it to displace the far more politically charged concepts of imperialism and neocolonialism should give us pause."[44]

But if we accept instead neocolonialism and imperialism as the realities of the moment, reactive strategies and local resistances and ontologies are not suspect. Anti-imperial and anticolonial resistances are necessarily reactive because they originate in opposition to an order that they wish to subvert. But the mode of these resistances is not determined by the logic of colonialism and imperialism because the resistances attempt to create different epistemologies and are geared to a different logic.[45] Local and familial traditions, as John Blassingame has shown in his research on slave communities in the United States, often become a locus of resistance to a colonial order like slavery.[46] More recently, as Nikhil Pal Singh suggests, the riots of the 1960s made the geopolitics of black power local and created a valorization of the ghetto as a site of resistance.[47]

On the other hand, it is imperative that concepts like local knowledge not be universalized as liberatory alternatives. Indeed, multinational corporations have long recognized the importance of connecting with small cultural units to market their products. Like the call for localization made by John Farrell, president of Coca-Cola's China division in Hong Kong, to the use of "glocal" as a marketing strategy in *Global Vision: Building New Models for the Corporation of the Future* (1994), local knowledge and local interactions are unquestionably seen as good business sense.[48] Capitalist globalization thus needs the local in order to proliferate, but it needs a specific kind of local, one that connects immediately with the global market but minimizes the significance of its cultural, social, and ethical linkages with the subnational, regional, or national. It is imperative, therefore, that the questions "Whose local knowledge?" and "To what ends?" continue to be asked.

Finally, much of globalization theory does not view racial difference as significant in the construction of contemporary subjectivity. Because the marking of Others is supposedly a regime of colonial modernity surpassed in the present, racial antagonisms and conflicts operate within what Hardt and Negri call fluid and amorphous masses instead of being fixed.[49] Taking the example of contemporary cultural forms such as rap and the renewed cult of Malcolm X among African American youth, Castells argues that ethnicity as community matters less than broader terms of identification, such as religion and class. As Castells puts it, "Race matters, but it hardly constructs meaning any longer."[50]

IMPERIALISM, NEOCOLONIALISM, AND POSTCOLONIAL THEORY

I have analyzed some of the problems of globalization theories because they have been clearly influential in thinking about culture since the 1980s and have ironically also affected some versions of postcolonial theory, a theory that came into being to provide an analytics of colonial difference. In this section I will mark the problematic conjuncture of globalization theory and language-based, poststructuralist versions of postcolonial theory and make a case for "resistance postcolonialism" as central to the study of U.S. culture. Through their cognizance of imperialism and colonial difference, world systems theories, I will argue, provide a better model for understanding contemporary U.S. culture than globalization theories or general calls for transnationalism and postnationalism.

Imperialism exists. Colonial difference matters. In 1920, Lenin formulated his treatise on the inevitable historical connection between monopoly capitalism and imperialism. Lenin prophetically wrote, "Capitalism has grown into a world system of colonial oppression and of the financial strangulation of the overwhelming majority of the people of the world by a handful of "advanced" countries."[51] The Comintern, urged by Lenin, transformed the 1848 slogan of Marx and Engels, "Workers of all countries unite!" into "Workers and oppressed peoples of all countries unite!" thereby including anticolonialism in the Third International.[52] This imperialist, colonialist aspect of capitalism, ignored by most Western Marxists and their latter-day left theorists of globalization, has been the centerpiece of third worldists or world systems theorists who, since the 1970s, have challenged the developmentalism of traditional Marxism[53] and have postulated the workings of capitalism through a single world system, the capitalist world economy. Immanuel Wallerstein suggests that because within this economy all states cannot develop simultaneously, the system works "by virtue of having unequal core and peripheral regions."[54] Unequal exchange between core and periphery is intrinsic to the system.[55] Samir Amin, another principal theoretician of world systems, explains the relations between center and periphery as being those of transfers of value from periphery to center; growth in the periphery, based on integration into the world market, Amin argues, is a development of underdevelopment.[56] As Amin recently explained, "imperialism has always been a component—and not as Lenin argued a stage—of capitalist development. Instead, it is the character of each stage of imperialism that has changed. The trend has been towards greater polarisation. . . . At the end of the day, however, what is essential is that there continues to be a growing gap between the centers and the peripheries."[57] Unlike the past in which imperialisms were in conflict with each other, contemporary imperialism is operating through a Japan-Europe-U.S. triad with the United States as hegemon, intervening powerfully in the societies of the periphery.[58]

Thus, while globalization theorists treat notions of center and periphery as outdated models, left over from colonial periods, world systems theorists explain the very functioning of contemporary capitalism through these notions. Of course since the U.S. invasion of Iraq in 2003, U.S. imperialism has once again begun to be viewed as central to political and economic analyses. David Harvey's *The New Imperialism* (2003), for instance, charts the United States' course from its attempts to control world markets following the collapse of Bretton Woods institutions to the clearly militaristic designs of the Project for a New American Century, while Chalmers Johnson's *The Sorrows of Empire* (2004) argues that U.S. militarism (with more than 725 military bases outside the country) is ending globalization.[59] Indeed the United States' aggressive stance after 9/11 has also generated debate in unlikely places. For instance, *Public Culture*, initiated as a journal analyzing the postimperial world of cultural globalization, devoted a 2003 issue to debating contemporary U.S. imperialism, paralleling the move of *Interventions*, a prominent journal of postcolonial studies. Few can dispute the country's imperialist stance since 2003; however, I want to argue that imperialism was alive and well in the 1980s and 1990s, but that recognizing it required a non-Eurocentric lens open to viewing imperialism and neocolonialism as central.

This is a perspective that is virtually absent from many theories of globalization. Thus, Castells's volume, *The Power of Identity* makes no mention of colonialism, neocolonialism, or imperialism. Apparently, the new global order buries questions of colonialism so much that even a strong indigeneity-based movement like the Zapatistas can be discussed largely as a movement of the network society without even a mention of colonial destruction or of Maya culture. Similarly, Anthony Giddens's theorizations of modernity and late modernity, which have been highly influential in thinking about globalization, simply exclude questions of colonialism and imperialism. While Giddens agrees that modernity is Western, he does not recognize the imbrication of modernity and colonialism.[60]

If, however, we are cognizant of the historical significance of colonialism and imperialism and of racial politics that buttress neocolonialism, we know that whereas imagining a world without Others is commendable, not recognizing Othering is an irresponsible, though undeniably "Western" gesture. For many theorists from the South, on the other hand, Othering and colonial difference are central to Western ontology. Walter Mignolo, who articulates a modern/colonial world system, explains the problem of not thinking in terms of inside and outside in the following way: "What the proposition asserts is that we should eliminate dichotomies from our vocabulary. And in this principle I do believe, since colonial discourse was one of the most powerful strategies in the imaginary of the modern/colonial world system for producing dichotomies that justified the will to power. . . . It is fine for me to eliminate dichotomies, or at least to try. What is more difficult to achieve is forgetting or eliminating the historical dichotomies that colonial discourse and epistemology imposed upon the world by inventing colonial differences."[61] Mignolo also suggests that arguments for eliminating inside/outside dichotomies are most often made by those who are clearly on the "inside," while many intellectuals in the third world believe in these distinctions.[62]

One could contend that Mignolo's position homogenizes the intellectual currents of the first or the third world. However, it is not accidental that the major proponents of world systems theories—Immanuel Wallerstein and Samir Amin—were both Africanist scholars who placed imperialism at the center of their theorizations. Amin has continued to raise the problems of neocolonial globalization and uneven globalization in *The Liberal Virus* (2004).[63] Perhaps culture can operate relatively autonomously from the economic sphere, but that argument holds only if one dissociates "culture" from the messy business of living, from an arena of struggle, and from the politics of neocolonialism and imperialism. But as postcolonial scholars have aptly demonstrated, colonialism and its aftermath have been central to the West's understanding of itself at least since the eighteenth century. And imperialism, as perspective, has been accepted as integral to studies of American culture since the 1990s, notably with the publication of *Cultures of United States Imperialism*, even though significant works on the history of U.S. imperialism such as R. W. Van Alstyne's *The Rising American Empire* were published in the 1960s.[64]

Interestingly, the mid-1970s, identified by Harvey as the beginning of the idea of globalization, also witnessed the beginnings of postcolonial theory in the U.S. academy, marked by the publication of Edward Said's *Orientalism* in 1978. Postcolonial theory brought to light the effects of Western colonialism on all fields of knowledge and the continuity of these effects in conditions of neocolonialism. The field offered renewed currency to the work of revolutionary anticolonial theorists such as Frantz Fanon and Amilcar Cabral and promised to open up further avenues for the analyses of U.S. minority discourse. Henry Louis Gates's collection, *"Race," Writing and Difference*, a compilation of essays written for *Critical Inquiry* in 1985 and 1986, and which included established African Americanist scholars as well as postcolonial critics, attempted to forge such an opening.

By the early 1990s, however, the general movement in postcolonial theory was away from models that focused on specific material conditions and foregrounded domination and exploitation to more linguistic models that focused on negotiatory analyses of colonialism.[65] Commenting on this shift, Benita Parry critiqued the turn in postcolonial theory that "celebrates globalism for the volatility of the cultural flows it brings about" while ignoring the implication of these flows in imperialism; such a turn, resultant on a disengagement from political theory and socioeconomic structures, dependent on the indeterminacies of language alone, dispenses with the notion of conflict.[66] Edward Said similarly denounced the effects of a "globalized, postmodern consciousness" on the field: "Anticolonial liberation theory and the real history of empire, with its massacres and exploitation, have turned into a focus on the anxieties and ambivalences of the colonizer, the silent thereby colonized and displaced somehow."[67] What bothers Said and Parry, and is articulated in a slightly different manner by Aijaz Ahmad, is that the specific problems of colonization and decolonization are being subsumed under the general theoretical concerns of poststructuralism,[68] a problem compounded by the fact that the two movements share a commonality in the critique of European humanism.

Despite the reservations of Said and Parry, the charge brought about by critics like Arif Dirlik that postcolonial theory has flourished only because of its complicity with global capitalism, or that its practitioners are overprivileged, is an overstatement that uncannily resembles the arguments of the Right against academics today.[69] (Indeed, I would argue that despite his dismissal of the term "postcolonial," Dirlik's analyses of regional, Pacific rim resistances to global capital are an important contribution to postcolonial studies.) In a useful intervention into debates about postcolonial theory's radicalism, Robert Young argues that postcolonial theory, which carries on the intellectual and political project of anticolonial movements, shares the anti-Western heritage of poststructuralism and combines it with the perspectives of writers from the formerly colonized countries.[70] However, despite Young's valuable recuperation of the political possibilities of postcolonial theory and his demonstration, say, of the imbrication of the anticolonial politics of Algeria and deconstruction, the privileging of a language-based poststructuralism within the work of some postcolonial theorists cannot be denied. This is the charge Vijay Mishra and Bob Hodge make against Helen Tiffin, Stephen Slemon, and other theorists of settler colonialism who regard postcolonialism as "already present in European thought" and who see no difference between the domination experienced by white settlers and natives in other colonies.[71] Following Mishra's and Hodge's differentiation between different kinds of postcolonialisms, I borrow the terminology of Ranajit Guha and suggest that we think of *resistance postcolonialism* and *collaborative postcolonialism*. Resistance postcolonialism takes seriously the existence of centers and peripheries and structures of colonial and imperial domination, is interested in the specific systems of oppression that these structures mete out in different locations, and attempts to forge oppositional strategies. Collaborative postcolonialism, reliant on a language-based poststructuralism that treats colonialism and imperialism as a series of exchanges, sees power dichotomies as theoretically unsophisticated, is interested in the fuzziness of boundaries, and privileges the language of colonial and imperial encounters over their material determinants.[72] Resistance postcolonialism is exemplified in the writings of anticolonial liberation thinkers such as Frantz Fanon, Amilcar Cabral, and N'gugi wa Thiong'o; analysts such as Edward Said, Benita Parry, and Anne McClintock; and subaltern studies scholars such as Partha Chatterjee and Dipesh Chakrabarty. Collaborative postcolonialism is represented primarily in the work of Homi Bhabha and the numerous others influenced by him (including diaspora theorists such as Iain Chambers), and in scholars such as Trinh T. Minh-ha, and Anthony Appiah.[73] While both types of postcolonialisms, as in Guha's paradigm, belong to the purview of the subordinated, resistance postcolonialism provides a more credible genealogy of anticolonial struggle, a relevant critique of colonial and imperial practices, and an epistemology for dealing with the highly charged question of internal colonialism in the United States. Resistance postcolonialism is "global" in its analysis of structures of domination, and in possibilities of resistance, but it conceives of the global through the lenses of imperialism and neocolonialism.

LOCAL STRUGGLES, RACE, AND POSTCOLONIAL RESISTANCE

> There was an insurrection in this city before,
> and, if I remember correctly,
> it was sparked by police brutality.
> We had a Kerner Commission report.
> It talked about what was wrong with our society.
> It talked about institutionalized racism.
> It talked about a lack of services,
> lack of government responsive to the people.
> Today,
> as we stand here in 1992,
> if you go back and read the report,
> it seems as though we are talking about what that report cited
> some twenty years ago,
> still exists today. . . .
>
> They picked my son up several times
> and dropped him in another project
> when he was just a little boy.
> They've done it to my kid,
> they'll do it to your kid.
> It's the color, because we're Black
> (Anna Deveare Smith, *Twilight Los Angeles, 1992*, pp. 160, 38)

Anna Deveare Smith's *Twilight Los Angeles, 1992* is a brilliant theatrical interpretation of the L.A. riots following the "not guilty" verdict about the police beating of Rodney King pronounced by the jurors of Simi Valley; it is presented as a series of interviews of a wide spectrum of people and rendered solely in the words of the interviewees themselves. The previous two excerpts from *Twilight*, the first from a speech given by Congresswoman Maxine Waters at the First African Methodist Episcopal Church in L.A., the second from Theresa Allison, founder of Mothers Reclaiming Our Children, powerfully demonstrate the significance of race and located knowledge in understanding the L.A. riots of 1992. Maxine Waters links the L.A. riots of 1992 and the Watts riots of 1965 to a genealogy of urban neglect and hopelessness. California's attempt to block the fair housing component of the Civil Rights Act by passing Proposition 14, the brutality of the Los Angeles Police Department (L.A.P.D.) toward African Americans, the poor schools in the inner city, and the despair of the residents created a politically volatile situation where a routine police arrest in 1965 could spark a major riot. A continuity of urban neglect ignited a similar riot in 1992. But, as with the aftermath of Hurricane Katrina, one can ask whether poor housing, high unemployment, and police brutality have much to do with imperialism. Are institutionalized racism at the national level and anti-affirmative action initiatives at the local level transnational concerns? Can the well-documented racism of the L.A.P.D. that Theresa Allison recounts be adequately understood through the lens of postcoloniality?

Clearly, both the L.A. and the Watts riots call for an understanding of the imbrication of race and inner-city politics brought to light most dramatically in the differences between the political culture of south central L.A. and Simi Valley. It was the L.A.P.D., for instance, that had been responsible for vicious attacks against the Black Panthers in the 1970s. Thus, to see the L.A. riots as an illustration of cultural and racial hybridity (collaborative postcolonialism) or to view Rodney King's beating simply as part of the suppression of blacks worldwide through the master trope of diaspora is not enough. As Sau-ling Cynthia Wong suggests, Rodney King was not beaten because he was part of the black diaspora but rather because he was a U.S. minority, an African American.[74] Wen Ho Lee was imprisoned because he was Chinese American and therefore, like all Asian Americans, seen as a perpetual foreigner and therefore potential spy. Sami Al-Arian was imprisoned because he was a Palestinian American who had openly declared his sympathy for the Palestinian cause. Yet although one minority experience cannot be substituted for another, imperial structures of racial dominance might be at play. However, these structures might operate in various ways in different racial sites. For instance, the preponderance of Korean Americans in the grocery store business might point to the exclusions of immigration policies for Asians, while the impetus for Korean immigration to the United States might be the result of U.S. military interventions in Korea.

Interestingly, the beginnings of globalization and postcolonial theory also coincided with a virtual renaissance in race studies. The advent of Critical Race Theory (CRT) in the field of legal academe, the emphasis on the centrality of race by sociologists, and the field of whiteness studies that interrogated whiteness as the norm, all contributed to a field collectively referred to as critical race studies. Prominent scholars in the field include Derrick Bell, Patricia Williams, Michael Omi, Howard Winant, Noel Ignatiev, David Roediger, and Cornel West.[75] All these scholars focus on national space, are insistent on the centrality of race in U.S. society, and refuse to reduce race to a manifestation of other supposedly more fundamental social relationships such as class or gender. Most important, CRT scholars valorize particularity as a challenge to the supposedly race-neutral scholarship of mainstream legal discourse. As Richard Delgado writes, "Most mainstream scholars embrace universalism over particularity, abstract principles and the 'rule of law' over perspectivism. . . . Critical Race Theory writers emphasize the opposite, in what has been termed the 'call to context.' For CRT scholars, general laws may be appropriate in some areas. . . . But political and moral discourse is not one of them. Normative discourse (as civil rights is) is highly fact sensitive—adding even one new fact can change intuition radically."[76] It is because general laws ignore the specificity of minority experience and favor the universalism constituted by whiteness that CRT scholars insist on context. This sensitivity to context has been central to critical race studies in general.

However, this insistence on particularity is not a Lyotardian postmodern denial of grand narratives, including those of emancipation, and a celebration of micro-truths alone.[77] Indeed, critical race studies is premised on the existence of racism as a negative grand narrative. However, unlike grand narratives that sought a totality, critical race studies does not posit itself as a universal because it is based on a different ethics and logic. The object of race studies' analysis is not a universalized idea of racism but rather race as a systemic form of oppression, legislated through the juridical apparatuses of the nation-state and normalized through social institutions such as schools. Here, race studies scholars have been joined by numerous scholars in U.S. minority studies. Lisa Lowe argues, for instance, that "Americanness" is a raced formulation based on the exclusion of Asian Americans from the body politic through specific juridical acts.[78] bell hooks's powerful indictment of Betty Friedan's universalization of the predicament of the bored housewife was based on the particularity of black female exploitation.[79] Recently, Houston Baker has recommended a "turning South" for American cultural studies in order to analyze the carceral network that has held the black-South body in imprisonment. Baker writes, "American 'history' thus reads out, in black-majority vocabularies, as enslavement, incarceration, imprisonment."[80] What Baker finds missing in an analysis of global modernity such as Gilroy's is the "specificity of time, place, and detail one requires to read (and, perhaps, empower) black United States modernism."[81] Here, in his critique of diasporic models of blackness, Baker has been joined by critics like Tiffany Ruby Patterson and Robin D. G. Kelley, who have critiqued the trend to homogenize all disaporic moments and erase local specificities.[82]

It is clear, therefore, that any analytics of race in the United States must be based on an understanding of the juridical structures of the nation-state through which the system of racial hierarchy is consolidated. For minority groups such as African Americans or Asian Americans, what I have called particularism or located thinking means thinking through the intersection of racial specificity and national (even regional) juridical apparatuses.[83] For other groups, locatedness might be more subnational. In the United States, located thinking has been recognized and most productively theorized in the work of Pacific Rim, Hawai'ian studies, and by Chicana/o scholars. Arguing that diasporic thinking reifies racial essentialism by focusing on origin and descent, Arif Dirlik makes a powerful case for what he calls a "place-based politics" premised not on exclusion but on refocusing attention on "building society from the bottom up" through the strengthening of community.[84] Similarly, Paul Lyons theorizes a located pedagogy for Hawai'ian studies that emphasizes the "cultural priorities, conversations, histories, and narratives of a particular place" but that becomes critical by seeing how vertical/horizontal structures engage with horizontal/contemporary movements in regional, national, and global configurations.[85] And writers such as Americo Paredes have long articulated the importance of the Southwest border as a key to understanding Chicano/a identity.

Likewise, in the work of subaltern studies scholars, European universalisms are constantly challenged through analyses of specific locations: Ranajit Guha's classic critique of dominant historiography's representation of the rule of British capital and of Indian nationalism as hegemony rather than dominance and Dipesh Chakrabarty's provincializing of concepts of European modernity through a focus on colonial Bengal.[86] Indeed, as Etienne Balibar suggests, while raced groups express specific demands for recognition, and are particularistic, they articulate their demands in universalist fashion in order to challenge the exclusions of what is accepted as universality.[87] In other words, Balibar finds the use of a strategic universality by specific groups especially important. In a similar vein, albeit fully challenging ideas of universalism, Zillah Eisenstein suggests the concept of a polyversal humanity and argues for "theorizing the specific as the means of allowing a polyunity to emerge."[88]

It is in this spirit of a polyunity of anti-imperialism that we can connect and theorize the specific agendas of racial justice to those of worldwide postcolonial liberation. Let us examine the links of the raced particular and local resistances with anti-imperial struggles from the perspective of scholarship, activism, and resistance literature. When we look at scholarship, we see that despite avowed differences, scholarly collections of postcolonial and race studies are remarkably fluid: witness Mae Henderson's "Speaking in Tongues" in Patrick Williams and Laura Chrisman's popular reader, *Colonial Discourse and Post-Colonial Theory* (1994), which earlier appeared in *Reading Black, Reading Feminist* (1990, edited by Henry Louis Gates); and essays by bell hooks and Wahneema Lubiano in another standard postcolonial reader, *Dangerous Liaisons: Gender, Nation, and Postcolonial Perspectives* (1997).[89] Collections commonly being used for critical race studies are similarly entangled with postcolonial theory. Theo Goldberg's anthology, *Anatomy of Racism* (1990), for instance, includes analyses of biological and cultural racism and features writings by Frantz Fanon, Edward Said, and Homi Bhabha. Henry Louis Gates's earlier and more literature-oriented anthology, *"Race," Writing and Difference*, included essays by prominent African Americanist scholars such as Hazel Carby, as well as ones by postcolonialists like Abdul JanMohamed and Gayatri Spivak. Yet Houston Baker's critique of the collection points to the different constituencies of postcolonial and race theorizing, especially if the postcolonial is seen as linguistic alone or what I have called collaborative postcolonialism.[90]

On the other hand, critical race studies is itself taking a transnational turn. Howard Winant's *The World Is a Ghetto* (2001) argues for a Wallersteinian global approach to race in the twenty-first century by positing a "new world racial system" in sharp contrast to the old structures of explicit colonialism and state sponsored segregation."[91] Evidence of this system today are the extreme disparities between the world's mainly white North and the mainly darker South.[92] And yet Winant's "global" approach functions through a comparative nationalism in which he analyzes the contemporary sociology of race by devoting separate chapters to the United States, South Africa, and Brazil; similarly the chapter on nineteenth- and early twentieth-century racial constructions is divided into different national sections. What is significant, however, is Winant's attempt to combine a located analytics of race with a transnational perspective and to theorize the latter in postcolonial terms.[93]

When we look at activism, we also see that progressive racial movements in the United States, as Nikhil Pal Singh recognizes in his analysis of the black power movement, have long articulated their visions in solidarity with the colonized and exploited people of color all over the world.[94] Today with the unilateralism and sheer military might of U.S. imperialism, the continual rollback of affirmative action programs, and the neoliberal moves to define the country as color-blind, it is more imperative than ever to recognize these resistances. As early as the late eighteenth century, African Americans like Prince Hall and John Marrant, for instance, claimed entry into the nation by linking their histories to those of African colonization.[95] Anticipating Fanon's category of "the wretched of the earth" and the capitalist racism of world systems theorists, W. E. B. DuBois early recognized the common degradation of people of color within and outside the United States, the sea of "human labor in China and India, the South Seas and all Africa," providing the foundation of modern industry, yet "despised and rejected by race and color."[96]

Similarly, the Third World Movement, which began in San Francisco State College in 1968, comprising African Americans, Latina/os, Asian Americans and Native Americans, all of whom declared ghettos and barrios to be internal colonies of the United States, combined two seemingly contradictory political trajectories. On the one hand, this movement was testimony to the fragments that haunted the nation and offered local-political potentialities irreducible to the nation-state, while, on the other, constituents of the movement used the language of nationalism as a rhetoric of radical dissent. But the nationalisms of black nationalism, Yellow Power, and La Raza operated from different paradigms than hegemonic nationalism or the modular forms of national society posited in the modern West as theorized by Benedict Anderson.[97] The raced nation challenged Benedict Anderson's idea of nationalism as fraternal comradeship; and the students of the Third World Movement looked outward, rather than to national print/visual cultures, modeling themselves after third world liberation struggles. Even while advocating a hemispheric concept of *familia* for La Raza, leaders like Rodolfo "Corky" Gonzalez linked the cause of Latina/os with those of indigenous peoples decolonizing their brethren.[98]

In like manner, the Black Panther Party, which was formed to claim social justice for African Americans, grounded its demands in a critique of U.S. imperialism and saw the subjugation of African Americans as analogous to that of the Vietnamese. The Vietnamese, in turn, provided modes of resistance. Huey Newton wrote: "The Black Panther Party for Self-Defense teaches that, in the final analysis the guns, hand grenades, bazookas, and other equipment necessary for defense must be supplied by the power structure. As exemplified by the Vietcong, these weapons must be taken from the oppressor."[99] As discussed in chapter six, Newton, in fact, changed the platform of the Black Panther Party from nationalism to what he called intercommunalism, because given U.S. imperialism's stranglehold on third world autonomy, there was a need to "ally ourselves with the oppressed communities of the world. . . . We must place our future hopes upon the philosophy of intercommunalism, a philosophy which holds that the rise of imperialism in America transformed all other nations into oppressed communities."[100] Indeed, Newton's solidarity with the Vietnamese drew the ire of other activists who felt embittered by Newton's offer to send African American troops for the Vietcong while their fellow African Americans were suffering in the slums of Los Angeles.[101] Even La Raza Unida (RUP), although operating as a third party, albeit a radical one within the United States, had activists who participated in the Sandinista revolution; RUP leaders in the 1980s saw parallels between their own struggles and those of the PLO.[102]

It is important to stress here the differences between radical race-based activism on the international level from the internationalism of both globalization theories and what I have called collaborative postcolonialism. Unlike globalization theory and the hybridity-inspired postcolonialism, theories like Huey Newton's are simultaneously committed to a version of national sovereignty (which for Newton has been undermined by imperialism), transnational anticolonial solidarity, and local resistance. Newton's invocation of communitarianism arises from his conviction that third world countries cannot have the prerequisites of nationalism such as economic independence, cultural determination, and territorial integrity under U.S. imperialism.[103] Anticolonial solidarity does not negate the significance of local thinking or the need for third world governments to consolidate a protective nationalism as a bulwark against imperialism. This is the spirit in which Subcomandante Marcos, although waging a guerrilla war against the Mexican government, argues for defending national sovereignty against the forces of global capitalism.[104]

Perhaps the most complex exposition of the relationship between nationalism and a worldwide anticolonial solidarity was formulated by Frantz Fanon, who was committed to anticolonial struggle and powerfully articulated the violent similarities of different colonial apparatuses. The colonial world, argued Fanon, is a "Manichean world" in which the native is not only suppressed by force but also painted as the quintessence of evil.[105] Because colonial domination suppresses native aspirations for cultural expression and national autonomy, Fanon insists on the importance and specificity of national culture: "every culture is first and foremost national . . . the problems which kept Richard Wright or Langston Hughes on the alert were fundamentally different from those which might confront Leopold Senghor or Jomo Kenyatta."[106] Obviously, national consciousness here is liberatory consciousness, not bourgeois nationalism. Indeed, liberatory nationalism looks outward: "it is national liberation which leads the nation to play its part on the stage of history. It is at the heart of national consciousness that international consciousness lives and grows."[107] Other theorizations of resistance literature and culture emphasize a similar dialectic between a subjectivity derived from a local historicity and a global solidarity of the oppressed. Edward Said, for instance, posits the awareness of "one's self as belonging to a subject people" as the "founding insight of anti-imperialist nationalism," but also argues that "It is best when Caliban sees his own history as an aspect of the history of *all* subjugated men and women."[108] Such a need for anticolonial solidarity explains why bell hooks begins her book on African American racial representation, *Black Looks*, with a lengthy epigraph, from Samia Hehrez, about decolonization.

In the United States, race has been both the primary means of social hierarchy as well as the site of the most significant resistances.[109] Loci of experience and enunciation have been central here. The power of a work like Gloria Anzaldua's *Borderlands* is its articulation of Chicana/o identity through linguistic, cultural, and geographical borders, demonstrated in the living conditions on the Texas–Mexican border. There is a distinctiveness to this experience, and the subsequent Chicana/o emphasis on shifting borders cannot be simply transposed to that of African Americans or Native Americans unless the specific histories of slavery and genocide mean nothing. Indeed, Anzaldua's book is most problematic in its occasional invitations for all who are "different"—from the squint-eyed to the mulatto—to participate in the borderlands; such equal opportunity differences, rather than disrupting power hierarchies, can have the insidious effect of silencing the oppressed because, after all, everyone can claim oppression through "difference."[110] In my own undergraduate class on women of color I have had students claiming a borderlands experience for reasons as varied as double-majoring or living at home while going to college.

Recent theorizations of the contemporary United States as postcolonial emphasize the importance of raced resistances. Thus, the editors of *Postcolonial Theory and the United States* see the "borders" school of race theorizing, one that emphasizes how shifting internal and external borders continue to create racial outsiders, as the site of productive exchanges with postcolonial studies.[111] Richard King, editor of *Postcolonial America*, who argues that postcoloniality needs to be reimagined in terms of change, decentering, and displacement, sees alternatives to colonial discourses in movements ranging from black power to multiculturalism.[112] However, King's dismissal of race as an analytical category and the use of supposedly unraced terms such as native, diasporic, and anticolonial, runs the risk of homogenizing minority groups.[113] Similarly, as I discuss in chapter three, while some feminist theorizing on race and gender problematically analogizes different kinds of oppressions, specific studies like Anne McClintock's on the particular connections between race, gender, and imperialism point to promising directions for U.S. race studies as well.[114]

But while the different oppressions of African Americans, Latina/os, Native Americans, and Asian Americans cannot be collapsed, these varied histories have the potential to provide alternatives to hegemonic Euro-American history without being universalizing, as long as the specificity of each history is maintained.[115] One of the best models for such alternatives has been formulated by the indigeneity scholar, John Brown Childs. In stark contrast to the idea of transnationalism, Childs posits the idea of transcommunality to explain interactions that occur among communities and organizations that maintain rooted affiliations and create broad constellations of cooperation that envision different forms of justice and challenge structures of oppression.[116] It should be clear, however, that anticolonial and anti-imperial resistance movements are not simply reversed mirror images of an imperial world order. As Walter Mignolo points out, "macro-narratives from the perspective of coloniality are not the counterpart of world or universal history, but rather a radical departure from such global projects." They are "narratives geared toward the search for a different logic," "an alternative to totality conceived as a network of local histories and multiple local hegemonies."[117] Mignolo chooses not to specify the relationships between networks of local histories and macronarratives from the perspective of coloniality, perhaps because doing so might risk universalization. I would argue, however, that antiracist, local resistances seek to link themselves with larger movements not only to build strategic alliances, but also to be seen as movements that speak to an anticolonial and anti-imperial logic. This logic, which has been a vitally necessary alternative to the narratives of modernity, postmodernity, and now globalization, has been a long-standing presence in the history of local resistances in the United States. An urgent critical task is to unearth and acknowledge the existence of such resistances, so that oppositional Post-Colonial narratives that relentlessly emphasize systemic inequalities can be sustained. This book culminates in an exploration of such possibilities within the current critical and political climate.

TRANSNATIONALISM AND AMERICAN STUDIES

How has the discipline of American Studies, emergent in the heyday of Cold War nationalism, and always in a politically sensitive position in relation to imperial nationhood, intervened in conversations about globalization? Clearly, there are calls for a movement from nationalism to postnationalism. Postnationalism in most of these arguments signifies a desire to reject the exceptionalism thesis of earlier American studies (that the United States was not, like Europe, a colonial power but defined instead by a commitment to freedom), to take seriously the critiques of *a* national culture offered by multiculturalism, and to give prominence to the histories of border nations that have defined U.S. nationalism. The writers of the introduction to *Post-Nationalist American Studies* (2000) capture well the appeal of postnationalism: "that adjective [postnationalism] does begin to describe the desire of those in our group to contribute to a version of American Studies that is less insular and parochial, and more internationalist and comparative. In this sense, our efforts to formulate a post-nationalist American Studies respond to and seek to revise the cultural nationalism and celebratory American exceptionalism that often informed the work of American Studies scholars in the Cold War era."[118] Postnationalism to this group largely signifies a dissent from normative ideologies of Americanism rather than an endorsement of a postnational political reality. Indeed, the writers acknowledge the powers of the nation-state and critique globalization theories' arguments about the demise of the nation.[119] Yet their very oppositions of insular/international and parochial/comparative reinforce the idea that the local is necessarily fixed and insular and that the transnational challenges hegemonic nationalism.

More important, there is a danger that the latest transnational turn in American Studies can augur a move away from the vitally urgent postcolonial critique of imperialism. Shelley Fisher Fishkin's otherwise exemplary 2004 presidential address to the American Studies Association, "Crossroads of Cultures: The Transnational Turn in American Studies," exemplifies my concerns. Although Fishkin's intent is to contest celebratory nationalist narratives by emphasizing borders and movements, her address eschews words like colonialism, domination, neocolonialism, and postcolonialism. Fishkin writes, "The United States is and always has been a transnational crossroads of cultures. And that crossroads of cultures that we refer to as 'American culture' has itself generated a host of other crossroads of cultures as it has crossed borders. . . . The story of these apparently 'American' phenomena—civil disobedience and jazz—are stories of transnational flows, as is the story of America itself."[120] Thus, despite her focus on decentering hegemonic U.S. nationalism, the systemic violence of colonialism and imperialism is displaced through the rhetoric of transnational flows and crossings, a rhetoric that disturbingly echoes that of global capitalism.

Other attempts to broaden the field of inquiry are based on a recognition that a nation-based perspective ignores the significance of other nations that are integral to the constitution of the United States. Thus, Carolyn Porter turns to scholars like Jose Saldivar and Roberto Retamar, whose "America" is a postcolonial connection of hybrid spaces connecting the Caribbean to the North, while John Carlos Rowe argues that the histories of border nations must be taken seriously within American Studies, the domain of which cannot be the nation alone.[121] Yet, as Rowe warns, comparative cultural studies can often contribute to cultural imperialism.[122] This is a warning that does not get taken seriously enough in the moves toward what is perceived as a more sophisticated internationalism. As Edward Said cogently pointed out in *Culture and Imperialism*, comparative literary study was Eurocentric, epistemologically organized as a hierarchy with European and Latin Christian literatures at the pinnacle. In the United

States, during the Cold War, the field, along with that of foreign languages, was promoted by the National Defense Education Act as one affecting national security.[123] Today, H.R. 609, The College Access & Opportunity Act, which has surreptitiously resurrected state surveillance of foreign language and Middle East studies, reflects well the exclusionary nationalism possible in comparative literature and area studies. Moreover, global American studies might well disturbingly parallel the globalization of American capital.[124] Furthermore, what I am suggesting is not a simple inversion of the proposition that transnational equals cosmopolitan, but rather a rethinking of the conception that particularistic and located analytics are necessarily provincial or fixed. Indeed, recent scholarship on early American subaltern studies demonstrates the potential of questioning the very terms of colonial modernity through a focus on the local.[125]

I see this book as contributing to the ongoing reinterpretation of U.S. culture through the lens of imperialism as demonstrated in the work of American Studies scholars, but, in its recuperation of a politics of locatedness and particularistic analysis in the tradition of critical race studies and subaltern studies scholars, it is also positioned in contestation with the valorization of postnationalism evident in contemporary American Studies scholarship. Furthermore, through its decolonizing of globalized analyses and its engagement with forms of Post-Colonial citizenship, the book argues the importance of imagining different kinds of identities to contest the imperatives of racism and imperialism.

The first part of the book demonstrates the crucial importance of racial specificity as perspective in two theoretical sites: African American cultural history and the difference of race within feminist theory. Chapter two analyzes the problematic role of postcolonial theory—what I have called collaborative postcolonialism—as an explanatory model for questions of race in the United States. Although in the writings of anticolonial liberationists such as Cabral, Fanon, and Cesaire, race was a fundamental category, the language-based, postmodern postcolonialism of today substitutes a universalized notion of marginality for the specificity of located racial analysis and resistance. What, for instance, is the effect of seeing middle passage as a metaphor for post-1960s South Asian professional immigration? At the same time, contemporary postcolonial theorists are increasingly becoming interested in the position of minorities in the United States. Through an analysis of some of the writings of Homi Bhabha, Gayatri Spivak, and Arjun Appadurai—whom I designate as South Asian postcolonial theorists in order to emphasize the positionality of enunciation of theory—I demonstrate how these theorists problematically recruit African Americanism into a homogenized notion of the global margins by dehistoricizing

African American experience and therefore dangerously eliding the effects of differential racism in the United States.

Chapter three takes up the question of racial specificity through an examination of Donna Haraway's postulation of the cyborg as a fluid figure, appropriate for rethinking feminism within global capitalism. It focuses specifically on the problematic appropriation of women of color into a universalized feminism through the use of the race/gender analogy and traces the continuity of the analogical mode of incorporation in Judith Butler's *Bodies That Matter* and Haraway's *Modest Witness@ Second Millenium*. Analogizing U.S. antinuclear demonstrators and third world factory workers, for instance, fails to address the positioning of the two groups of women within late capitalism. This chapter thus emphasizes the political necessity of nurturing critical vocabularies of race and resistance postcolonialism as alternatives to Western feminism in the United States.

The next two chapters move from theory to literary and cultural production, charting a movement within Asian American texts from what I call global imperialism to Post-Colonial resistance. I argue that narratives of cultural globalization are intimately related to (a) narratives of imperialism, and (b) U.S. narratives of race that privilege and normalize whiteness. Chapter four thus turns the lens to three contemporary narratives of globalization. In order not to universalize my own analysis, I examine texts authored by diasporic South Asians who have been part of the post-1965 immigration to the United States: Pico Iyer's travelogue, *Video Night in Kathmandu* (1988), Meena Alexander's memoir, *Fault Lines* (1993), and Bharati Mukherjee's novel, *Jasmine* (1989). All three works rest on tropes of mobility, hybridization, and cultural syncretism. Appadurai hails *Video Night* (a text now routinely used in courses on globalization) as exemplifying the irrelevance of cultural centers and peripheries in the age of globalization. I use *Video Night* to make a simple point: the incessant use of the gendered trope of Orientalism (with its binaries of West/East, male/female) in a text so self-conscious of power dynamics and that strives to emphasize shifting cultural boundaries and the racial hybridity of the narrator, points to the imperialism inherent in many narratives of globalization. I also demonstrate how Iyer's ostensibly mixed global world rests on a normalization of both whiteness and heterosexuality. Similarly, Meena Alexander's *Fault Lines*, which emphasizes an agonistic and shifting construction of racial subjectivity for the displaced female subject of globalization, relies on a problematic self-subalternization and an appropriation of blackness by the privileged academic; in addition, the narrator's diasporic identity depends on an Orientalizing of the homeland (India) that, in accordance with imperialist temporality, is relegated to the past. In contrast to Iyer's and Alexander's texts, Mukherjee's novel details the violent imprintings of imperialist globalization on the landscape and bodies of her characters and suggests that the performance of Orientalism is necessary for the survival of the immigrant; yet the very repression of blackness in Mukherjee's text questions the multicultural horizon she posits. Although I do not wish to draw large conclusions from these three texts, I want to suggest that fetishizations of movement qua movement, hybridity qua hybridity, whether celebratory or otherwise, are caught within the discourses of imperialism for two major reasons: they deny the limits and restraints on the unprivileged subjects of global capital, and they operate through a logic of Orientalist Otherness in which mobility rests on a geopolitical imagining of the developing world through the tropes of stasis, pastness, and/cultural authenticity.

Chapter five positions the photographs of Tseng Kwong Chi, specifically his self-portraits with backdrops of famous U.S. monuments like the Statue of Liberty, against debates about transnationalism as a perspective in Asian American studies. Intervening in this debate, I suggest that Asian American subjectivity, while mobile and transnational, formulates a crucially important resistance through local racial interpellation. Taking the case of Tseng Kwong Chi, a diasporic Taiwanese and putatively Asian American photographer, I demonstrate how Tseng's photographs with national monuments draw upon and critique the construction of the Asian American as inscrutable and outside the national body politic, part of an internal colony, even as the photographs gesture outside the nation, toward China. I thus suggest that the arguments by Asian American critics to discard the ostensibly limited and provincial "claiming America" perspective forged by critics such as Frank Chin and Jeffrey Chan can problematically collude with the "white" racial politics of positioning Asian Americans as perpetual foreigners in the United States.

The postcolonial critique enacted in Tseng's photographs demonstrates the importance of using a specific raced identity as a locus of resistance against the racial project of the nation-state. The final section of the book builds on Tseng's critique and moves to analyses of racial activism. Are there possibilities for anticolonial and anti-imperial solidarity emanating from within the United States that do not preempt the urgent questions of race and local context? Or, to flip the question, do located struggles for racial justice recruit anti-imperial alliances that are urgently needed as alternatives to narratives of globalization? Are anti-imperialist resistances relevant in what is being seen as a decentered world? Can local struggles be useful in formulating anti-imperial movements? The last three chapters delineate moments of anticolonial and anti-imperial solidarity that have been part of the history of located resistances in the

United States and map the structure of a few contemporary resistances that are anticipated in prior historical configurations. Implicitly, this section makes a case for possibilities of located resistances and anticolonial solidarities creating possibilities for Post-Colonial citizenship today.

Chapter six examines the articulation of Post-Colonial citizenship in an energizing moment in the history of racial unrest: the post-civil rights momentum of black liberation struggles of the 1970s. Here I focus particularly on Assata Shakur, who wrote her autobiography as a deliberate political intervention. Shakur's theorizations about resistance offer a compelling alternative to what have been seen as polar oppositions of filiative and affiliative, rooted and rhizomatic, resistances. I would argue that these oppositions, offered by much of postmodern theorizing, are gendered as well. (The frequency with which contemporary black women novelists like Toni Morrison and Gloria Naylor write resistance narratives that figure powerful mother–daughter relationships should be cause enough to question the filiative/affiliative dichotomy.) Refusing to buy into these gendered dichotomies, Shakur emphasizes both the filiative and affiliative nature of black liberation. Black liberation, rooted in African American history, nurtured through the structures of the family, simultaneously achieves self-consciousness and sustenance from worldwide anticolonial and anti-imperial struggle. Assata Shakur, who ends her autobiography by writing for her daughter, for instance, refers to herself as a twentieth-century escaped slave. In the 1970s, anti-imperial struggles thus become both the causes and goals of black liberation. In its ability to enlist both the local, familial, and raced particular, as well as its openness to several third world revolutionary discourses, Shakur's version of black nationalism offers ontologies of resistance theorizing and practices of Post-Colonial citizenship that can be particularly useful today.

From the turbulent politics of black nationalism in the 1970s, chapter seven turns to Native American activism. I use Leslie Marmon Silko's *Almanac of the Dead*, a highly political novel strongly indicting the five hundred years of European colonialism in North America and prophesying an insurrection of the indigenous and other oppressed groups, to examine the mechanisms of Silko's revolutionary politics. At the heart of the novel is a commitment to Native American survival and resistance, conceived through a pan-tribal solidarity. Using the Benjaminian imperative to seize moments of the past in their revolutionary potential, Silko conceives of an almanac as a counterpart to the Mayan codices that survived Spanish destruction. The almanac, the preservation and living history of which becomes central, records the history of colonial conquest and portends the end of European rule. Simultaneously, the present of the novel seethes with revolutionary possibility and imagines a Post-Colonial future. The Indian followers of spiritual leaders Tacho and El Feo join forces with Marxist-indigenist leader, Angelita, and ex-con Barefoot Hopi who raises funds for the return of Indian lands. In turn, Silko envisions cross-racial alliances with Africans who have overthrown European rule, with African Americans in the United States, and with other disinherited peoples. As in Shakur's autobiography, a rooted, filiative allegiance to a racially specific history—that of Native American resistance—becomes the basis for transracial alliances and affiliations and for a critique of the nightmarish present of organ harvesters and transnational land speculators. Contemporary capitalist globalization, as manifested in North America, with Tuscon as a site, becomes not simply a new phenomenon but a continuation of the process of colonization and disinheritance of the Natives that began five centuries ago. Therefore, wresting revolutionary moments in Native American history and bringing them to bear on coalitional insurrections become Silko's tools of enacting a Post-Colonial citizenship in the present. Such coalitional politics, I argue, were prefigured in the work of nineteenth-century Native American activist William Apess and, in different ways, in the memoir of American Indian Movement radical Mary Crow Dog.

In the conclusion, I emphasize the importance of foregrounding key terms such as "race," "imperialism," "oppression," and "postcolonialism" for the understanding of contemporary U.S. culture. I then briefly attempt to map the structures of three types of contemporary resistances in order to chart different kinds of possibilities for Post-Colonial citizenship emanating from them. I first turn to the anti-imperial potentialities of racial activism by examining the contours of the reparations movement and that of the the Partido Nacional La Raza Unida (PNLRU). Emphasizing their outsideness to the nation in terms of rights, groups demanding reparations have emphasized anticolonial solidarities with other constituencies such as indigenous peoples. Next, I turn to the possibilities of anticolonial and anti-imperial movements as exemplified by the International Solidarity Movement that organizes around very specific sites to enlist a Post-Colonial solidarity. By examining the raced discourses surrounding the death of Rachel Corrie in April 2003, I argue that such activists challenge U.S. imperialism by claiming local space and implicitly critiquing the universality of whiteness. However, I do not want to suggest that resistance is possible only when there are highly charged life-and-death or incarceration choices; there are other local resistances that enlist us to support the marginalized and disempowered—migrant workers, domestics—through ethnic or professional affiliations and that participate in postcolonial critique. Here I examine the workings of a New York–based South Asian domestic workers' organization called Workers'

Awaaz as well as a net-based activist group, the campaign to Stop Funding Hate (SFH) directed at charities that funnel monies from the United States to Hindu fundamentalist organizations in India. My argument is that these movements, which are urgently connected to specific racial groups and local struggles, are important in creating anti-imperial solidarities because they engage us at the nodes of imperial power where most of us live our daily lives and where the exercise of imperial power is experienced most directly. These kinds of local struggles are effective in the long term in challenging imperialism because they articulate specific types of resistances and global solidarities that contest the nexus of the national and global raced order today.

A word about the organization of chapters is in order here. All the chapters in the first two parts can be understood on their own, although it would be helpful to read the introduction. What the reader would miss reading the chapters independently is the way the chapters converse with each other. The chapters in the last part follow a chronology, but they also make sense as arguments about resistances at different historical moments. However, the trajectory of the book from theory to practice is an important one and, in that sense, the chapters move in a progression. The fact that Asian American and African American contexts occupy more space than others reflects my own research interests. I do not claim to offer a comprehensive minority study. Nevertheless, the arguments about racial politics and Post-Colonial citizenship derived from these contexts can, with particularist modifications, be useful for thinking about other racial groups as well.

Part One

RACIAL ERASURE IN GLOBAL THEORY

CHAPTER TWO

Expunging the Politics of Location

Articulations of African Americanism in Bhabha, Appadurai, and Spivak

> Whereas the critique posed by African American studies and the alternative (non-Eurocentric) worldview asserted by Afrocentricity cut uncomfortably close to home, postcoloniality seems to offer its opposition from a distance, as Gayatri Spivak might say, "in other worlds."
>
> —Ann Ducille, "Postcolonialism and Afrocentricity"

> To be forced to cross the Atlantic as a slave in chains, to cross the Mediterranean or the Rio Grande illegally, heading hopefully North, or even to sweat in slow queues before officialdom, clutching passports and work permits, is to acquire the habit of living between worlds, caught on a frontier that runs through your tongue, religion, music, dress, appearance, and life. To come from elsewhere, from 'there' and not 'here,' and hence to be simultaneously 'inside' and 'outside' the situation at hand, is to live at the intersections of histories and memories.
>
> —Iain Chambers, *Migrancy, Culture, Identity*

> His foreparents came to America on immigrant ships; my foreparents came to America on slave ships.
>
> —Jesse Jackson, 1988 Address to Democratic Convention in Atlanta

It's ironic that Ann Ducille would take the title of Spivak's 1987 collection, *In Other Worlds*, as a metaphor for postcolonial theory's disengagement from materiality because the trajectory of Spivak's book is explicitly designed to move from the superstructure of Section One (titled "Literature") to the base of Section Two (titled "Into the World") to the resilient, unassimilable reality of the third world of Section Three (titled "Entering the Third World"). Perhaps postcolonial theory's opposition seems distanced to Ann Ducille because few, if any, of its practitioners had dealt with African American culture or U.S. culture at large in 1994, when Ann Ducille published her piece. The influential collection, *The Empire Writes Back* (1989), had declared the United States as the first postcolonial nation, but few had pursued this lead. Edward Said had positioned the United States as a latecomer to Orientalism and had dealt briefly with the United States in both *Orientalism* and *Culture and Imperialism*. Although Said had pointed to the importance of 1960s social movements in challenging imperialism, postcolonial theorists paid little sustained interest to minority cultures in the United States. Shortly thereafter, however, issues surrounding African American literature and culture, and U.S. racial politics generally, began to surface in the writings of postcolonial theorists.

Yet the critique pointed to by Ann Ducille begs further scrutiny. Is it possible that in some versions postcolonial theory, particularly often in what I have called collaborative postcolonialism, the "post" in the postcolonial begins to mark a universality that renders irrelevant the specificities of the raced local? Or has contemporary globalization really produced a worldwide diaspora that we can talk about simply through a language-based common master vocabulary—despite differences between the comfort of work permits and the rigors of surreptitious border crossing—as Iain Chambers does?[1] Does it not matter, as Jesse Jackson reminded Michael Dukakis, what kinds of ships brought people to North America? Do people who've come on very different ships because of racial difference really end up in the same boat? I suggest that homogenized (too often purely linguistic) ideas of global diaspora, migration, and postcoloniality, all of which are being increasingly deployed as emancipatory paradigms, often beyond race, in fact meet their limits when we introduce the question of race.[2] Indeed, Carole Boyce Davies's rejection of postcolonial theory, albeit hasty and reductive, is based partially on some of the theory's recent repudiation of race as an analytical category.[3] Yet U.S. academic postcolonialists, formerly interested largely in European colonization and its aftermath, are now intervening in debates about multiculturalism and ethnicity in the United States. Many are particularly eager to incorporate minority experiences into theorizations of postcolonial, migratory subjectivities that transcend the national. This chapter offers a close examination of the terms of this incorporation by analyzing the conceptualization of race and the representation of African Americans in selected writings of three prominent South Asian postcolonial theorists: Homi Bhabha, Arjun Appadurai, and Gayatri Spivak.

I use the term "South Asian" not to designate a national point of origin, even though the three theorists are disaporic South Asians, but rather to mark their major geopolitical research interests. The major context for Bhabha's theories is the British colonization of India; Appadurai is a South Asian anthropologist; Spivak, who began her career as a Francopohone theorist and critic of British literature, has long since turned her energies to the Indian context. Moreover, for all three critics, India functions as a productive catachresis, a site through which they theorize questions of nation, colonialism, and globalism. Through a brief comparison with the theorizations of race in the works of some influential critical race studies scholars—Omi and Winant, Noel Ignatiev, and Patricia Williams—I consider how the marginalization of locatedness in both the representations of African Americans and the interpretation of race in the writings of South Asian postcolonialists might unwittingly reproduce the racism of a liberal multiculturalism that effaces power relations. The object of my critique is certainly not to condemn all of postcolonial theory or even the theorists examined in this chapter, but rather to demonstrate how an intellectual alignment with diaspora, migration, and transnationalism on the one hand, and on the other, a refusal to take seriously the specificity of racial identities in the United States, in this case even African American identity in the broadest sense, positions these theorists at odds with the project of racial emancipation in the United States. The larger intent of my analysis, as demonstrated in the final part of this book, is to argue that the intellectual concerns of what I have called resistance postcolonialism and those of critical race studies need to come together in order to effectively wage an anti-imperial resistance from the bottom up.

In the context of racial politics in the United States it is useful to note some interesting and conflicting genealogies. Issues of internal racial oppression and colonialism have not, in fact, always been disparate. The 1965 Immigration Act, which radically de-racialized new immigration, was politically related to the Civil Rights Act of 1964, which, in turn, was related to the contradictions of U.S. foreign policy during the cold war.[4] As mentioned in chapter 1, the Third World Movement of the late 1960s combined a critique of internal racial oppression with a critique of colonialism.[5] This movement, we know, did not last long. On the other hand, the growth of hybridity-inspired, collaborative postcolonial theory in the academy since the late 1980s—a period of intense affirmative action backlash and a shift in the social sciences from radical paradigms of race (associated with rights and inequalities) to safer paradigms of ethnicity (cultural difference)—has been nothing short of spectacular.[6] I am by no means suggesting a simple race conspiracy theory for the prestige of postcolonial academic theory in the United States, although I am interested in the problematic erasure of the raced local in some versions of the theory. I am arguing, however, that the production of collaborative postcolonial theory must be analyzed, not only in relation to global capitalism as Arif Dirlik and Aijaz Ahmad have done, but, as importantly, in relation to issues of race and racial politics.[7] Thus, my unusual designation of Bhabha, Appadurai, and Spivak as South Asian postcolonial theorists is a polemical one, designed to localize and racialize theory production and to situate these theorists among other South Asians of the post-1965 migration to the United States.

The trajectory of Homi Bhabha's ideas is captured in his 1994 collection, ironically titled *The Location of Culture*. Most readers of Bhabha are familiar with his concepts of ambivalence, hybridity, interstitiality, liminality, and splitting, all of which are rehearsed in almost every essay in the collection. What is interesting for our purposes, however, is how this collection attempts to incorporate African American theory and culture into postcolonial theory and posits a seamless identity between the two. A look at the back cover of *The Location of Culture* points to the happy marriage of postcolonial and African American. The two endorsements—both of which praise Bhabha as a postcolonial and postmodern theorist—come from Edward Said and Toni Morrison, signifying the merging of postcolonial and African American constituencies both outside and inside the book. A similar theoretical enterprise demonstrably frames the book and is evident in both the introduction and conclusion. In the introduction, Bhabha posits a postcolonial modernity or contra-modernity that emerges from the writings of the migrants, transnationals, and dispossessed. This writing, emanating from interstitiality and unhomeliness, and creating cultural hybridities, interrupts the progressive linear time of modernity through a Benjaminian present of astonishment. From these interstitial and border spaces, Bhabha suggests that politically empowering calls for solidarity and community can be made. Instead of a world literature constituted by different national traditions, the literature of the border might well constitute world literature. At stake is not simply the writing of alternative histories because this would keep intact a binarism between the empowered and disempowered, but an interruption of modernity via disjuncture. For readers familiar with Bhabha's work on mimicry, stereotype, and nation, none of these ideas is particularly new except the manner in which Bhabha now uses these concepts to interrupt the idea of modernity. What is striking about the introduction, however, is the way in which Bhabha uses African American texts as generative for these ideas. Toni Morrison's *Beloved*, in particular, becomes an ur-theoretical text in *The Location of Culture*. The unhomely moment that can be heard in 124 Bluestone Road relates "the traumatic ambivalences of a personal psychic history to the wider disjunctions of political existence."[8] Morrison, like Gordimer, demonstrates the "contemporary compulsion to move beyond, to turn the present into the 'post'" (180). And *Beloved* provides the heading for the last section—"Looking for the Join," the desire for social solidarity.[9]

The very last chapter of *The Location of Culture* is titled "'Race,' Time and the Revision of Modernity," clearly suggesting for Bhabha the centrality of race in the interruption and construction of modernity. Beginning with Fanon, whose performance of displacement interrupts modernity's progressive myth of man, to Houston Baker's reading of the Harlem Renaissance as a 'deformation of mastery,' Bhabha goes on to locate the colonial space as the 'non-space' from which the ideology of modernity as beginning and new starts (237, 241, 246). He critiques Foucault and Anderson, two theorists of modernity, for placing racism outside of modernity (249). Again the interruption of modernity's time, "the time-lag of postcolonial modernity" that "moves forward, erasing that compliant past tethered to the myth of progress," (253) is exemplified in black vernacularism, in Cornel West's construction of a prophetic pragmatic tradition, in Sonia Sanchez's poem, and, most important in *Beloved*. Beloved's presence, "which is profoundly time-lagged, moves forward while continually encircling that moment of the 'not-there' which Morrison sees as the stressed, dislocatory absence that is crucial for the rememoration of the narrative of slavery" (254). The chapter ends with Bhabha making DuBois the precursor for his discourse on the time lag. In this chapter, postcolonial and black become rhetorically interchangeable. Bhabha writes, "subalterns and ex-slaves" seize the spectacular event of modernity (246); "The intervention of *postcolonial or black critique* is aimed at transforming the conditions of enunciation at the level of the sign—where the intersubjective realm is constituted" (247, emphasis mine).

Clearly, Bhabha wants to privilege and centralize African American theory, literature, and art in his text. But since Bhabha is concerned with the expulsion of race from modernity's time in Foucault and Anderson and because the title of the chapter, "'Race,' Time and the Revision of Modernity," signals an urgency about the category of race, we should ask what race really means in *The Location of Culture* and how it is deployed in relation to African American cultural critique. Let us detour a moment to Fanon—another central figure for Bhabha. Working from the epigraph of "The Fact of Blackness," "'Dirty nigger! Or simply, Look, a Negro!'" Bhabha links the effect of this racial interpellation to similar effects in Palestine, Zaire, or Antwerp. "Wherever I am when I hear a racist, or catch his look, I am reminded of Fanon's evocatory essay" (236). Here, what a racist look means or what constitutes racist talk seems incontrovertible and unambiguous. Racism is simply that which marginalizes and condemns on the basis of race. But what Bhabha wants to emphasize about Fanon is a generalized, interstitial positionality of oppression. Fanon, Bhabha writes, "talks not simply of the historicity of the black man, as much as he writes in 'The fact of blackness' about the temporality of modernity within which the figure of the 'human' comes to be authorized" (236). For Bhabha, the particular historicity of the black man about whom Fanon agonizingly writes is not as important as Fanon's questioning of modernity's construction of the human. "Not simply . . . as much as" is also the logic of the chapter titled "Interrogating Identity: Franz Fanon and the Postcolonial Prerogative," in which, by emphasizing "want" in Fanon's "What does the black man want?," Bhabha makes a case for valorizing Fanon simply for his use of the psychoanalytical language of demand and desire and for rarely historicizing the colonial experience (42). Little wonder that Bhabha avoids mention of Fanon's references to the Antilles and that he never deals with *The Wretched of the Earth* or *A Dying Colonialism*. Transnational power relations and materiality are clearly not important. Bhabha writes: "Colonial and postcolonial texts do not merely tell the modern history of 'unequal development' or evoke memories of underdevelopment. I have tried to suggest that they provide modernity with a modular moment of enunciation" (251).

There is nothing wrong with the argument that articulations of colonial experience address central concerns of modernity. Indeed, this kind of generalizing move is a powerful demonstration of continuum between local and global and suggests that colonialism concerns everyone. However, there is something profoundly Westernizing and colonial in the idea that the discursive constructions of the colonized are significant *primarily* insofar as they challenge concepts like modernity, which, for Bhabha, remains, in its origins, a purely abstract and linguistic Western concept that is *thereafter* challenged by Fanon. Just as we are now suspicious of interpretations of theorists that dismiss their overt racism and ethnocentrism by arguing that such minor details are unimportant to the general outlines of speculative theory, so should we be similarly suspicious of readings of colonial experience that dismiss historicity. For instance, we do not simply think of Cecil Rhodes the humanitarian without thinking of Rhodes the imperialist, or of J. S. Mill's *On Liberty* without thinking of his Filtration theory of colonization, or, as Gayatri Spivak has pointed out, Marx without the Asiatic mode of production.[10] It seems like a singular colonial inversion, then, to prize in Fanon simply interventions into narratives of modernity. Kumkum Sangari's argument about how to read postcolonial literature applies also to Bhabha's reading of Fanon. Sangari writes that only celebrating [postcolonial literature's] difference from the center relegates the "'Third World' to the false position of a permanent yet desired challenge to (or subversion of) a suffocating Western sovereignty."[11]

Yet, like many postcolonial critics, including Said, and theorists of nation such as George Mosse, Bhabha also suggests that racism be seen as integral to modernity, and from here he attempts to create a position for postcolonial agency. Racism, he argues, should be viewed "as part of the historical traditions of civic and liberal humanism that create ideological matrices of national aspiration. . . . Such a privileging of ambivalence in the social imaginariness of nation*ness*, and its forms of collective affiliation, would enable us to understand the coeval, often incommensurable tension between the influence of traditional 'ethnicist' identifications that coexist with contemporary secular, modernizing aspirations" (250). Despite the polemic of centering racism, Bhabha still sees an opposition between a secular, rational modernity and ethnicist identification that is supposedly atavistic. Here it is appropriate to consider briefly the differences between Bhabha's approach to race and that of scholars in British cultural studies such as Stuart Hall and Paul Gilroy. While Bhabha shares with them an emphasis on hybridity, syncretism, and cultural fluidity, and particularly with Hall an emphasis on mobile, urban subjects as constitutive of the global-hybrid moment—all reflective of immigration to the center by Britain's formerly colonized—his approach to race differs considerably from that of Gilroy.[12] Gilroy interprets modernity as constitutively black. For Gilroy, racial slavery is "internal to modernity and intrinsically modern" and the specificity of slave experience marks blacks as the first truly modern peoples. The particularities of slave experience, that is, constitute modernity.[13]

It is also important to note how in the previous quote by Bhabha, race is collapsed into ethnicity that is then conflated unproblematically with religion. Race is clearly not an analytical category and the specific operations of racism are not important, even though Bhabha points out that the project of mapping out an enunciative present for interrupting modernity has a descriptive history in African American critics such as Hortense Spillers, Deborah McDowell, and Houston Baker (178). What Bhabha's analysis attempts is a harnessing of the particularities of African American experience and history to a generalized celebration of the postmodern (rerouted as "contramodern") and to a critique of modernity, through the tropes of liminality, interstitiality, hybridity, and ambivalence. The project resembles, in many ways, Deleuze and Guattari's postmodern excitement about the molecular and the rhizomatic, both of which rely on a problematic East–West divide.[14] Moreover, the deep structural resemblances between Bhabha's contramodernity and what Rob Wilson has called simply textual and white-bread postmodernism (in contrast with a particularized, located postmodernism) make any located analysis on Bhabha's terms difficult at best.[15]

My purpose here is not to rehearse the solid critiques of Bhabha's celebration of an ahistorical and purely linguistic hybridity made by critics such as Ella Shohat, Benita Parry, Robert Young, Pheng Cheah, or most recently Hardt and Negri in *Empire*, or to point out the obvious structural resemblances between postmodern marketing strategies and cultural hybridity, but rather to see how these problems affect the manner in which the signifiers of African American history and critique get circulated in Bhabha's texts.[16] This brings us again to Toni Morrison and *Beloved*, the text that for Bhabha exemplifies the liminal moments in which he is interested. In "By Bread Alone," *Beloved* becomes the springboard for a discussion of the possibilities of panic in opening up an interstitial, borderline experience that breaks down the binaries of inside and outside. The repetition of 124 in *Beloved*, as sign of the undecidable, serves as a segue into a discussion of the role of rumor and panic as signs of the agency of the sepoys in the Indian Mutiny as evident in Sir John Kaye's history of the mutiny. There is no discussion of the historicity of the circulation of 124 (whether it takes place during or after Reconstruction is irrelevant), only a marking of it as an affective moment that then gets linked to the circulation of rumor by sipahis of the Indian Mutiny.[17]

This denial of historicity and the privileging of space alone becomes even more problematic in the introduction where *Beloved* is again a major text. Using *Beloved* to illustrate the transnational sense of the hybridity of imagined communities, Bhabha writes: "Toni Morrison's *Beloved* revives the past of slavery and its murderous rituals of possession and self-possession, in order to project a contemporary fable of a woman's history that is at the same time the narrative of an affective, historic memory of an emergent public sphere of men and women alike" (5). Morrison's agonistic representation of slavery opens up the present moment of utterance, although Bhabha does not say how the public sphere will be specifically altered by the haunted presence of slavery. Bhabha continues, "What is striking about the 'new' internationalism is that the move from the specific to the general, from the material to the metaphoric, is not a smooth passage of transition and transcendence. The 'middle passage' of contemporary culture, as with slavery itself, is a process of displacement and disjunction that does not totalize experience" (5). Here we get to the crux of Bhabha's methodology, a belief that the located, historico-specific must and does always get translated to the general, the material to the metaphoric/linguistic in order to interrupt modernity. But at this point it is not misplaced to ask: What are the elisions and suppressions that must be carried out in order to so metaphorize middle passage? What could the middle passage of contemporary culture be? Even if one argues that the brutality of middle passage was not homogenous, as a moment it cannot be simply equated with other contemporary oppressions (or with equivalent oppressions of gender, sexuality, and class through the logic of the comma so prevalent in cultural studies). *Beloved*, with its centering of haunting and interruption of time, is obviously a useful text for discussions of interstitiality and hybridity as long as one brackets racially specific moments that are undeconstructible: the "Sixty Million and more" to whom the novel is dedicated; the moment when Sethe picks up the ice pick to attack Bodwin (322). And, in turn, one must be open to the possibility that what is differentiated and deferred, in the Derridean sense, through interstitiality and unhomeliness might be more than racial essentialim, which is easy to dismiss. It might be black experience (though particularized), which, as Paul Gilroy suggests, functions as the "*changing* rather than an unchanging same," something different from ideas of essentialism or anti-essentialism.[18]

To move from Bhabha's use of the African American voice as an exemplification of a world literature from the margins or a new internationalism that ruptures modernity to Appadurai's conception of a decentered modernity is to enter a celebration of diasporic pluralism in the age of globalism. Although Appadurai is far less invested in claiming an African American constituency than Bhabha is, the strategy by which this constituency is included, and the positionality of this inclusion, need further scrutiny. I will focus particularly on Appadurai's essay, "Patriotism and Its Futures," first published in *Public Culture* in 1990 and subsequently reprinted in a shorter version as "The Heart of Whiteness" in *Callaloo* in 1993. Despite the fact that "The Heart of Whiteness" was solicited by Tejumola Olaniyan in a special issue on "Post-Colonial Discourse," I want to remark on the specific ways in which Appadurai's theory "travels," to use Edward Said's term, from the trans-ethnic diasporic concerns of *Public Culture* to the racially specific concerns of black African American, African, and African diasporic cultures of *Callaloo*.[19]

Most of Appadurai's ideas about the appearance of a global culture without discernible center and periphery, working through global flows, marked by the fact of immigration, were captured in his essay "Disjuncture and Difference in the Global Cultural Economy," which first appeared in *Public Culture* in 1990. In this essay, Appadurai rejects the local as epistemologically helpful. Ethnicity, he writes, "once a genie contained in a bottle of some sort of locality (however large), has now become a global force."[20] In "The Heart of Whiteness," which is largely a reprint of "Patriotism and Its Futures," Appadurai retains this theoretical emphasis on the global and transnational, but, interestingly enough, adds the problematic category of "personal experience" to localize the workings of race. And he argues for the importance of extending the focus of postcolonial studies to include concerns of nation, particularly the United States. It is here, in the attempt to see the local simply as an instance of the global and transnational, that problems become evident:

> Postcolonial discourse studies need to be alert to the ever present danger that they might become another way to contain the unruliness of the postcolony while satisfying the endless appetite of the Western academy for colorful topics. One way to avoid this danger is to ensure that the study of postcolonial discourse should include the United States, where debates about race, urban violence and affirmative action index more general anxieties about multiculturalism, about diasporic diversity and thus about new forms of transnationality.[21]

But in what way, one should ask, are debates about affirmative action really about new forms of transnationality? Does the new transnationalism that Appadurai refers to implicitly assume a post-1965 immigration of professionals (who actually ceased to be the dominant South Asian group since the 1980s) who are repeatedly conjured as illustrative migrants in *Modernity at Large*?[22] Is it useful to index affirmative action debates through the immigration of professionals whose physical and sometimes virtual mobility (in contrast to the immobility of the urban poor of the United States or the peasants of the third world) ensures a constant transnationalism? Might the politics of affirmative action and liberal multiculturalism be entirely opposed? These are questions that cannot be answered in his essay because of Appadurai's theoretical foreclosure of the local and of race as a systemic category that needs to be retained in thinking about African American culture.[23]

The essay, in both versions, is a powerful invocation of a postnational, cosmopolitan culture, utopian in its vision of transnational, progressivist affiliations, but premised on class-specific and nation-specific assumptions. Deterritorialized diasporas, ones in which neither home nor nation are fixed, are the markers of the contemporary world for Appadurai. Such a postnational rethinking of the world is necessary, Appadurai writes, in order to recognize the difference between the United States "being a land of immigrants and being one in a postnational network of diasporas. In the postnational world that we see emerging, diaspora runs with, and not against, the grain of identity, movement, and reproduction. Everyone has relatives working abroad."[24] The two different scenarios Appadurai sketches here—the land of immigrants versus the postnational network—do not of course cover the realities of U.S. society, although the immigrant model is still one espoused by conservative ethnicity theorists. Werner Sollors's model of consent versus descent to describe ethnicity as it develops in the United States (via consent), as opposed to the descent-based ancestral ethnicity of immigrants, depends on a presumed whiteness in which acculturation and assimilation are simply matters of choice.[25] Even though Appadurai, unlike Sollors, is concerned with immigrants of color, the immigrant/postnational model falls far short of accounting for the different nonwhite populations of the United States. Immigration is obviously irrelevant for Native Americans who were the original inhabitants and continue to be colonized, for many Chicana/os who never moved while national borders did, or for most African Americans whose ancestors were forcibly brought on slaveships. And, of course, "everyone" does not have relatives working abroad.[26]

The privileging of immigration and the interpretation of immigration largely as mobility in contemporary U.S. culture explains Appadurai's interpellation of African Americans within a generalized diasporic movement that forecloses attention to the locus of racial enunciation through the linguistic logic of the hyphen and the comma. As I discuss in chapter three, this strategy is similarly used by universalist feminist critics to subsume race under gender. Appadurai writes,

> The formula of hyphenation (as in Italian-Americans, Asian-Americans, and African-Americans) is reaching the point of saturation, and the right-hand side of the hyphen can barely contain the unruliness of the left-hand side. . . . The politics of ethnic identity in the United States is inseparably linked to the global spread of originally local national identities. For every nation-state that has exported significant numbers of its populations to the United States, as refugees, tourists or students, there is now a delocalized *transnation*.[27]

Voluntary mobility and forcible movement, as well as different groups, are problematically mixed here into a generalized idea of transnation. Yet it is only when race (as systemic) is foreclosed that purely diversionary forms of identity such as Italian American can be equated with African American, a trick that liberal theorists of ethnicity (as opposed to radical theorists of race) have well learned. Race in the practice of everyday life is irrelevant here. And while contemporary Asian American communities might be considered part of a delocalized transnation, African Americans of slave descent cannot similarly be theorized as a delocalized transnation. As David B. Wilkins writes, "while black Americans can claim African culture, we have never had the luxury of relying on our African heritage to provide a set of common symbols and beliefs within which we can organize our lives. This history separates us from every other group of hyphenated Americans."[28] Middle passage so muddied the "origins" of African Americans that the question "Where are you from?," for instance, cannot be asked of them as it can be, for instance, of Asian Americans. But just as Bhabha saw African American writing as quintessentially a postmodern border writing of the world, albeit unsettling and disruptive, Appadurai sees African American identity as similar to all diasporic, hyphenated identity constructions—productive, creative, pluralistic.

Appadurai's privileging of a worldwide diaspora as an explanatory paradigm for racial grouping in the United States again undergirds his purely linguistic conceptualization of double hyphenation that is generated by specifying nation. The hyphenated American, Appadurai suggests, "might have to be twice hyphenated (Asian-American-Japanese or Native-American-Seneca or African-American-Jamaican or Hispanic-American-Bolivian) as diasporic identities stay mobile and grow more protean."[29] Here the universalizing logic of globalism encounters a logical dead end. One can see how while immigration patterns, for instance, might invite an intragroup specificity that necessitates a category such as Asian-American-Japanese, the category African-American-Jamaican is really a noncategory. For if Jamaican immigrants need to be interpellated as specifically from Jamaica, they cannot, at the same time, be absorbed into the category "African American" (Jamaica is not in Africa) unless, of course, for African American we substitute "black"—a far more powerful political and racial category, which Appadurai's globalist narrative precludes. Yet, even within Appadurai's own system, the category African American seems to resist incorporation into a generalized double-hyphenation. Appadurai writes, "Or perhaps the sides of the hyphen will have to be reversed, and we become a federation of diasporas, American-Italians, American-Haitians, American-Irish, American-Africans."[30] American Haitians, we note, are differentiated from American Africans and thus the category African American resists double hyphenation.

I have referred to Appadurai's bracketing of the specificity of African American culture and of racial oppression, which obviously occurs through the subjects' location within the complex set of national legal and social racial structures, as foreclosure in the Freudian sense rather than simply exclusion because even in the original essay, "Patriotism and Its Futures," these specificities are present as excesses that need to be vigorously denied in order to put forward a globalist multiculturalism. Thus, it is not surprising that in the *Callaloo* essay, "The Heart of Whiteness," racial oppression and the local emerge as part of the Real in a quasi-hallucinatory form.[31] Remembering an encounter with the Dotbusters (a white New Jersey–based hate-group targeting immigrants from India via the Hindu women's practice of wearing *bindis*/red dots on their foreheads), Appadurai writes,

> I and my fellow migrants from India, had arrived. Someone out there hated me. The stakes of my own diasporic existence here had somehow changed; I was certainly American now. . . . I am now well advanced on the road to becoming a person of color. It's not exactly that I thought I was white before, but as an anglophone academic born in India and teaching in the Ivy League, I was certainly hanging out in the field of dreams, and had no cause to think myself black.[32]

In this use of personal experience, Appadurai invokes the very categories of "white," "black," and "person of color," categories linked through a normalized power-knowledge system of racial oppression in the United States, and the ones he vigorously foreclosed in the celebratory narrative of universal hyphenation in the global diaspora. Appadurai's essay leaves us with the unanswered, yet urgent questions: What does it mean to *think* oneself black in the United States? Is the imaginative identification as black by an upper-class diasporic working in the Ivy League an act of solidarity or a denial of brown privilege? Why is a relationship with blackness central to immigrant groups?

While for Bhabha and Appadurai, questions of race and the political constituency of "African American" are indexed through their interest in migrancy and global diaspora respectively, for Spivak they are indexed through her concerns with the third world and the superexploitation of third world labor in the global economy of neocolonialism. Although Spivak's comments about race and racism are scattered through many of her essays, her two most focused analyses are in the published version of her interveiw during the Cultural Construction of Race Conference in 1985 and in her review essay, "Race Before Racism," originally published in 1993. In both texts, Spivak's project can be described as one of "provincializing" blackness and the black-white racial hierarchy in order to look at "larger issues." Provincializing, as in Dipesh Chakrabarty's provocative use, suggests a deemphasizing, a restriction of the domain of.[33] My brief analysis of both texts asks where this provincializing positions Spivak in relation to race and African American culture.

Spivak critiques the trend of multicultural studies that problematically conflate problems of imperialism with those of immigration and reduce third world problems to problems at home. To illustrate, Spivak points out how at the African Literature Association conventions,

> Black Americans are much more interested in the question of any Black tradition, whereas the Continental Africans are much more interested in the problems that they and their colleagues are making for themselves, in the problems of the various African nations, in the problems existing between European language productions in Africa, and what is happening to African languages as it's all getting organized into philosophy, the discipline of literature, and so on and so forth. What you really mark, is that it is the ones with United States passports who are trying to identify the problems of racism in the United States with what is happening in decolonized Africa.[34]

In the racial concerns of black Americans in a transnational context, Spivak sees a subsumption of the third world by the first. Although not misplaced, this critique depends on a problematic categorization of black Americans within a worldwide system of imperialism. Black Americans are marked as "the ones with United States passports" as if the DuBoisian double-consciousness of being black and American, being subject to a local racial hierarchy, is somehow irrelevant, as if carrying U.S. passports actually gives African Americans de facto citizenship. African Americans simply become citizens of a neocolonial power.[35]

To focus on race, for Spivak, is to indulge in what she calls a "simple chromatism" that participates in the same epistemic violence of colonialism by ignoring the collusion of third world comprador capitalists and the "white" world. Spivak writes:

> The international division of labor does not operate in terms of good whites, bad whites, and blacks. . . . To simply foreclose or ignore the international division of labor because that's complicit with our own production, in the interests of the black-white division as representing the problem, is a foreclosure of neocolonialism operated by chromatic race-analysis.[36]

There are several unresolved problems in the mutually exclusive positions Spivak maps here, not the least of which is the easy slippages of terms. For Spivak, "race," "chromatism," and the "black-white division" are problematically identical. But, as we all know, in the United States questions of citizenship, rights, and national character have been fundamentally tied to race, which, in turn, is related to, but not totally coincident with, skin color. *Plessy v Fergusson*, the famous case that legitimated Jim Crow laws, for instance, was definitely about race, but only incidentally about skin color or chromatism. Homer Plessy was visibly white. The black-white division that Spivak mentions refers both to identity categories and to power apparatuses, but, as the prolific literature on passing suggests, cannot be tied to chromatism. Similarly, although the problems with the international division of labor and those of race in the United States might be very different, they might not be mutually exclusive. As Immanuel Wallerstein suggests, national cases are also part of a world system in which there is a basic division between whites and nonwhites (180);[37] today, the difference between the North and the South is also arguably racialized. Even if we suspend the national and world connection for a moment, let us reverse Spivak's proposition and ask whether the exclusive focus on the neocolonial relation of the United States (U.S. passport holders) to third world labor and a dismissal of race ignores completely the problem of African American oppression and denies, in fact, how revolutionary African American writers from David Walker to Angela Davis have, in fact, affiliated themselves with resistance movements in the third world. Spivak, that is, misses the opportunity of seeing how local racial identities can productively intervene in critiques of neocolonialism.

If I seem to belabor the obvious, it is only because Spivak is minutely aware of the different racial positioning of minorities in the United States and yet often chooses to interpret U.S. racial identities through the prism of the third world, or, more narrowly, South Asia, and thus paradoxically denies the politics of location and the specificity of race in the United States. For instance, Spivak's "Race Before Racism" is a laudatory review of Jack Forbes's *Black Americans and Native Americans*, a work that pays attention to racial mixture and thus offers resistance by questioning the state's legal grouping. Spivak praises Forbes's demonstration of the heterogeneity subsumed under racial markers, the legal reduction of this heterogeneity to a white and nonwhite distinction in the United States, and the structural problem of minorities replicating the power structure by constructing themselves as the Other of the dominant group. Concluding her review, Spivak writes, "Given that, in the literally postcolonial areas such as Algeria or India, white racism is no longer the chief problem, Forbes's historical reasoning is yet another way of bringing together the intuitions of global resistance."[38] Again, Spivak's reading of U.S. race relations through third world postcolonial cultures is problematic because it does not address the problem of specific racialization in the United States. Most obviously, the argument suggests that just because white racism is not a problem in India and Algeria, this "post" of racism should function as a premise in the United States as well. But at this point one is compelled to ask how racialized unequal access to resources within the country can be addressed simply by dismissing white racism.

Yet, although Spivak disallows race as a category of analysis by dismissing it as chromatism, race enters through the back door, as it were, when Spivak writes about the locatedness of South Asians in the United States. Because of the post-1960s brain-drain immigration of Indians in the United States, Spivak writes, "we don't share the same history of oppression with the local Blacks, the east Asians, and the Hispanics; on the other hand, our skins are not white, and since most of us are postcolonials we were trained in the British way, so there is a certain sort of Anglomania in the United States, we can be used as affirmative-action alibis."[39] It is the *nonwhite skins* of Indians, along with their white-associated British (read: privileged) training, that allows Indian immigrants in the United States, particularly those recruited as "professionals," to be used as evidence against affirmative action. Just as Frank Chin had written two decades earlier about Asian Americans functioning as being "not black," Spivak here sees Indian immigrants manipulated in order to serve the needs of a power structure that thrives on black racial oppression.[40] Although the Indian immigrant is obviously constructed by imperialism and her entry into the United States is obviously a product of the international division of labor, within the local space of the United States, that immigrant also functions within a racial hierarchy. Blackness, Spivak recognizes here, cannot simply be provincialized in relation to the "larger" concerns of the third world. Lenin needs to be tempered by Fanon.

Because most of Spivak's oeuvre is insistent on a scrupulous historicity, her work has the possibility of offering valuable insights into the functioning of race in the United States through a local-global dialectic and of productively linking antiracism in the United States with anti-imperialism, the animus of postcolonial critique. There is potential, for instance, in the occasional moment of comparative analysis such as the one in the essay, "The Political Economy of Women as Seen by a Literary Critic" in which she argues the importance of maintaining distinctions between the subjects of "post-modern neocolonialism" who are reentering a "feudal mode of power" and ethnic subjects in the United States who are "still caught in some way within structures of colonial subject-production . . . especially, from the historical problem of ethnic oppression on First World soil."[41] At present, however, such analyses remain incidental in her work.[42]

Unlike the conceptualizations of race in the writings of South Asian postcolonial theorists previously discussed, the work of critical race theorists (despite variations among their formulations) offers a fundamentally different approach. These differences, in turn, point to both the problems and possibilities of incorporating specific minority identities, resistances, and exclusions within a narrative of globalized diaspora or transnational capitalism. Interestingly, none of the postcolonial theorists discussed above maintains any engagement with, or awareness of, critical race studies.[43] At the outset, because it has become the straw man for those seeking to negate the significance of race, it bears reiteration that, for these theorists, race is not biological or fixed, but sociocultural and fluid. It is a postfoundational concept. As Omi and Winant point out, race is "*an unstable and 'decentered' complex of social meanings constantly being transformed by social struggle.*"[44] As discussed in chapter 1, this does not mean that racial categories do not have decisive and painful effects. Thus, the second most important characteristic of race studies: all agree about the centrality of race in U.S. society. Omi and Winant's concept of racial formation, which has proven indispensable to cultural critics, depends on this centrality. Racial formation refers to "the process by which social, economic, and political forces determine the content and importance of racial categories, and by which they are in turn shaped by racial meanings. Crucial to this formulation is the treatment of race as a central axis of social relations which cannot be subsumed under or reduced to some broader category."[45]

Seeing race as central, however, does not mean denying the importance of other identity categories such as gender, class, or religion, but it does mean seeing every identity, institution, and social practice in the United States as being saturated with race. Thus, Noel Ignatiev's pioneering study, *How the Irish Became White*, positions itself as a corrective to works by labor historians that either ignore race or see race simply as a disguise for class. Ignatiev demonstrates how the Irish, themselves fleeing caste oppression, adapted to a society in which "color was important in determining social position" by choosing to become white by embracing white supremacist positions.[46] Ignatiev sees no use for the term "racism," which denotes only individual prejudice; he focuses instead on racial oppression and demonstrates the centrality of race to the formation of an American working class. Moments when an anticapitalist coalition becomes a real possibility are not realized, he demonstrates, because of the "alliance with capital on the basis of a shared 'whiteness' "on the part of some workers."[47] Similarly, David Roediger sees whiteness as a psychological wage that white workers accept in lieu of better wages.[48]

Privileging race for critical race theorists does not mean embracing a racial essentialism or static binarism. Indeed, Patricia Williams's project of race(ing) the color blindness of law is also, and as important, a critique of the hypostatization of exclusive categories that mark legal understanding in Anglo-American jurisprudence: "rights/needs, moral/immoral, public/private, white/black."[49] Thus, Williams challenges the traditional legal understanding of redhibitory vice (a defect in merchandise which renders it useless), based on a perfect/defect distinction, by invoking an 1835 case in Louisiana in which the redhibitory vice was the alleged craziness of Kate, a slave whom the plaintiff had purchased for $500.[50] Indeed her own paradoxical social interpellation as black and nonblack simultaneously questions clear racial dichotomies and emphasizes the importance of racial categorization. For instance, Williams notes how she is interpellated as nonblack when colleagues include her as part of "us," urging her not to make too much of her race because they don't even think of her as black, and how she is viewed as (good) black when another (troublesome) black woman colleague engages in an unsuccessful tenure battle.[51]

Finally, as discussed in chapter 1, critical race studies privilege locatedness or what Richard Delgado terms the "call to context" that challenges the traditional juridical preference for universalism over particularism and abstract principles over perspectivism.[52] This critique of universalism is of course not news to anyone since the 1960s. Poststructuralism's challenging of Western metaphysics as based on a structure of hierarchical binary oppositions, French feminisms' focus on the gendered versions of these oppositions, feminists of color's critiques of the raced construction of woman in white feminism, subaltern studies' provincializing of the concepts of Western liberal democracy are all challenges to universalism. However, postcolonial theory, in what I have called its collaborative versions, has, despite its poststructuralist bases, created its own universalisms that, while not claiming the humanism of the Enlightenment or the progressive teleology of modernity, serve to ignore the locatedness necessary when thinking about race. At the same time, as my analysis of Bhabha, Appadurai, and Spivak reveals, what seem to manifestly be generalizations about diaspora and transnationalism often turn out to be implicitly about the South Asian diaspora or, specifically, Indian colonization. A postcolonial homogenization operates in such moves: Bhabha's notion of a new internationalism based on migrancy, Appadurai's dismissal of the global-local dialectic in favor of a global diaspora, and Spivak's privileging of what she terms the third world at large.

How does this foreclosure of the local in these theorists' thinking about race position the theory itself in relation to contemporary U.S. culture? At one level, there is a structural resemblance between the idea of white as norm and of a normative idea of migrancy. At another level, the very presence of narratives of race and the African American presence in South Asian postcolonial theory suggest, as Toni Morrison has pointed out about whiteness in *Playing in the Dark*, that these theorists construct themselves in some way in response to blackness.[53] It remains to speculate on what the nature of this construction is. Is the relationship of this theory the one first outlined by Frank Chin and reiterated by many other

Asian American critics that the function of Asian Americans is to be not black?[54] Clearly this question cannot be answered in the affirmative. Bhabha's positioning of *Beloved* as a master text in the interruption of modernity and his linking of it to diasporic South Asian texts like Rushdie's *The Satanic Verses*, as well as other diasporic texts, suggests a commonality of the marginalized; Appadurai's hyphenated Americans together form a broad community that includes African Americans; Spivak points to a community constructed by imperialism, even though she recognizes the model minority function of South Asians. But this move to solidarity still poses the further question of whether South Asian postcolonial theory formulates possibilities for progressive identifications and alliances with African Americans and a basis for critiquing racial oppression. These possibilities are present in the theories to be sure, but are also undermined, I contend, when the theorists make linguistic similarity rather than historical difference the basis for an alliance.

At another level, these questions have to do with the relationship of postcolonial theory to African American studies. Although, as chapter 1 has suggested, neither of these fields is a unified monolith, existing absolutely apart from each other, and although many thinkers such as W. E. B. DuBois, Martin Luther King Jr., Angela Davis, and Richard Wright have seen a continuity between African American and other struggles of the colonized, the political trajectories of African American and postcolonial studies have been different. The problematic treatment of race in the work of some postcolonial theorists, at times a denial of race as an analytical category, despite the brilliant articulations on race by Fanon, have resulted in theoretical blind spots that have made connections between the fields tenuous.[55] On the flip side, there has been the assumption that while African American studies naturally intersects with the field of black diaspora, it has little connection with issues of colonialism, imperialism, and neocolonialism outside of Africa. This is an assumption that has recently been challenged in works like Vijay Prashad's *Everybody Was Kung Fu Fighting* and Bill V. Mullen's *Afro-Orientalism*. And possibilities for theoretical cross fertilization are being articulated by scholars such as Kenneth Mostern who are demonstrating the persistence of postcolonial tropes and the inseparability of postcolonial and racial concerns in the writings of African American intellectuals far predating the advent of postcolonial theory.[56]

CHAPTER THREE

Border Crossing, Analogy, and Universalism in (White) Feminist Theory

The Color of the Cyborg Body

While theorizing a transnational feminist practice, Inderpal Grewal and Caren Kaplan call attention to the problems of a global feminism predicated on a "relativistic linking of 'differences'" and articulate the need the need to address the concerns of women "in the historicized particularity of their relationship to multiple patriarchies as well as to international economic hegemonies."[1] Grewal and Kaplan, that is, sound a cautionary note against postulating a feminism without attention to the specificity of power relations. Racial difference remains an important challenge of historical specificity to an age that is being theorized as one of global flows and border crossings. However, it might seem as if located concerns of race have, in fact, long been adequately addressed within feminist theory. Since the 1970s, when African American and Latina feminists challenged the universality of white feminism, it seems to have been understood among feminist theorists that questions of race, colonialism, and imperialism that require attention to the historical particularities of oppression in different locations were being suitably addressed within gender studies. Indeed in the early 1980s, Adrienne Rich issued an injunction to Western, white feminists to interrogate whiteness, to recognize "our location, having to name the ground we're coming from, the conditions we have taken for granted," intimating that feminist theory could no longer be uncritically universalist.[2] Since then, an inclusion of a chapter on race in nearly every book on feminist theory in the United States has become standard fare. It has also become a given that works in gender/sexuality studies acknowledge multiple axes of oppression or invoke the mantra of race, class, gender, and sexuality. In the age of global capitalism when the language of globalization places a premium on the rhetoric of border crossing, hybridity, network, and flows, feminist theories have also focused on a destabilization of the boundaries of gender and sexuality, often through the vector of racial difference. Yet, as Caren Kaplan notes, "The theoretical celebration of difference and pluralism that marks much of feminist poststructuralist criticism in the United States more often has led to a relativism that masks appropriation."[3]

But how has the celebration of difference indeed been an appropriation? What are the terms of this appropriation? It is imperative to push further into the means of appropriation, to understand the methodology by which racial difference gets incorporated into and bracketed under gender difference, locatedness under a generalized language of border crossings if we are to understand the continuity of the project of universalism within feminist theory, even as universalism is ostensibly being challenged as imperialistic. In a remarkably prescient analysis of sexism and racism, with particular reference to black women, Elizabeth Spelman referred to the critical practice of seeing as extra the racial burden that black women had to bear, as "additive analysis." Spelman writes, "An additive analysis treats the oppression of a black woman in a sexist and racist society as if it were a *further* burden than her oppression in a sexist but non-racist society, when, in fact, it is a *different* burden."[4] Additive analysis, in other words, seeks to incorporate particularities and differences as additions to a common universalist narrative. Two decades since the publication of Spelman's essay, additive analysis still continues, albeit in different forms. By examining the terms of racial incorporation in a major essay that positions itself within the globalized society of late capitalism—Donna Haraway's "A Cyborg Manifesto: Science, Technology, and Socialist-Feminism in the Late Twentieth Century"—I argue that this essay offers the dominant paradigm of a problematic incorporation of the woman of color in contemporary gender/sexuality studies: incorporation by analogy. Indeed, as my analysis of Haraway's essay will suggest, the acontextual celebration of hybridity and difference as markers of a global, marginalized sisterhood resembles South Asian postcolonial theorists' incorporation of African American difference into a narrative of diaspora and migration.[5]

I focus on this essay written twenty years ago, not because of a desire to pigeonhole white feminism in a time warp, but for several important reasons. First, Haraway's essay remains an influential treatise on feminist theory as configured through what are seen as key elements of globalization: the porosity of borders and transnational connections. Second, Haraway's methodological emphasis on border crossings and hybridity resonates with much of globalization theory and globalization-inspired postcolonial theory or collaborative postcolonialism. Finally, because it proleptically configures the pervasive mode of analogical racial incorporation that continues, albeit with significant changes, till today and because this dangerous project of universalism continues within the rhetoric of globalization, diaspora, migration, and hybridity. My critique of Haraway is thus made in the spirit of advancing feminist theory toward a progressive affiliation with critical race studies and what I have called resistance postcolonialism. It is in this spirit that I turn briefly at the end of the chapter to recent key texts of feminist theory in which race has been addressed. I argue that while Judith Butler's *Bodies That Matter* and Donna Haraway's *Modest Witness @ Second Millennium* substantially further feminist theory's investigation of race, they simultaneously continue to include race analogically, thus subsuming the located concerns of race under what are deemed as more important rubrics—those of sexuality for Butler and those of border crossing for Haraway.

THE COLOR OF THE CYBORG BODY

Donna Haraway's utopian meditations on human-machine borders in "A Cyborg Manifesto" pose important questions about the relationship between feminist/sexuality/gender studies and questions of race. In the tradition of a located feminist politics, Haraway calls attention to her own raced subject position, stringently critiques the idea of a common feminist language, uses the insights of some men and women of color for her theory, and frequently marks the position of women of color as a site for her conception of a cyborg identity. But it is precisely because Haraway invokes women of color so frequently in her essay and because the cyborg myth has been received so enthusiastically by poststructuralist feminists and seems to speak so adequately to the needs of globalization, that we need to understand and interrogate the relationships between the cyborg myth and women of color.

What is a cyborg? Haraway provides different descriptions, all of which emphasize its partial, shifting, nontotalizing, and subversive nature:

> A cyborg is a cybernetic organism, a hybrid of machine and organism, a creature of social reality as well as a creature of fiction.[6]

> The cyborg is resolutely committed to partiality, irony, intimacy, and perversity. It is oppositional, utopian, and completely without innocence. (151)

> . . . holistic politics depend on metaphors of birth and invariably call on the resources of reproductive sex. I would suggest that cyborg have more to do with regeneration. . . . We require regeneration, not rebirth, and the possibility for our reconstitution includes the utopian dream of the hope for a monstrous world without gender. (181)

The cyborg is a resource for two major domains: the new computerized and globalized mode of production, and the need for a broad, though not totalizing, feminist solidarity. The idea of the cyborg, derived from the human-machine figures of science fiction, provides a resource, Haraway suggests, for combating the information-based society of late capitalism that has intensified domination in increasingly new ways. She argues that the preponderance of computer technology in creating antilabor home economies and globalization can be significantly challenged by embracing the breaching of the human-machine border signified by the cyborg. For feminism, the cyborg promises possibilities other than those based on the maternal, the pre-Oedipal, or the universalizing. The cyborg provides "pleasure in the confusion of boundaries" and critiques the imperialism of a common feminist language. Haraway's aspiration is to provide an image for a politics that can "embrace partial, contradictory, permanently unclosed constructions of personal and collective selves and still be faithful, effective—and, ironically, socialist-feminist" (157).

There is nothing particularly new or different about the politics Haraway articulates if one compares it to different versions of French poststructuralist theory or to postcolonial theory in its postmodern, linguistic guise (what I have called collaborative postcolonialism). Ernesto Laclau and Chantal Mouffe's ideas of resistance, for instance, are based on radical pluralism, the blurring of frontiers, and the unsutured character of the social.[7] For Deleuze and Guattari, the schizophrenic (like the cyborg) ruptures wholeness and puts disjunctions to affirmative use. "He is and remains in disjunction."[8] Deleuze and Guattari's later concepts, such as rhizomatic thought and the nomadism, are similar attempts to name disruptive ontologies. Similarly, Haraway's politics has much in common with Homi Bhabha's valorization of interstitial and border spaces as sites for solidarity and his celebration of hybridity as a metaphor for postcolonial writing, colonial discourse, and colonized identities.[9] Finally, Haraway's utopian proclamations about cyborg possibilities anticipate Hardt and Negri's theorization of the multitude, although the latter is problematically devoid of gender consideration.

The danger here lies in feminist theory simply repeating the universalizing knowledge claims of Western colonialism, the universality of global capitalism, and even the ubiquity of U.S. cultural hegemony, by celebrating an ahistorical and acontextual, indeed almost purely linguistic, blurring of boundaries. For instance, might the blurring of racial boundaries be an obfuscation of the systemic racial oppression and racial hierarchies that continue to affect women's lives? Indeed, Haraway herself seems to recognize the necessity of context-specific theory much in the manner of critical race theorists in her own paradigm of situated knowledge. Positing an alternative to a value-free relativism that she declares to be the "perfect mirror twin of totalization," Haraway suggests an alternative that is "partial, locatable, critical knowledg[e] sustaining the possibility of webs of connections called solidarity in politics and shared conversations in epistemology." "Our problem, is how to have *simultaneously* an account of radical historical contingency for all knowledge claims and knowing subjects, a critical practice for recognizing our own 'semiotic technologies' for making meanings, and a no-nonsense commitment to faithful accounts of a 'real' world, one that can be partially shared."[10]

It is in the spirit of Haraway's own call for partial and locatable knowledge that I mean to examine the relationship between Haraway's concept of the cyborg and the women of color who figure so prominently in the essay. Such an analysis also reveals the problematic nature of the concept of woman of color as used by Haraway. I have already mentioned the overly celebratory nature of Haraway's cyborg myth as a means of resisting the domination of a thoroughly technologized information culture and as a description of that culture. Haraway writes, "By the late twentieth century, our time, a mythic time, we are all chimeras, theorized and fabricated hybrids of machine and organism: in short, we are cyborg. The cyborg is our ontology; it gives us our politics. . . . This chapter is an argument for *pleasure* in the confusion of boundaries and for *responsibility* in their construction" (150). The cyborg enables a productive blurring of the binaries such as male/female, self/other, culture/nature that have sustained Western cultural hierarchies.

Just as the cyborg provides the means whereby to resist repressive dichotomies through unnatural fusions and illegitimate couplings, Haraway suggests that the political constituency of women of color offers a means of constructing a political solidarity out of coalition and affinity rather than essential identity. Unlike identities based on sameness or unity, this postmodern identity is premised on "otherness, difference, and specificity" (155). Chela Sandoval's model of 'oppositional consciousness,' which suggests a mode of articulation seized by those denied stable identities of race or gender, demonstrates to Haraway the subversive potential of the coalition, women of color. Thus, women of color becomes for Haraway a cyborg identity, "a potent subjectivity synthesized from fusions of outsider identities" (174). By the end of the essay, the analogous relationship of women of color to the illegitimate and hybrid fusion of the cyborg is clear. Haraway moves to delineate aspects of the cyborg myth by looking at "two overlapping groups of texts . . . constructions of women of color and monstrous selves in feminist science fiction" (174). What follows are illustrations of subversive political identities formulated by women of color such as Audre Lorde and Cherrie Moraga and feminist science fiction writers such as Joanna Russ, Samuel R. Delaney, James Tiptree, Jr., Octavia Butler, and Vonda McIntyre.

Tracing a partial trajectory of Haraway's complex essay still leaves us with a few nagging questions: Why are women of color needed to formulate a cyborg myth centrally based on the monstrous fusion of human and machine? Who are the women of color referred to in the essay? Let us attempt to answer the second question first. Clearly the term "women of color" (it usually appears in quotation marks in the essay) alludes to radical African American, Chicana, Native American, and Asian American feminists who constituted themselves as a group apart from white U.S. feminists. Chela Sandoval's formulation of oppositional consciousness that Haraway cites was preceded by the formation of Kitchen Table: Women of Color Press and the publication of the influential anthology *This Bridge Called My Back: Writings by Radical Women of Color*, edited by Cherrie Moraga and Gloria Anzaldua in 1981. Subsequently, the term women of color gained widespread critical and pedagogical usage.

Let us now see how Haraway explains the first question. Haraway regards the writings of women of color as postmodern resistance writing or cyborg writing. Like all colonized groups, women of color seize the power to write in order to resignify hegemonic Western myths: "The poetry and stories of US women of color are repeatedly about writing, about access to the power to signify; but this time that power must be neither phallic nor innocent. . . . Cyborg writing is about the power to survive, not on the basis of original innocence, but on the basis of seizing the tools to mark the world that marked them as other. . . . Figuratively and literally, language politics pervade the struggles of women of color" (175). Haraway's claims for the writings of women of color are similar to the arguments of scholars who see minority writing or postcolonial writing as resistance writing alone. However, such an argument not only reifies the very binaries of center and margin, colonizer and colonized, that Haraway as poststructuralist wishes to blur, but also homogenizes, through a colonial imperative, the margin itself, a tactic strongly critiqued by feminists like Chandra Mohanty.[11]

Let us revisit, for a moment, the two groups of texts Haraway compares: "constructions of women of color and monstrous selves in feminist science fiction." The one includes a variety of texts (presumably including autobiographies, novels, poetry, and drama) by a racially marked group; the other deals with grotesque bodies in a specific genre. One would be hard-pressed to find similar generalizations about white U.S. women's writings, but women of color become fair game here as did all third world texts in Frederic Jameson's much contested claim about these texts being national allegories.[12] Here, I would argue in similar fashion to Aijaz Ahmed that many texts of women of color are not about access to the power to signify or about subverting either the central origin myths of Western culture or myths of original innocence.[13] Indeed, the very assumption that texts of U.S. women of color are centrally *about* subverting Western myths suggests that minority texts are significant only insofar as they relate to the center. Many texts of U.S. women of color—Toni Morrison's *Beloved* and Fae Myenne Ng's *Bone* are powerful examples—are not fundamentally about subverting Western myths. Morrison's and Ng's texts, specifically located within African American and Chinese American histories, speak to questions of culture and survival within those communities and are not primarily positioned against some putative Western ontology. Further, simply to suggest that writings about women of color are "repeatedly about writing" is to simply reiterate the discursive postmodern truism that all fiction is metafiction. Moreover, the very distinction between women of color and feminist science fiction writers begs the obvious question: Is Octavia Butler (who is included in the category of feminist science fiction) not a woman of color?

I have already pointed out the similarities between the politics of the cyborg myth and that of poststructuralist politics. I would argue that the similarity also extends to the proclivity of some poststructuralists, in their attempts to question and destabilize Western ontologies, to view the East, in a kind of reverse Orientalism, as a repository of horizontality, multiplicity, and difference. Thus, Deleuze and Guattari's rhizomatic model is derived from the East (Oceania in particular) while the idea of the plateau comes from Gregory Bateson's work on the non-orgasmatic libidinal economy of Balinese culture.[14] Poststructuralist feminism of course has a long history of romanticizing the East. Luce Irigaray's recently translated *Between East and West* (2002), which looks back to pre-Aryan India as a golden age of gender in a manner reminiscent of colonial British Indologists, is in line with Julia Kristeva's earlier analysis of footbinding as a strong cultural recognition of the phallic mother.[15] I am not suggesting that Haraway's deployment of women of color is coded with the degree of nostalgia as are the uses of the East by Irigaray and Kristeva, but the need to locate a homogenized non-Western Other onto which fantasies can be projected, precisely in order to subvert the hierarchies of Western metaphysics, is an overdetermined Western, and I might add neocolonial, gesture that Haraway is implicated in.[16]

If the constituency "women of color" names somewhat problematically the writing practices of these U.S. women, Haraway's broader use of the term to similarly encompass female workers in multinationals in third world countries as well as in the Silicon Valley bespeaks an indiscriminateness that dangerously elides cultural, political, and class differences. Haraway's gesture here is similar to the absorption of African American difference within formulations of race by South Asian postcolonial theorists. Haraway's women of color include "unnatural cyborg women making chips in Asia" (154), women in the Silicon Valley, "young Korean women hired in the sex industry" (174), and the "real-life cyborg (for example the Southeast Asian village women workers in Japanese and US electronic firms. described by Aihwa Ong)" (177). Of course one must praise Haraway as a feminist for drawing attention to the most oppressed of workers within the circuit of multinational capitalism. It is also scintillating to have these workers brought together in a subversive, oppositional moment with U.S. women writers of color. But juxtaposition does not translate into a connection or a relationship. Indeed, the obfuscation of the differences between the two denies not only class differences but also the distinction between what Spivak calls the subjects of "Postmodern neocolonialism" who are reentering a"feudal mode of power" and ethnic subjects in the United States who are "still caught in some way within structures of colonial subject-production; and especially, from the historical problem of ethnic oppression on First World soil."[17] So while one might agree with Haraway that the alliance between Asian women workers making microchips and antinuclear demonstrators spiral dancing in a Santa Rita jail would be energizing and powerful, it cannot be articulated without an acknowledgment of the historical and political difference of the demonstrators that positions them, in however weak a fashion, as simultaneous beneficiaries of globalization even as they protest it, and with different interests than Asian women laborers who, in the interests of feeding their families, might not always join the protesters against multinationals. Indeed, although the need for forging anti-imperial, postcolonial connections is ever more imperative today, I suggest that such connections are most useful when located resistances within the nation articulate specific connections with other resistances and then link together macrologically both within and outside the nation to create a dynamic exchange of ideas, strategies, and political solidarity. The last part of this book maps out the potentiality of some of these located, race-based resistances in the United States.

I have focused at length on the deployment of the category "women of color" because Haraway's attempt to articulate an oppositional ontology and politically effective strategy for feminism that includes women of color is to be lauded. Yet if the practice entails a disregard for historical specificity and locatedness, it avails itself of the universalizing and unmarked privileges of whiteness, a problem that also dogs much of globalization theory. It also runs the risk of becoming simply linguistic. As Abby Wilkerson suggestively points out, it might be worth asking "whether many white feminists have enthusiastically taken up the cyborg myth precisely because of what it does not say about race."[18] Wilkerson argues that taking up the hybrid identity of the cyborg might well be a way of not assuming responsibility for whiteness while appropriating the identity politics of women of color.[19] Ontologically, the move resembles globalization and diaspora postcolonial theorists' problematic homogenizing of racial differences under an umbrella category of immigration, while appropriating African Americanism. The same might be said of similar universalizing gestures animating the poststructuralist theorists' use of the East discussed earlier.

We can now understand the relationship between the cyborg and women of color. At one level, there is no relationship, only oneness. Since in the informatics of domination we cannot all help being cyborgs, women of color are cyborgs. But the ultimate relationship is again analogical. Just as the cyborg is a fusion of human and machine, a monstrous and illegitimate fusion, so, the argument goes, is the constituency of women of color, forged as it is without identity. Thus, is it not surprising that race sometimes figures in Haraway's essay as part of an undifferentiated, analogical series in which the different matrices governing race and gender/sexuality are not recognized: "Race, gender, and capital require a cyborg theory of wholes and parts" (181). "The causes of various women-headed households are a function of race, class, or sexuality" (167). "Some of the rearrangements of race, sex, and class rooted in high-tech-facilitated social relations can make socialist-feminism more relevant to effective progressive politics" (165). Cyborg identities, mediated through the politics of women of color, help defuse, or, to use Wilkerson's terminology, deny the responsibility of working with whiteness and white feminist social and historical location. Haraway's stated reasons for turning to women of color make this clear. Haraway writes:

> For me—and for many who share a similar historical location in white, professional middle-class, female, radical, North American, mid-adult bodies—the sources of a crisis in political identity are legion. The recent history for much of the US left and US feminism

> has been a response to this kind of crisis by endless splitting and searches for a new essential unity. But there has also been a growing recognition of another response through coalition—affinity, not identity. (155)

The coalitional politics through which white women join forces with women of color while continuing to treat race and gender as analogous modes thus suggests that racial analogy within (white) feminist theory helps whiteness retain its privilege by being uninterrogated.

PERFORMANCE AND ITS OTHERS

Since the mid-1980s, the gender/race/sex analogy has only proliferated in feminist theory even as new paradigms for conceptualizing gender have been put forward. Arguably, the most influential model has been the model of performance, articulated by Judith Butler in 1990 in *Gender Trouble*. Indeed, her work continues to garner paramount critical attention within gender studies today where performance is seen as central to the construction of identities that are mobile, shifting, and hybrid, identities central to a postnational world. It is important, therefore, to trace the workings of race within Butler's theorizations of performance. I do not intend this analysis to be by any means an exhaustive critique of Butler's impressive oeuvre, but rather a focused examination of her theorizations about race and gender in a few limited moments. Because Butler has, in fact, made sustained attempts to think productively about race and gender, an analysis of her theories reveals both the limits of adding race as a vector within gender and queer theory and the need for progressive possibilities resultant on a historically specific intersection of the two.

In *Gender Trouble*, Butler proposed the idea of gender as a performance, constructed in the very act of performing and a challenge to the ubiquity of gender categories. Although at moments Butler alerted readers to the punitive system of gender performances within compulsory social systems, the book proliferated the idea of gender as infinite, individualistic performance, as rebellious carnival, without much attention to the pains and problems of performing.[20] Considerations of race are virtually unaddressed in the book. However, at the end of the book, Butler confronts the epistemology of theories that "elaborate predicates of color, sexuality, ethnicity, class, and able-bodiedness" and "invariably close with an embarrassed 'etc.' at the end of the list."[21] Butler suggests that the "etc." should not be read as a sign of failure but as a sign of the "illimitable process of signification itself," the "excess that accompanies any effort to posit identity once and for all."[22] Problematically, what Butler questions here is only the idea of an identity prior to signification, not the analogizing of vastly different vectors such as able-bodiedness and color.

In *Bodies That Matter* (1993), a book that begins, significantly with an epigraph from Haraway's "A Cyborg Manifesto," Butler begins to ponder the problems of the analogical model, although race is arguably still added to theorizations about gender and sexuality. The bulk of the introduction theorizes the constructedness of "sex" and interrogates the critical assumption of a prior, unmarked category of sex onto which gender is culturally imposed. Instead of constructedness, Butler proposes the notion of matter, a process that "*produce[s] the effect of boundary, fixity, and surface we call matter*."[23] Sex and the contours of the body, Butler argues, are regulated by the heterosexual imperative. It is only much later in the introduction, after the theorizations of the body, sex, and matter have been made, that Butler presents, as part of her chapter summaries, the idea that "normative heterosexuality is clearly not the only regulatory regime in the production of bodily contours."[24] Structurally, that is, body, sex, and matter are constituted as the main items of theory to which race is added. As Butler argues, race is not simply another domain separable from sexual difference "but that its 'addition' subverts the monolithic workings of the heterosexual imperative as I have described it so far."[25] Although Butler is clearly aware of the problems of simply adding race to the understandings of the body and of sex, her own positioning of race in the introduction is nonetheless additive. Yet Butler goes on to suggest a focus on the specificities as well as intersections of race and gender construction:

> It seems crucial to resist the model of power that would set up racism and homophobia and misogyny as parallel or analogical relations. The assertion of their abstract or structural equivalence not only misses the specific history of their construction and elaboration, but also delays the important work of thinking through the ways in which these vectors of power require and deploy each other.[26]

Butler's attention to the problems of analogizing, though a small portion at the end of the introduction, is a welcome turn in gender theory, and indeed a crucial, methodological process that must be sustained if the located concerns of race are not to be marginalized within what are often perceived to be the "larger" questions of gender. Butler's decision to focus on texts such as *Paris Is Burning* and Nella Larsen's *Passing* is also an important step in theorizing conjunctures, convergences, and relationships between race and gender. Yet, in the spirit of furthering rigorous analysis into these very areas, I want to suggest that Butler's analyses need to be interrogated through the critical paradigms she herself has set up at the end of her introduction.

Let us focus here specifically on questions of race and appropriation, particularly brought to light by bell hooks's criticism of *Paris Is Burning* to which Butler responds. Butler considers the ways in which drag is a site that questions the manner in which hegemonic heterosexuality reproduces itself through imitation and performance. Reading Venus Xtravaganza's desire to become a "real" woman and drag performance as a "contesting of realness," Butler argues that such performances expose the norms that regulate realness and also the fact that "norms of realness by which the subject is produced are racially informed conceptions of 'sex.'"[27] hooks's critique of the film centers on Jennie Livingstone's role as a white lesbian woman ethnographer, photographing subjects of color, but imperialistically concealing her own standpoint in the film. Butler accedes to the problem of the raced gaze, but offers a reading that presents itself as problematically analogical. Butler writes, "hooks is right to argue that within this culture the ethnographic conceit of a neutral gaze will always be a white gaze . . . . But what does it mean to think about this camera as an instrument and effect of lesbian desire?"[28] Butler, that is, rewrites the question of race as a question of sexuality, the underlying assumption being that one can be substituted for the other. Thus, although Butler suggests that to an extent the camera assumes the place of the phallus, she suggests that the cinematic gaze is not simply white and phallic *because* the occasion of drag balls constructs kinship relations outside the heterosexual family. Being outside heterosexuality, by analogy, means being outside whiteness. Butler writes, "If the signifiers of whiteness and femaleness . . . are sites of phantasmatic promise, then it is clear that women of color and lesbians are . . . excluded from this scene."[29] I am not arguing that whiteness as hegemony does not greatly legislate heterosexuality as norm that, in turn, excludes lesbians from many articulations of whiteness, but that does not mean that lesbians are excluded from whiteness in a manner similar to women of color.[30] What the analogy also excludes is the possibility that some lesbians might enjoy their access to the phenotypical privileges of whiteness at the same time as they are denied access to other aspects of white privilege. Indeed, as the case of openly gay right-wing Netherlands politician Pim Fortuyn made clear, sexual minorities can well be proponents of racial hatred. However, the indiscriminate equation of all forms of "difference" as subject to and resisting a hegemonic order elides crucial divergences that remain necessary to be recognized.

The argumentative equivalence of race and gender in the analysis of *Paris Is Burning* is mirrored, in turn, in analogical descriptions that the film cannot sustain. Questioning the results of the denaturalization of gender and sexuality by Venus, Butler writes, "As much as she crosses gender, sexuality, and race performatively, the hegemony that reinscribes the privileges of normative femininity and whiteness wields the final power to *re*naturalize Venus' body."[31] However, although one might well argue that Venus desires whiteness and its privileges, she never attempts to pass as white; she does not cross racial lines in the film (as she does gender lines) unless we, through a complete substitution of race by gender, consider any drag to be a subversion of whiteness in which case whiteness becomes, as Richard Dyer powerfully argued, everything and nothing at once.[32]

The subsumption of race under gender/sexuality via analogy, despite Butler's intentions to the contrary and the near absence of race in discussions of normative and radical kinship in *Antigone's Claim* (2000), suggests that feminist/gender/sexuality theories have far to go before recognizing the racial projects to which we, particularly the formerly colonized, have all been subjected to since modernity. Although *Antigone's Claim* does not warrant extended discussion here because it does not invoke the race/gender analogy, it is worth pointing out that it does make universalized claims about kinship systems without being sufficiently cognizant of its West-centered perspective. While challenging the heterosexual imperative of the Oedipal configuration for the family, for instance, Butler suggests a different familial configuration caused by such factors as migrations, divorces, and blended families. However, the extended family structure endemic to many Asian cultures, and which third world theorists such as Ashis Nandy have argued challenges Oedipal configurations (although not heterosexuality), is never mentioned.[33]

Interestingly, when in *Precarious Life*, Butler turns the lens to considerations of contemporary U.S. imperialism, particularly following the invasion of Iraq in 2003, she no longer posits a race/gender analogy. Under the pressure of historical specificity, of located analysis, the universalizing spatial terms of globalization rhetoric—hybridity, border crossing, flows—give way to a recognition of differences that need not be metaphorized out of existence. Pondering the question of differences among feminist groups, Butler writes, "We could have several engaged intellectual debates going on at the same time and find ourselves joined in the fight against violence, without having to agree on many epistemological issues. We could disagree on the status and character of modernity and yet find ourselves joined in asserting and defending the rights of indigenous women to health care, reproductive technology."[34] Here there is no universalization of marginality or difference, but rather a recognition of connections forged through specific sites of activism.

CODA: ON LOCALIZATION AND VAMPIRISM

Is it possible to theorize race and gender in any way other than analogically? Is analogy destined to be the predominant mode of thinking race and gender, particularly within discourses of globalization that operate from the perspective of a first world universalism? To the extent that feminist theory—white or otherwise—refuses historical specificity, there is always a danger of analogizing. Take, for instance, Chela Sandoval's attempt to articulate an oppositional politics in *Methodology of the Oppressed* (2000). Although Sandoval critiques Haraway's appropriation of the methodologies of women of color into examples of cyborg feminism,[35] her book remains indebted to Haraway's construction of the cyborg as a generalized locus of difference and contradiction. Perhaps that is why the predominant mode of analysis in the book is analogizing different forms of dissident consciousness such as Barthes's punctum, Anzaldua's *mestizaje*, and Haraway's cyborg feminism. While it might well be important to demonstrate the undeniable structural similarities among these concepts, the very methodology of generalization and analogy might blind us to problems apparent only through localized readings. For instance, to read Anzaldua's deployment of *mestizaje* only as a challenge to strict racial definitions is problematic because Anzaldua articulates her concept in the context of the U.S.–Mexican border. In this context, the use of *mestizaje* as Mexico's official policy of amalgamation, adopted in order to disempower indigenous blacks, needs to be recognized and Anzaldua's celebratory use of it needs at least to be interrogated. Sandoval's investment in an ahistorical and acontextual, almost simply linguistic universality of the margins, however, precludes such a needed interrogation.[36] The analogical model might also preclude a recognition of power relations that might be at work among different categories.

However, I would argue that while the analogical model continues to proliferate, there are other models that have emerged from more localized studies. Patricia Hill Collins demonstrates, for instance, how an emphasis on the *interconnection* of race, gender, and class has important ramifications for African American women who, by forcing courts to see them as doubly or triply oppressed, can claim better protection under Title VII of the Civil Rights Act of 1964.[37] Collins's theoretical argument is bolstered through, indeed emanates from, context, in the tradition of critical race studies. Similarly, postcolonial feminist Anne McClintock, in her brilliant analysis of Victorian imperialism, argues that race and gender "come into existence *in and through* relation to each other—if in contradictory and conflictual ways."[38] And it is the contradictory and conflictual relationship that

McClintock stresses. Different forms of fetishization such as the fetishization of white skin, of national flags, of lesbians cross-dressing as men, McClintock argues, cannot simply be lumped under "a single mark of desire without great loss of theoretical subtlety and historical complexity."[39]

An important critique of the race-gender analogy has been offered by Siobhan B. Somerville, who argues that simple analogies between race and gender/sexuality actually perpetuate a separation between the two and obscure the ramifications of a specific history of analogizing at a particular historical moment. Somerville's project is to demonstrate that such analogies have a specific history, that "the formation of notions of heterosexuality and homosexuality emerged in the United States through (and not merely parallel to) a discourse saturated with assumptions about the racialization of bodies."[40] The discourse on race, that is, facilitates the discourse on sexuality. So I speculate that the possibilities for decolonizing (white) feminist/gender/sexuality theories and of forming progressive affiliations, might lie precisely in analyses grounded in a specific, local moment for then these analyses would begin the work of undoing universalism. Zillah Eisentein's theorizations about differences are useful here. She argues that not only is identity multiple, but so are differences and "the more multiple, the more possibility for partial connections which are similarly different and differently similar."[41] But it is through such partial connections, rather than analogical equation within a presumed affiliation, that there can be a basis for what Eisentein calls "polyunity" or "polyversality."[42]

It is fitting to conclude my speculations on the disruptiveness of localization to the race/gender/sexuality analogy by briefly examining Haraway's analytics of race in *Modest_Witness@Second_Millenium*. Although the essay on race, "Universal Donors in a Vampire Culture," begins with a numbingly familiar series of analogies—"Race, like nature and sex, is replete with all kinds of rituals of guilt and innocence in the stories of nation, family, and species," "race, like sex, is about the purity of lineage; the legitimacy of passage"[43]—the bulk of the essay derives its interpretive impetus from historically specific articulations. Through a table that periodizes twentieth-century kinship categories through key objects of knowledge—race, population, and the genome—in three periods in the twentieth century, Haraway both contextualizes the categories of race, sex, and nature and suggests related discontinuities and unfamiliar connections along the chart by seeing the chart as a hypertext. The most insightful of Haraway's observations derive from rigorous localized analysis. Thus, Haraway demonstrates both the humanist impulse behind the Human Genome Project and the raced, colonial workings through which indigenous peoples were once again the objects of knowledge rather than partners in a research agenda.[44] In a brilliant analysis of an advertisement by Premed, Haraway traces the unmistakable ways in which the picture of a white male doctor, ostensibly marrying a gorilla clad in bridal white, invokes the worst of racial stereotypes in order to causally link the African American woman to the overburdening of the health care system.

However, it is when Haraway moves from localized analysis to generalized metaphors as explicators of different kinds of groups either marginalized by the nation, or straining the categories of the nation, that the problems of universalism begin to erase the systemic violence of race. To trouble the categories of biological kinship and racial purity, Haraway draws on the figure of the vampire. The vampire "both promises and threatens racial and sexual mixing" and "feeds off the normalized human."[45] Like the cyborg, the vampire is a figure for border crossing and hybridity; spatially it evokes unfixity or the *unheimlich*. Suggestive of violence, pollution, and mixing, the vampire becomes for Haraway a figure for the alien, the immigrant, the cosmopolitan, the queer, and is embroiled in racism, sexism, and homophobia. Historically associated with the figure of the Jew accused of polluting Europeans, "the vampires are the immigrants, the dislocated ones, accused of sucking the blood of the rightful possessors of the land. . . . So, in an orgy of solidarity with all the oppressed, one identifies firmly with the outlaws. . . . The vampire is the cosmopolitan, the one who speaks too many languages."[46] The figure of the vampire clearly facilitates Haraway's inquiry into leakages among kinship categories. Yet, like the cyborg, or Sandoval's notion of oppositional consciousness, the figure also tends to become, like whiteness, everything and nothing at once. What kinds of differences, for instance, are suppressed when the alien and cosmopolitan are brought together in a solidarity of the oppressed? More important, for our purposes of analyzing the problems of the analogical model, what kinds of power relationships get obscured when sexual difference like queerness gets equated with the racial difference of the Jew? Such an analogical model disavows the possibility of the racially marginalized perpetrating sexual marginalization or, vice versa, the possibility that gays and lesbians, while marginalized, might well enjoy some privileges of whiteness. Indeed such a model would all but forestall well-worn discussions about the varieties of heterosexism practiced within racial minorites such as African American, Latina/o, and Asian American.

Contemporary multiculturalism, Haraway presciently recognizes, naturalizes racial categories with their histories of violence into safe forms of consumption. Haraway asks in response to *Time* magazine's 1993 cover of a morphed portrait of a woman's face created by a computer mixing of different races, a figure she labels SimEve, "Nothing here is scary, so why am I trembling?"[47] However, in a similar manner, I ask about the figure of the vampire, "Everything is so messy, so why am I so suspicious?" My suspicion arises from the ease with which Haraway's use of the vampire allows us to be on the other side of kinship and the dramas of identity and reproduction. As Haraway concludes in her chapter, "I believe that there will be no racial or sexual peace, no livable nature, until we learn to produce humanity through something more and less than kinship. I think I am on the side of the vampires, or at least some of them."[48] But where and how, within the specific matrices of racial and gendered/sexual oppression, can vampirism be a choice? I suggest that, like the postmodern figure of the cyborg, the vampire, recuperated metaphorically for illegitimacy and racial crossing, can function to erase the specificities of race and sex out of existence as it, in the language of globalization, celebrates universalized border crossings of immigrants and cosmopolitans and possibly makes room for analogy.

Part Two

FROM THE GLOBAL IMPERIAL TO THE POST-COLONIAL

CHAPTER FOUR

Globalization and Orientalism

Iyer's *Video Night in Kathmandu*, Alexander's *Fault Lines*, and Mukherjee's *Jasmine*

> The subaltern lies outside the circuit of the international division of labor and must bear the impact of global-systemic neocolonialism . . . . Such actions of survival cannot easily be romanticized or recuperated as hybrid resistance.
>
> —Pheng Cheah, "Given Culture: Rethinking Cosmopolitan Freedom in Transnationalism"

In fall 2003, Wendy's aired a radio advertisement for their mozzarella chicken sandwich that ran as follows: a smug and satisfied Wendy's customer, pleasantly satiated after a calorific meal, wonderstruck at the combination of chicken and gooey cheese, exultantly rattles off the ingredients of the burger—the soft bun, the tender chicken, crisp lettuce, fresh tomato, sticky melted mozzarella cheese—not just as providing carnal satisfaction but as deeply spiritual, edifying for the soul. After all, he explains to his friend, the burger was brought to him by his "guru." To the background music of the sitar, metonym for India, spirituality, and hippiedom, the customer drools over the juiciness of the chicken and the texture of melted cheese, marveling at the metaphysical pleasures of this ostensibly hedonistic delight. The burger is indeed food for the soul. The advertisement ends with an ironic twist when the customer's friend learns that the guru purveying the food is not a spiritual guide but rather the customer's colleague, a guru of technology, a techno-guru. Such an ad might seem like a poster for the unpredictable cultural syncretism generated by globalization. Western fast-food culture beckons to and incorporates the East through the incongruous combination of burgers and sitars. The word guru becomes a polyvalent term: it signifies at once the guru as teacher, evoking India as the land of ancient wisdom; America's fascination with alternative religions as satirized, for instance, in the 2002 blockbuster movie, *Guru;* and, more recently, the twenty-first century Indian as techno-guru with the ability to capitalize on the software industry and outsource jobs out of the United States.[1] In this way, one might argue that the polarities of West and East, West and the rest, North and South, have been undermined in the cultural arena by globalization's diffusion of these dichotomies into an unstable and complex process of mixing.

And yet I would hesitate to celebrate the Wendy's advertisement as an undermining of imperial power relations for several reasons.[2] First, it would obviously be a mistake to deny the incorporative strategies by which the foreign, here India (closer to the target, Indian American, the majority of whom are vegetarians) is summoned as market for U.S. fast-food. Large corporations were, in fact, the first to see the benefits of operating through the logic that everywhere is home, that instead of "us" and "them" there is only the "us" because in the world of hypercapitalism that interpellates people through consumption rather than production, we are all consumers. Second, despite its challenging of stereotypes, the advertisement is still predicated on hierarchies that become perceptible when we try and imagine the scenario in reverse: an advertisement for chicken curry with a typically white genre like country music playing in the background. We would do well to remember (despite the empire furiously cooking back in Britain) the furor in the British media in 2001 over the remark of a member of parliament that chicken tikka masala was the national dish of Britain.

The point I am making is that despite the undeniably fast movement of cultures and people across borders and the collision and contact among cultures in Western metropoles, erstwhile colonial and current imperial power relations (of which the current U.S. occupation of Iraq is the most obvious) undeniably leave their mark on cultures and peoples. Postcolonialism, in the version of resistance postcolonialism, which, as I have explained earlier, takes seriously the existence of centers and peripheries, and offers a critique of colonial and imperial power dynamics, is particularly relevant here even if it must be reoriented to map the effects of cultural globalization. The first part of this book has dealt with the problems of erasing the perspective of the race and the biopolitical imperatives of the racialized nation-state within postcolonial and feminist theory. Implicitly, it has suggested the collusion of language-based hybridity theories and globalization theories in expunging the historical specificities of systemic racism. This chapter shifts the focus to narratives of globalization by migrant writers in order to chart the complex ways in which the valorization of cultural globalization intersects with ideologies of whiteness and imperialism. It maps the workings of imperialism as marked through the vectors of race, gender, and time in texts by Pico Iyer, Meena Alexander, and Bharati Mukherjee, often taken to be exemplary of concerns of migrancy and globalization. I will begin by turning to what has become a classic in cultural globalization studies—Pico Iyer's travel narrative, *Video Night in Kathmandu* (1988)—and trace the imperial underpinnings of Iyer's analysis of the contact between American and Eastern cultures. By examining Iyer's assumption of the standard colonial trope most powerfully demonstrated by Edward Said, the East as seductress or woman awaiting penetration, I will tease out the raced and gendered implications of this for the ostensibly unraced, heterosexual narrator, bound within Orientalist temporalities. Next, I will turn to *Fault Lines* (1993), a memoir of migrancy by Meena Alexander, to analyze the complicity between the shifting and indeterminate narratives of movement on the one hand, and the gendered, bipolar narratives of modernity and tradition, West and East, that insistently mark the memoir. Similarly, I will also examine the contradictory relationship between Alexander's interpellation as black in the United States and her assumption of colonial dichotomies. Chronopolitics will be central to our understanding of migrant subjectivity here.

Finally, I will briefly turn to Bharati Mukherjee's novel, *Jasmine* (1989), as a complex critique of celebratory transnationalism, a demonstration of the power of imperialism in the subjectification of migrants in the United States, and a mapping of a newly racialized postcolonial community that rests on a problematic appropriation of blackness. My larger argument is that migrant narratives of cultural globalization in the United States, are often complicit with (a) narratives of imperialism that function through dichotomies of race, gender, and time and (b) U.S. narratives of race that privilege and normalize whiteness and without which narratives of imperialism cannot function unimpeded. Cultural exchange, I suggest, is carried out on a clearly unequal terrain. I have chosen specifically to deal with texts authored by post-1965 immigrants of the Indian diaspora for several reasons. First, the 1965 Immigration Act, with its contradictory imperatives of racial inclusion and neoliberal capitalist imperialism, marks a moment when, in part due to this immigration, U.S. cultural hegemony begins to overshadow that of former European empires and the United States becomes the metropole of the third world. Thus, in the cultural, historical, and political imaginary of the writers under consideration here, it is the United States rather than Britain that functions as the hegemonic West. Second, because the post-1965 immigration is popularly read as a strategic and savvy choice of mobility by educated professionals, texts by writers of this immigration are particularly useful in analyzing the restrictions and workings of cultural fluidity. My selection of texts authored by writers of the Indian diaspora is meant to localize and historicize, in a way, the idea of migration and to avoid homogenizing third world migrants. This geospecificity of origin does not mean, however, that there is a uniform "Indianness" or "Indian American" experience that these works represent. (Indeed, all three writers have very different histories of immigration and naturalization ties to the United States.) Rather, I am suggesting that these works partake, in some way, in a particularized racial interpellation in the United States and in specific imperial positionings manifested in immigration laws and the dictates of capital.

GLOBALIZATION AND SEDUCTION: *VIDEO NIGHT IN KATHMANDU*

Has globalization produced a heady mix of cultures and a borderless world? Are we all equally participants of "Planet Reebok"? Is the planet of Planet Reebok simply a further arrangement of the world as consumers of American goods and popular culture? Ever since its publication in 1988, *Video Night in Kathmandu*, Pico Iyer's travelogue, propelled by his desire to assess the impact of American pop culture on Asia, has been hailed as an important text in understanding globalization. In the now classic essay on cultural globalization, "Disjuncture and Difference in the Global Cultural Economy," Arjun Appadurai used *Video Night* as testimony to a new global culture. Appadurai writes, "Iyer's own impressions are testimony to the fact that, if *a* global cultural system is emerging, it is filled with ironies and resistances, sometimes camouflaged as passivity and a bottomless appetite in the Asian world for things Western. Iyer's own account of the uncanny Philippine affinity for American popular music is rich testimony to the global culture of the hyperreal."[3] *Video Night*, Appadurai contends, gives lie to the notion that the globalization of culture is simply Americanization.[4] Appadurai's acclamation of *Video Night* no doubt heightened its standing as an exemplary text on globalization. Even now, the book is being taught in college courses on culture and globalization or postmodernity and globalization and Iyer's stature as the guru of global culture has been further established with the publication of another journalistic memoir, *The Global Soul* (2000) and his most recent publication, *Abandon*, a novel whose action spans the globe from Syria to Spain to Iran to India. As one reviewer put it, Iyer is "a global soul and an apt symbol of multiculturalism."[5]

Indeed Iyer's description of himself as a "global village on two legs" suggests a mobile subjectivity, not anchored to nation or place.[6] *Video Night* similarly presents itself as a text articulated from a perspective of constant displacement. Iyer writes:

> What results, then, is just a *casual traveler's* casual observations, a series of first impressions. . . . The only special qualification I can bring to my subject, perhaps, is a boyhood that schooled me in *expatriation*. . . . I spent eight months a year at a boarding school in England and four months at home in California—in an Indian household. As a British subject, an American resident and an Indian citizen, I quickly became accustomed to cross-cultural anomalies and the mixed feelings of *exile*. Nowhere was *home*, and everywhere.[7] (emphases mine)

Travel, expatriation, exile, home. Iyer's prefatory remarks encapsulate what have become the dominant tropes of contemporary globalization and, as Caren Kaplan has noted, the dominant tropes of critical theory as well.[8] But instead of travel and displacement being widely different, if not oppositional registers of movement, the one denoting privilege and leisure and the other marking colonial and imperial histories, the two are brought together in a cosmopolitan, postmodern diasporic space where questions of power, of center and periphery, and of racial difference are suspended if not outmoded. The narrator's access to British and American subjecthood seems problematically unfractured by race, a subjectivity that has arguably proven useful in Iyer's position as an essayist for *Time* and a writer for other mainstream magazines. A raced, yet reassuringly unraced cosmopolitanism can alleviate racial-cultural anxieties at the very moment when U.S. imperialism and racism are operating in powerful synergy. Like Hardt and Negri's postulation of a nondichotomous realm of empire, Iyer in *The Global Soul* suggests that an international empire has replaced the erstwhile empires of colonialism.[9] Himself a child of the age of globalization, Iyer is a "nowhereian."[10]

In the course of his travels through Asia, Iyer discovers a similar subversion of imperial dichotomies in the realm of culture:

> I was interested to find out how America's pop-cultural imperialism spread through the world's most ancient civilizations. I wanted to see what kind of resistance had been put up against the Coca-Colonizing forces and what kinds of counter-strategies were planned. . . .Yet the discovery I made most consistently throughout

> my travels was that every one of my discoveries had to be rejected or, at best, refined. And as I got ready to leave the East, I began to suspect that none of the countries I had seen, except perhaps the long-colonized Philippines, would ever, or could ever, be fully transformed by the West. Madonna and Rambo might rule the streets, and hearts might be occupied with secondhand dreams of Cadillacs and Californians; but every Asian culture I had visited seemed, in its way, too deep, too canny or too self-possessed to be turned by passing trade winds from the west. (5, 357)

Indeed, Iyer argues that "the East was increasingly moving in on the West" (359). With his last chapter titled, "The Empire Strikes Back," which details the culinary as well as literary inroads of Asians in the United States, Iyer seems to exemplify the kind of postcolonial writing back embodied in works such as Coetzee's *Foe* and Achebe's *Things Fall Apart* and that Rushdie immortalized in his phrase, "the Empire writes back to the Centre."[11]

I have juxtaposed the two lengthy quotes from Iyer's text to make the simple point that cultural globalization and its critical theorizations are not divorced from the dichotomies of neocolonialism and imperialism; indeed they are deeply invested in these dichotomies, even in the act of negation. Moreover, the very slippage in the second passage between "America" and "West" (where "West" functions as a synonym for "America") and between "Asia" and "East" speaks to the power of Orientalist categories that are intimately related to U.S. imperialism.[12] But is *Video Night* simply a writing back? Or does globalization and its diasporas take us into a post of the postcolonial, a post-postcolonial in which even terms like syncretism or hybridity are irrelevant because there are no polarities that are then hopelessly mixed? Hardt and Negri criticize Bhabha's concept of hybridity precisely because it assumes that power works only through the dialectical and binary structure characteristic of modern sovereignty; postcolonial theory, they argue, is thus incapable of dealing with the new form of rule dictated by empire.[13] As I have argued earlier, I part company with Hardt and Negri's postulation of the irrelevance of postcoloniality. Instead, I would argue that imperialism continues to exist and opposition to imperialism cannot be mounted from the perspective of universal migration, worldwide diaspora, or permanent displacement because it is the very universalizing of these categories that erases the material conditions under which most people become displaced and a few assume mobility. Thus, to privilege displacement as such, either in a celebratory or angst-ridden manner, without attention to the material conditions of displacement (such as colonialism or imperialism), or to the politics of mass migrations, is to simply reiterate the aestheticized modernist trope of exile, which, as Caren Kaplan has demonstrated, was profoundly Eurocentric.[14] Paradoxically, then, universalized ideas of migration, which are the staple of cultural globalization theories, provide us with no better ideologies than the highly individualistic, thus depoliticized, modernist notion of exile and, furthermore, problematically write the foreign as essentially ethnic.[15] The privileging of displacement in the texts of globalization under consideration here—*Video Night*, *Fault Lines*, and *Jasmine*—exists in a paradoxical, often mutually constitutive relationship to the imperial dichotomies of gender and time that are intimately bound with the racial hierarchies of the texts.

In her superb analysis of the politics of travel writing in *Imperial Eyes*, Mary Louise Pratt describes the genre as apt vehicle for Eurocentered forms of planetary consciousness manifested in narrative conventions such as the "monarch-of-all-I-survey" scene, a convention that continues undisturbed from the sixteenth century to Anglo-American travel writers like Paul Theroux, even in sentimental anticonquest travel narratives.[16] Iyer's treatise on globalization and resistance seems to consciously resist this imperial trajectory. As mentioned earlier, Iyer's stated purpose is to track the vectors of Coca-Colonizing forces and find arenas of cultural resistance, the latter of which are overwhelmingly in evidence at the conclusion of the text. In fact, Iyer turns the conventions of Western travel writing around in the final chapter by offering, in the genre of Oriental travel letters, the observations of a Chinese traveler who finds in New York not signs of wealth, progress, and presentness, but rather an old history and third world despair. Joe, whom Iyer had met in Guangzhou and to whom he had given $25 to take the TOEFL, delightedly reports to Iyer his excitement about having seen really old buildings, beggars, prostitutes, and filth in New York City. The very titles of the chapters also reveal Iyer's intent to consciously postulate an oppostional postcolonialism. The chapter on Bali, for instance, is subtitled "On Prospero's Isle"; Hong Kong is labeled "The Empire's New Clothes," and the concluding chapter is titled "The Empire Strikes Back."

Globalization's increasing proximity of cultural interactions would seem to have made possible room for an energetic critique of imperialism. But how then do we read the persistent mapping of cultural encounter as gendered heterosexual encounter? Of Western travel as cultural seduction? Edward Said's description of the structures of Orientalist thought, particularly what Said describes as latent Orientalism, is useful: the Orient as woman—sensual, willing, eager, supine, representing backwardness and the past, apotheosized in Flaubert's picture of Kuchuk Hanem.[17] Clearly, the introductory chapter, "Love Match," sets up the gendered parameters of West and East that continue throughout the rest of the text.

Yet Iyer argues that his use of heterosexual romance undermines its power as a metaphor for conquest. Presenting cultural encounters through the trope of heterosexual romance as a means of individualizing dichotomies of power, Iyer suggests that personal encounters between people challenge systemic inequalities. Rambo's falling in love with a Vietnamese girl is evidence that the cultural encounter resembles a "mating dance."[18] "Whenever a Westerner meets an Easterner," Iyer writes, "each is to some extent confornted with the unknown. And the unknown is at once an enticement and a challenge" (21). Using *The Tempest* to map the experience of the Westerner in Bali, Iyer writes:

> And almost every foreign writer on the island . . . had, sooner or later, found himself playing Ferdinand to some enchanted nine-year-old Miranda, recording his worship in flowery prose and sunstruck diction. On my very first night in Bali . . . an Indonesian girl came up, and sat down beside me, and said, not glibly, but with an eerie, penetrating intensity, "I had a dream last night. I found two flowers and put one of them in my hair. That flower was you." (36)

In "China: The Door Swings Both Ways," Iyer records, in gendered terms, China's new relationship with the West:

> The New China is well aware that her longtime seclusion has only inflamed the romantic illusions of the West, adding the lure of the long-forbidden to the appeal of the mysterious. The New China also knows that many a dreamy admirer will spare no expense at all to catch a long-denied glimpse of her mist-wreathed pagodas and jade mountains; a courtesan's expensiveness is, after all, part of her seduction. (103)

And finally, in Thailand, where the narrator is continually propositioned by pimps, he also discovers that the standard couple of Bangkok—"the pudgy foreigner with the exquisite girleen"—might well subvert the power dynamics of buyer and seller, subject and object (300). Some couples stayed together for months, with the Western suitor being "the mature and sophisticated companion she had always lacked" and the woman being the "demure and sumptuously compliant goddess of his dreams" (301). Often, however, a real exchange of emotions would prompt a marriage. Thus, Iyer argues, "my tidy paradigm of West exploiting East began to crumble. Bangkok wasn't dealing only in the clear-cut trade of bodies, it was trafficking also in the altogether murkier exchange of hearts" (301).

Clearly, Iyer is hyperconscious of using the trope of the male penetrating East/woman as used in male Western travel writing and literature about the East. The trope, although most powerfully crystallized in the discourse of Orientalism, had been widely used by male travel writers from Columbus to H. Rider Haggard in what Anne McClintock has aptly termed "an erotics of ravishment."[19] Iyer continues to use the gendered parameters of Western-male and Asian-female but attempts to imbue them with a difference. No longer will the Eastern woman simply be the pliant object of Western fantasy, a Madame Butterfly whose suicide was made desirable and beautiful by Puccini. Instead, Iyer's Eastern woman is the active agent who turns the narrator into a dream object; she is the woman who demands an exchange of hearts and the permanence of marriage; her actions critique imperial power relations and render ideological borders murky. Perhaps, most importantly, she is the well-versed seductress, the courtesan who choreographs the moves of her Western lover.

But how does attributing agency to the trope of East as woman affect the ideological structures of imperialism? I would argue that while it denaturalizes these structures through the very act of attempting to refashion them, it does not fundamentally undermine them because although Iyer vigorously attempts to contend against the subjugation that the gendered trope implies, his efforts are problematically individualistic and grounded in a wholehearted acceptance of the permanence of the mind-body logic of imperialism's heterosexual, gendered dichotomies. As he writes in *The Lady and the Monk*, published three years after *Video Night*, "the pairing of Western men and Eastern women was as natural as the partnership of sun and moon. Everyone falls in love with what he cannot begin to understand."[20] In the chapters on China, Bali, and Thailand in *Video Night*, the West is figured as male, the East as female; the male is stable and permanent, the female is fickle and changing; the Westerner wishes to sample the mysteries of the Orient-woman and pry into her seclusion; the Westerner, incarnated as American-Rambo is the good imperialist who is rewarded with the love of the good (read: nationalist-hating) Vietnamese woman. The American as male might be enraptured or confused, but he is still active, exploring, scopic, the agent of history. Here it is appropriate also to consider Iyer's collusion with the narrative of imperialism in his erasure of the role of the State in the production of gendered hierarchies. Bali, the least developed of Indonesia's islands, and its largest source of tourism revenues, routinely advertises itself in Orientalist terms as the enchanted isle designed to seduce the western tourist, indeed a space unto itself. Iyer's representation of Bali as seductive woman, with hardly a mention of Indonesia or a recognition of Bali as part of Indonesia, reproduces the denial of the state that the packaging of Bali for Western tourist consumption requires.

Even in chapters that acknowledge briefly the economic imperatives of the state, however, the raced and gendered dichotomies continue. Yet the problem with accepting these hierarchical gendered constructions is evident even to scholars who have attempted to attribute agency to the Eastern woman's fetish of the white man as representative of a liberated lifestyle. Karen Kelsky, for instance, views Japanese women's use of white men as agents of liberation as a demonstration of agency, but also acknowledges the problems, thus, of confirming imperialism's race and gender dynamics.[21] Iyer's use of imperialism's gendered trope also intersects with the chronopolitics of empire through representations of Eastern indolence and stasis. For instance, the narrator watches Chinese people en masse bicycle with "hasteless equanimity" while along a "noiseless riverbank" an old man sits in "thoughtful repose" and on the main street men and women "languidly" battle shuttlecocks (117). Note that this is the same China that the narrator has attempted to characterize as a powerful courtesan. We might see Iyer's problem as similar to that of Indian nationalists that Chatterjee analyzes in his perspicuous critique of postcolonial nationalism: they refuse to accept the West's Orientalist notion of the East as inferior but continue to distinguish India from the West in the terms set out by Orientalism: spirituality versus materiality; passivity versus activity.[22] Similarly, while Iyer's problematic, to an extent, is the reverse of Orientalism because as an unhomely, displaced figure and, to some degree, a postcolonial intellectual, he does not wish to privilege the perspective of American/Western as representative of empire, his thematic (the justificatory structure he uses to question this privilege) is largely Orientalist.[23] After all, it was the power implicit in this gendered hierarchy that generated fables of romantic love between white U.S. servicemen and Asian women as allegories of empire after World War II.[24]

Iyer's attempt to change the power hierarchy of gendered categories of empire also raises the question whether a figure like the courtesan can pose an effective challenge. I hasten to add that I am not interested in making any essentialist claims for or against this figure, but rather on its usefulness in the particular context of U.S. imperialism and Orientalist critique. If Iyer's reworking of East as woman via the courtesan questions, to an extent, stereotypes of Eastern passivity and thus challenges imperialism, it nevertheless problematically rests on a sexualization of power that has been the basis of male dominance.[25] As Ann Laura Stoler has argued, sexual control was more than a metaphor for colonial dominance; the very categories of colonizer and colonized were defined through forms of sexual control.[26] Iyer's courtesan beckons the intrepid American possibly to bend to her wishes but only while she promises sexual fulfilment, or the American wills the courtesan into performance. (Current American fascination with geishas, as evidenced by the stupendous sales of Arthur Golden's *Memoirs of a Geisha*, followed by the film version and an accompanying motley of geisha cosmetics, feeds into this power fantasy.) Either construction affirms Anglo-American privilege and the ubiquity of gender categories and power hierarchies rather than confusing the categories altogether. The brilliance of David Henry Hwang's rewriting of *Madame Butterfly*, for instance, is not simply that Renee Gallimard/Pinkerton becomes manipulated as butterfly, thus reversing the power dynamics of Orientalism, but that throughout the play gender categories are so ambiguous (Song is at once man, woman, cross-dresser) that it becomes impossible to reroute the trajectories of power.

In this context, Iyer's sound affirmation of the heterosexual matrix of latent Orientalism (despite the narrator's many encounters with men in the text and given the tradition of homosexuality and gender confusion in travel writers such as Richard Burton and T. E. Lawrence) bears further scrutiny.[27] I would argue that the insistent heterosexuality of *Video Night*, reiterating the gendered power dynamics of Orientalism, requires an active suppression of homoeroticism and gender confusion so that the power dynamics necessary to Iyer's metaphor of cultural seduction can be maintained. In Bali, paradise island and testing ground of the dynamics of the colonial encounter, the narrator, woken by a native while sleeping on a railway bench, describes his exchange with the native as follows:

> I now, so it seemed, had not only a roommate, but also a benchmate. Eyes flashing, my slim-hipped new friend asked me where I came from. New York. His ardor noticeably dimmed. "AIDS!" he pronounced, and moved back a little. Firmly believing that this might not be the ideal time for a tete-a-tete, I nodded vigorously. But my potential companion was not so easily deterred. Did I like men? In certain contexts. And women? Sometimes. Ah, he said, snatching up his own word as if it were a prompt, there are two kinds of woman, the soft and the hard. And so . . . I was treated to a most persuasive treatise on the two kinds of woman. (44–45)

Here in the midst of a chapter rife with descriptions of Balinese sensuality embodied by women, the narrator, in response to being propositioned by an attractive native male, reveals his own shifting and uncertain sexuality. The native's brilliant eyes and slim body arouse sexual energies in him. Possibly bisexual, he is attracted to both men and women. No sooner does this sexual confusion interrupt the narrative of heterosexuality, however, than it is rerouted as heterosexuality and the gendered hierarchies of Orientalism continue. A similar interruption marks the introductory chapter, "Love Match" in which the narrator, in return for the tea served him by Burmese black marketeers, teaches them the words "lesbian" and "skin flicks." (14).

Yet this rechanneling of bisexual energies is necessary to produce the narrator himself as heterosexual as well as the generator of the hierarchical, heterosexual Orientalist narrative of seduction. I am not suggesting here that homosexuality or bisexuality are the privileged venues for upsetting the power dynamics of Orientalism—racial hierarchies can continue within homosexuality—but rather that given the gendered racial narrative set up by Iyer (Western: male, Eastern: female), it is not surprising that the narrator's own sexuality is one that affords privilege in the United States: that of the heterosexual male. It is a privilege that the Iyer is loath to relinquish and which also extends itself through a privileged racial-cultural identification. I use the term "racial" here not to signify some unchanging biological essence but to point to the material, social, and intellectual valences attributed to long-standing racial typologies. While the nineteenth-century Orientalist, as Said points out, would have found support for his observations about Asian degeneracy in popular theories of racial classification, the twentieth- and twenty-first century expert relies on accepted cultural categorizations to reach similar conclusions: Asians who have excelled in technology are said to have Westernized or Americanized well.[28] Of course, focused on Europeans and white Americans writing about the Arab world, Said is dealing largely with the coincidence of the cultural and racial: Europe and the United States are collectively defined as Western and presumed to be white.

Within the contemporary United States, however, questions of the coincidence of racial, cultural, and national identification are more complex. Whites are usually interpellated as nonhyphenated, Western, American, and the norm; blacks are hyphenated, quasi-Western, quasi-African, American, and Other; Latina/os are hyphenated, largely seen as Mexican, illegal immigrant, and neighboring Other; Asians are hyphenated, Eastern, foreign, and another Other. One might argue, as with the case of Iyer, that a person's sense of racial-cultural identification can be different from that of a larger social interpellation. But can one write or will oneself out of racial interpellation in the United States where the state (as discussed more fully in the last part of the book) continues to oppress racial minorities? Clearly, phenotypical interpellation cannot be willed away (although Iyer comes close to claiming that in *The Global Soul*), but can the racial-cultural?[29] What, for instance, is at stake when an Asian American like Iyer denies racial interpellation and identifies herself solely as Anglo-American? At one level, this identification is a powerful critique of a culture that has denied its own impurities and mixtures, that has sought to resist the fracture between phenotype and cultural identity. At another level, however, the identification also seeks to deny the violence with which an idea of the West-white as norm has been maintained in the United States at the expense of non-whites.[30]

All these complex questions need to be brought to bear on Iyer's own identifications in *Video Night*. Despite the migrant, homeless, global identity Iyer overtly charts as his qualification, presumably for a decentered perspective, the "I" of the text presumes a Westernness and whiteness that is geopolitically located but does not need to specifically mark itself as such. It is a privileged cosmopolitanism that can position itself as unmarked. When Iyer writes, for instance, about the possibility of our not simply being comically deluded Titanias abroad but also Mirandas with faith in the new world, the subject "we" can include nonwhite travelers but only if we suspend the racialization of Miranda (23). Through most of the text Iyer continues to presume an identification with a Western perspective: "Why did she not like Indonesian boys, I asked Wayan when I met her the following day. To Western eyes they seemed the very picture of gentleness and beauty" (55). When Indian producer Romesh Sippy talks exasperatedly of the lowbrow tastes of Indians, Iyer writes, "But in the West we also have E.T. And Jaws. And R2D2" (250). The connection between "the West" and the narrator (and the power accruant to Westernness) is seamless, though unspoken. Finally, close to the end of the text, the narrator describes himself upon return to New York as a "Rip Van Winkle awakening to the lineaments of a new order" signified by the eruption of Koreatown, Little India, and Japanese and Thai restaurants (359). Like Washington Irving's Rip, who had so identified himself with the British colonial order that the Revolutionary War passed him by in his sleep, Iyer, perhaps unwittingly, associates himself with the smug, provincial white American except that, unlike Rip, the narrator isn't the object of satire.

Interestingly, the text reveals that although Iyer as tourist had constantly been interpellated as Indian in Asia and barraged with queries about Bollywood stars, Iyer as narrator limits his discussion of this interpellation to two paragraphs in the chapter on India, much of which is taken with an analysis of Bollywood films and is titled "Hollywood in the Fifties." Thus, the Western identity of the narrator, like his heterosexual identity, is only temporarily destabilized, not fractured by his interpellation as Indian, and it is ultimately this privileged Western identity that enables the narrator, in turn, to draw on Orientalism to structure his text. As Traise Yamamoto argues in her analysis of Iyer's *Lady and the Monk*, "Iyer's own positioning in relation to British and American culture is rendered invisible, particularly the extent that he can identify himself as the arbiter of Western cultural values."[31] In addition, the seemingly unraced nature of the narrator in much of the text also implicitly uses what has been recognized in the context of the United States as a white prerogative, that of assuming white as a norm that does not have to be recognized as raced.[32]

MIGRATION, GENDER, AND CHRONOPOLITICS: MEENA ALEXANDER'S *FAULT LINES*

In contrast to Iyer who celebrates an expansive global identity, albeit one produced through expatriation, Alexander in *Fault Lines*, registers the pain of the migrant subject's fragmentation and displacement.[33] Part memoir, part essay, *Fault Lines* traces the trajectory of the author's life as it moves from reminiscences of her birthplace and ancestral home in Kerala, India, to her adolescence in Khartoum, Sudan, her college education in England, her stints of working in Hyderabad and Delhi and her life in Manhattan as writer, mother, and wife of a white American Jew. As the title of the book indicates, and as the narrator painstakingly charts through the various meanings of her central metaphor—fault lines—she is marked by different dislocations and splittings: spatial, temporal, and subjective. But despite the multiple migrations that the narrator constantly reiterates, the narrative energy of the text, like that of Iyer's, rests on a constant set of Orientalist oppositions that are often self-consciously structured as such by the narrator: past and present; fixity and movement; continuity and disjunction; tradition and modernity; Kerala and Manhattan. In Alexander's text, these dualities cannot be mapped isomorphically to the narrator's identity as displaced subject, raced other, and as a woman because the dualities function differently for the narrator as immigrant, Indian American, or woman writer and wife. Yet being mined from the discourses of colonialism and imperialism, they point to the ubiquity of these discourses even within narratives of migration.

Alexander's mapping of these dualities occurs early in the text. Alexander writes:

> That's all I am, a woman cracked by multiple migrations. Uprooted so many times she can connect nothing with nothing. Her words are all askew. . . . Till my mind slipped back to my mother—amma—she who gave birth to me, and to amma's amma, my veliammechi, grandmother Kunju, drawing me back into the darkness of the Tiruvella house with its cool bedrooms and coiled verandas; the shelter of memory.[34]

If history has traditionally prized a narrative of linearity or at least evolution even after Marx, thus explaining the discontinuities of revolution, modernity has similarly located its breaks with the past within history and has further seen these breaks themselves as constitutive of, and characteristic of Western progress, often justifications for the colonial enterprise.[35] Theorists of globalization as well as postcolonialists like Bhabha see migrancy as challenging this Eurocentric temporality of modernity. Appadurai argues, for instance, that global cultural flows challenge the hegemony of Eurochronology, making the past function synchronically as a warehouse of cultural scenarios rather than a simple place to return to.[36] Similarly, Bhabha suggests that "postcolonial time questions the teleological traditions of past and present, and the polarized historicist sensibility of the archaic and the modern" and, through the creation of a disjunctive present, introduces the time lag that modernity attempts to normalize.[37]

However, as we see in Alexander's rendition of herself as migrant subject, the migrant as displaced seeks to insert herself within a linear temporal schema that is made possible only when the past is seen diachronically, stabilized through memory. She seeks a constituency unavailable within the present, which is figured as a narrative of discontinuity and nonconstituency and possible only in a stabilized figuration of homeland as home. Often figured as pre-Oedipal sensuality or the pre-symbolic maternal, this home challenges the temporal logic of modernity. But it does so by buying into a developmentalism that locates this home outside of modernity's time. Some postcolonial critics have challenged the temporality of modernity by demonstrating the limits of its Western ontology. Ashis Nandy argues, for instance, that in an Indian and decidedly non-Western conception, the past is open-ended and leads to choices in the present.[38] Alexander, however, does not radically reconceptualize her use of the past. By not interrupting the present of modernity this past does not undermine the structure of modernity's present in the United States. Indeed in locating her identity in an unvarying past in contradistinction to the changing spatialities and temporalities of the metropole, Alexander writes a narrative of modernity that reifies hierarchical differences between the archaic and the modern.[39] As Alexander notes toward the end of the text, "In India, I rest, I just am, like a stone, a bone, a child born again" (176). In India, she is a being outside of history, whereas, in Manhattan, "Things are constantly falling apart. The city is dispersing itself, jostling, juggling its parts" (177). Alexander's echo of Yeats' modernist angst here and T. S. Eliot's earlier (in "she can connect nothing with nothing") are duplicated in her fetishization of the native/past as stable and unthreatening.

But while Alexander as migrant attempts to take refuge in a consciously constructed, fixed Indian past, often figured as maternal, Alexander as woman strives to break free of the patriarchally constructed, ossified gender roles for middle-class Indian women. The contradictions of this role were set into motion in India's early nationalist period. As Partha Chatterjee has powerfully demonstrated, nationalism in India was attained in the realm of home by writers and intellectuals who sought to keep a domain of Indian tradition protected from and inaccessible to British influence. This domain of nation was attained by postulating a separation between spiritual-Indian and material-Western spheres, the former being embodied in the figure of the educated middle-class housewife, the socio-symbolic bearer of nationhood.[40] Ironically (and Chatterjee does not fully interrogate the implications of this), postcolonial modernity and nationhood predicated on the "inner" realm were premised on the Orientalist thematic, which, in its U.S. configuration, demarcated and continues to demarcate the spiritual India of the past from the material, present-Oriented United States or its latest progeny, the Americanized techno-guru.

Alexander constantly negotiates with this nationalistic construction of the woman as signifier of nation in India. Her diary entry, "'If you want me to live as a woman, why educate me?'" and her rumination, "The fault lay in the tension I felt between the claims of my intelligence . . . and the requirements of a femininity" (102) speaks to the contradictions of the educated housewife ideal of nationalists, an ideal arguably active in present-day India. Essential to the requirements of femininity, writes Alexander, "was an arranged marriage. It was the narrow gate through which all women had to enter, and entering it, or so I understood, they had to let fall all their accomplishments, other than those suited to a life of gentility: some cooking, a little musical training, a little embroidery, enough skills of computation to run a household. In essential details and with a few cultural variants, the list would not have differed from Rousseau's outline for Emile's intended" (102). Reiterated variously throughout the memoir, this idea of middle-class femininity becomes a metonym for national culture. As Alexander's comparison to Rousseau suggests, this is India in a time warp, outside of the globalized present, outside of modernity, but part of modernity's progressivist teleology. In the narrative logic of the text, the United States' past is India's present. But should the vector of gender be the site for what Alexander postulates as a progressive developmentalism? The answer is not simple, despite colonialism's deployment of narratives of development because to deny progress and change regarding women's issues would be to bury the feminist project wholesale. The point I am making is that uneven developmental trajectories need to be recognized within each culture, Western or not, as much as between them. In the contemporary United States, the increasingly strong voices that have slowly chipped away at abortion rights since the 1980s demonstrate that feminists have by no means come to center stage. Alexander seems to recognize the limits on women's agency in the United States. Pregnant with her first child, the narrator of *Fault Lines* finds kinship with the characters of Tillie Olsen and writes, "I felt I would never get to write the real stuff of my life. I knew I was one of those women, mouths taped over, choking on her own flesh" (161). However, despite the narrator's agonized identification with women whose creativity has been suppressed by the strictures of American womanhood, Alexander does not associate women's sphere in the United States, as she does with India, as past. Even to her as a mother, Manhattan offers "the pleasures of sheer motion to the migrant" (205). Indexed through gender, thus, the narrator's rendition of Indian society functions through chronopolitics, what Johannes Fabian has called a denial of coevalness, the refusal to recognize that the native and Westerner coexist in the same time, and which has been a strategy fundamental to Western anthropology's othering of the native.[41] Thus, both the embrace of the Indian past as stable and the rejection of India as past rest paradoxically on colonial and imperial temporalities that position India outside the present and the United States as the very embodiment of it.

The only possibility of moving beyond Orientalist temporalities in *Fault Lines* comes from the vector of race and in a complex series of negotiations that involve the cognizance of objecthood as well as the postulation of a racialized identity. Fanon describes the moment of racial interpellation as an existential one when he is locked out of the present and sealed into an objecthood that exists outside of historical time, in the permanence of racial stereotypes. In *Fault Lines*, Alexander registers an analogous instant. Strolling with her son, at one with the tranquility of a Minneapolis summer, the narrator is jolted outside of the time-space of the scene through the imprecation of a white motorcyclist, "You black bitch!" The instant of racial naming plunges the narrator into a transhistorical identification with the targets of the New Jersey Dotbuster skinheads as well as the "Unwhite in America" (169). In contrast to Iyer, who sees liberating possibilities in the workings of stereotypes, Alexander points to the pain of those subject to the objectifications of stereotyping.

Racial interpellation challenges the idea of the perpetual present that the narrator associates with the ideology of newness through which she defines American national character and to which she was introduced through the writings of Emerson. But presentness, as we know, is also the ontology of postmodernity as analyzed through the axis of consumption by Frederic Jameson or through the axis of gender by Judith Butler. While, for Jameson, postmodernity's production of the perpetual present is a sign of the inability to face the past historically, for Butler, the trope of performativity rests on discontinuous acts or performances that construct gender as mobile and shifting.[42] Theorists of the globalization of culture similarly characterize the manufacturing of syncretic cultures as taking place in a hitherto unprecedented, fluid moment in which cultures are ruptured from their past associations. Migrancy, particularly from third world to metropole (here the United States), or North to South, participates in this culture of the present in which, as with popular applications of the idea of performativity, identities are always being remade. But the process of subjectification in which corporeality becomes identity participates in a well-known history of racism that shatters the idea of America as present: "I can make myself up and this is the enticement, the exhilaration, the compulsive energy of America. But only up to a point. And the point, the sticking point, is my dark female body. I may try the voice-over bit, the words-over bit, the textual pyrotechnic bit, but my body is here, now, and cannot be shed" (202).

The darkness and blackness of her body and the sociocultural interpellation it maps out for her both ruptures the idea of the redemptive present and suggests possibilities, though inchoate, of a community of the subordinated. It is the "violence of racism" that evokes for Alexander the idea of a shared political identity with African American activists such as Frederick Douglass, Harriet Jacobs, Audre Lorde, and Toni Morrison, an identity one might think of as participating in Post-Colonial citizenship. Yet Alexander's postulation of this citizenship is inchoate because there is no sense of what this citizenship or community might entail for thinking about contemporary culture or racialized subjectivity or indeed what it might mean particularly for a relatively privileged South Asian to identify herself with a past of slavery. Like Haraway's postulation of a cyborgian identity for North American peace demonstrators and workers in third world factories, community is sutured over through analogy. It is also problematic that this identification, like that of Iyer's with many of his Asian friends, remains individualistic and does not produce any meaningful ties with an African American community in the present. One might think of Alexander's postulation of marginality and displacement, following R. Radhakrishnan's skepticism about hybridity, as marginality skin deep, one not connected in any viable manner to a critical inventorying of the traces of marginality on Alexander as a historical subject.[43] A similar claim might be made for Alexander's master trope, "fault lines."

To that extent, Alexander's "blackness" also reiterates racially, the modernist idea of displacement that precludes community. Even in *Manhattan Music*, where Alexander creates the character Draupadi (named after the mythological heroine of the *Mahabharata)*, a New York immigrant whose Indian ancestors were brought to Fiji as slaves by the British, and who as a performance artist identifies with and enacts the imprisonment of Harriet Jacobs, taking on identities seems to be a mark of style consonant with consumer culture. As Draupadi explains to Rinaldo,

"I was born in Gingee, most part Indian, part African descended from slaves, pride of Kala Pani, sister to the middle passage. Also part Asian-American, from Japanese, Chinese, and Filipino blood."[44] There is, however, no development in the novel of the consequences of this particular hybrid identity. Rather, it is presented simply as yet another version of liberal multiculturalism's concept of multiple selves, a concept that cannot deal with the specificity and violence of racial difference. Indeed, the articulation of racial identity here resembles, structurally, the mapping of consumer identity early in the novel: "Born in America, I must have seemed the epitome of newness, all she [the aristocratic, totally Indian Sandhya] might one day be—leather jacket, Benetton sweater, short black hair, subtle eyeshadow, the lot."[45] Someone like Frank Chin, in contrast, urges Asian American identification with African Americans for reasons ranging from resistance to the state, cultural nationalism and masculinity, to the forging of a unique racial aesthetic.[46] Thus, although by associating the United States with the continuous legacy of racism, Alexander attempts to demonstrate how race as a vector of migrant identity can challenge a hegemonic, raced nationalism, her rendition of the present as property of the metropole problematically reifies an imperialist chronopolitics.

Fault Lines thus demonstrates the problems inherent in the very idea of "migrant" as a category challenging the hierarchies of neocolonialism, imperialism, and racism. I am not suggesting that the migrant is an empty signifier or a floating signifier in the postmodern sense; I am simply arguing that all the axes of migrant identity are not positioned analogously vis-à-vis the metropole. The cross-hatching of these different vectors might produce a weave that is not consistent but instead jagged and contradictory. In some ways, the middle-class third world migrant may not be deterritorialized at all because she might, in the new space of the metropole, reproduce both the bourgeois nationalism of her native country and the internalization of the racial hierarchies of colonialism that is often part of this nationalism. Indeed Indian Americans have often bought into Orientalist dichotomies that allow them to be positioned as superior to blacks.[47] Being on the racial-cultural margins of the new nation-state might not be subversive in a significant ideological sense. At the same time, the assertion of new racial identity or solidarity through Post-Colonial citizenship might challenge, significantly, narratives of nation and the democratic and emancipatory narrative with which the metropolis advertises itself. In *Fault Lines*, for instance, the geopolitical imagination of the narrator is in different ways, colonized, and reproduces Orientalism, at the same time as her corporeal identity and the significance she attaches to it, have the potential to subvert imperial temporalities.

TRANSNATIONALISM, MOBILITY, AND RECOGNITION IN *JASMINE*

I want to approach *Jasmine*, Mukherjee's much celebrated and reviled novel, neither from the viewpoint of falsely sugarcoating immigrant experience that has preoccupied much of the criticism of the novel, nor from the perspective celebrating movement qua movement, dissociated from both constraints and luxuries, but rather as a complex, multileveled allegory for third world transnational mobility in the age of globalization, a mobility that is often predicated on a restricted recognition of the migrant subject. I take Fanon as a starting point for thinking about the idea of recognition because notwithstanding the very different cultural scenario mapped in Mukherjee's novel, Fanon's articulation of the colonial dynamic remains central to understanding the politics of cultural recognition and the uses of this recognition in a landscape crossed over with multiple migrations. In his complex meditations on the idea of the self, Hegel postulated that "self-consciousness exists in and for itself when, and by the fact that, it so exists for another; that is, it exists only in being acknowledged." Surprisingly, being-for-itself emerges through the process of recognition that "is possible only when each is for the other what the other is for it."[48] Writing about his experience of being objectified and hence shattered by being interpellated as "negro," Fanon comments on Hegel's theorizing: "There is of course the moment of 'being for others' of which Hegel speaks, but every ontology is made unattainable in a colonized and civilized society."[49] Fanon, that is, gives voice to the unequal or impossible process of recognition in colonialism in which the colonized subject cannot ever have Hegelian self-consciousness or being-for-itself because she does not exist as another in the eyes of the colonizer. Although the process of contemporary migrations to the United States creates unexpected and new solidarities and constituencies, the mobility (cultural, social, economic) of the migrant subject is predicated on a restricted recognition of her, a process complexly allegorized by Mukherjee in *Jasmine*. And whereas the politics of recognition occupy a minor role in Alexander's memoir, they become central in Mukherjee's novel.

In representing migrant metropolitan subjectification as a sphere of increasingly narrow choices, I am going counter to the spirit of arguments of critics such as Louisa Schein, Bonnie Honig, and Bruce Robbins who argue variously in *Cosmopolitics* that contemporary transnationalism fueled by transcultural encounters and migrations from East to West, South to North, create conditions for "radical cosmopolitanisms from below."[50] I am going counter to the "spirit" rather than the matter of these arguments because although I believe migrations are undoubtedly changing—in a way that we cannot univocally and definitively map—cultural conditions in the metropole, the celebratory readings of this migration miss the crucially important fact of unequal cultural exchange that underlies these migrations. Let us return to the trope of India as spirituality, with which this chapter started. As Daisy von Scherler Mayer's blockbuster movie, *Guru*, makes crudely clear, upward mobility for Indian migrants requires a performance of what has been a persistent Anglo-American association of India with spirituality, divorced from contemporaneity and history, epitomized in the works of Whitman and Emerson and which continues to today.[51] Indeed, the central character, Ramu Gupta (played by Jimi Mistry), who runs a dance studio in India, and is a hustler of sorts, finds that he can fulfill the American dream and attain stardom only by strategically combining ideas of spiritual India with the more generalized idea of the East as sexuality to become the "Guru of Sex."

Bharati Mukherjee's *Jasmine* forces on its readers the fact that migrant mobility, especially cultural, moves along national-racial vectors and that the upward mobility of migrants rests, to an extent, on this restricted cultural mobility.[52] In making this claim for *Jasmine*, I am not arguing that the novel doesn't engage in a celebratory Americanism or that it doesn't perpetuate the colonial-imperial binaries of Asian oppression and American freedom, imperial chronopolitics of Asia as past and the United States as present as Iyer's and Alexander's texts do and which troublingly reiterate U.S. imperial encounters in Asia. To an extent, the novel engages in both. I don't think one needs to decide whether a novel such as this simply extols the idea of America and promotes imperial ideologies or whether it excoriates the unfreedoms of the metropole for the migrant. Indeed such either–or options (which have engaged much of the critical attention on the novel) are sure to miss any dialectical connections between the two and to impoverish practices that need to keep contradictory readings at play. I suggest instead that the novel maps the mutually constitutive yet contestatory terrains of imperialism and transnationalism, mobility and restriction, in a manner that reveals the raced biopolitical control over migrant experience without reducing the experience to a simple allegorization.

The novel deliberately deconstructs the idea of the East as backward, past-oriented and oppressive, indeed a monolithic East, by dramatizing the differences between Hasnapur and Jullundhar, country and city, feudalism and modernity. Even within Hasnapur, the forces of tradition and modernity, personified by Pitaji who wishes to terminate Jyoti's education, and Masterji who fervently pleads her case (with support from Jyoti's mother) to Pitaji, clash, just as in her previous novel, *Wife*, Mukherjee drew attention to the differences between the flirtatious Ratna Das and the self-sacrificial model wives. Indeed, Jyoti/Jasmine's husband Prakash is the most progressive of her male protectors, encouraging her to read, fix electronics, and imagine her subjectivity outside of the maternal. The fact that both these men are murdered by Sikh militants (called Khalsa Lions), thus rendering Sikhs responsible, figuratively, for the death of secular, modern India is certainly problematic, particularly given the politics of Hindutva (Hindu fundamentalism) today; however, this rendition doesn't erase the heterotemporality with which the cultural landscape is endowed and out of which the eponymous heroine emerges.[53]

It is this complexity and present-day historicity that have to be suppressed in order for the heroine to make her way in the United States, an accommodation that requires Jasmine to follow a scripted racial performance. Jasmine's gruesome encounter with Half-Face allegorizes the circumscribed path that new immigrants, interpellated through U.S. imperial encounters, must follow to be mobile in social space. Half-Face, captain of the boat on which Jasmine is smuggled, is a Vietnam veteran whose scarred face represents the disfigurement of his moral psyche by the country's imperial war. Half-Face precedes his rape of Jasmine by furiously commanding her to recognize herself as part of a backward, pretechnological Asia and forbids talk of Prakash and electronics repair. With Lillian Gordon, the fairy godmother benefactress, Jasmine has no past and is simply interpellated as a wretched, though special, immigrant. For her next protector, Taylor, Jasmine is the epitome of foreignness, a difference he eroticizes and wishes her to maintain even as he remains ignorant of her bloody past till she decides to leave New York City. Finally, in Iowa, the rural heartland of America, Jasmine is exoticized by intrepid farmer Darrell as an "Indian princess," an interpellation to which she adeptly acquiesces as she makes her home with Bud Ripplemeyer. "Bud courts me because I am alien. I am darkness, mystery, inscrutability. The East plugs me into instant vitality and wisdom. I rejuvenate him simply by being who I am."[54] Here we get to the final point of the zero-sum game of recognition. Jasmine discerns the Orientalist stereotype of the East in the popular U.S. cultural imaginary with herself recognized as personification of it; she fashions herself on this recognition at the same time as she casts off from self-consciousness (being) whatever is not recognized because we as readers know that the being ("who I am") of Jasmine far exceeds her role as mysterious sex goddess. Jasmine's mobility depends on her enacting her role as Oriental woman within well-established and raced colonial dichotomies.

The irony of Jasmine's success being dependent on her peddling of Orientalism is that the virtual and material landscape that Jasmine inhabits in the United States is unmitigatedly multicultural, crisscrossed with transnational connections.[55] In fact, on almost every page of the novel there is a reference to another, usually third world country. Even rural Iowa isn't experientially white: it teems with doctors from Asia; Hmong children populate the public schools; Bud Ripplemeyer has visited China on a banker's delegation; the mailman has spent a month in Kathmandu; a distraught pregnant woman in Iowa confesses her love for the Ricky Ricardo doll; and the local Lutherans and Mennonites raise money for Ethiopians.[56] It is a global world where hair from the heads of Hasnapur women helps American meterologists. As Jasmine exclaims, "Nothing was rooted anymore. Everything was in motion" (152). Yet Mukherjee is careful to underline the fact that the contemporary multicultural medley of the United States is strongly connected to its imperial ventures abroad and to the forces of capitalism. Mr. Skola, Du's history teacher, was probably a Vietnam veteran as was the scarred Half-Face; Du Thien, the adopted son of Bud, is a refugee from Vietnam. And Mukherjee presents contemporary migration to the United States as a latter-day version of the slave trade, with the only difference being the ostensibly voluntary movement of present-day migrants: "In the New World, on a shrimper . . . four of us bound for the Gulf Coast of Florida slept under the tarp. You learn to roll with the waves and hold the vomit in" (104). As Half-Face, the captain with the generic white male name, Bubba, says, his job is "nigger-shipping" (111). The evocation of middle passage is a stringent critique of nation as racialized and suggests that the landscape of contemporary transnationalism is engineered through the familiar, if updated vectors of racism and imperialism. Perhaps it should not surprise us, then, that the heroine is propelled along through the dynamics of imperial recognition and concomitant self-fashioning.

It is in fact Mukherjee's creation of Jasmine as a character whose mobility depends greatly on her cashing in on Orientalized fantasies that has provoked the ire of many critics. Debjani Banerjee, for instance, sees Jasmine's acquiescence to her own exoticization and her selective presentation of her past as symptomatic of Mukherjee's and the heroine's first world leanings.[57] But such a critique surely misses the overdetermined narrative of imperialism that the novel also exposes. Symptomatic of the lowest rung jobs available for poor third world women and the fascination with Asian women—geisha girls or Filipino mail-order brides—are the two options for survival spelt out in the novel: the nanny, a modern version, as Taylor jokingly points out, of "dark-skinned mammies" (169) or the as exotic, eroticized Oriental woman. The conflation of the two roles in the heroine points to the limited script afforded the South Asian woman in the metropole.

Critics less concerned with Mukherjee's complicity with first world ideologies have paid attention to her use of the romance plot of the English domestic novel. Both Bruce Robbins and Patricia Chu variously see Mukherjee's revision of the plot of the domestic novel, as exemplified in *Jane Eyre*, as a critique of the assumptions of the plot. While Robbins sees Mukherjee challenging ideas of upward mobility and replacing them with lateral mobility, Chu finds in Mukherjee's difficulty of mapping the British plot to exigencies in contemporary America, a demonstration of her critique of the Cinderella myth inherent in it.[58] In fact, Robbins argues that *Jasmine* as well as Kinkaid's *Lucy* exemplify the genre of au pair narrative with its landscape of multicultural nannies that embodies solidarities and possibilities of relationships outside old binaries and that spell a new internationalism. I concur with Chu and Robbins about Mukherjee's revising the domestic plot and with Robbins' ascertaining of new solidarities, but with a difference. The very gross improbabilities of the plot signal to us that Mukherjee is also parodying the well-worn melodramatic conventions of the Bollywood blockbuster that capitalizes on the production of the purest forms of devotional motherhood and wifehood. Overplaying the part of grieving widow, Jasmine decides to commit *sati* (contrary to what the novel implies, this is not common practice in contemporary India), but instead of doing it on her husband's funeral pyre, she plans to travel overseas to enact it. While the traditional Bollywood movie mandates suicide *over* a life of dishonor after rape, Mukherjee has her heroine contemplate but reject this option.

Perhaps the most persistent criticism of the novel is its celebration of an Americanism comprising assimilation, access to mobility, an endorsement of liberal individualism and a denial of the material realities of third world immigration.[59] Mukherjee's own explanations about her change from expatriate status in Canada to immigrant status in the United States, from the racism of the Canadian cultural mosaic to the heady transformation of identity in the United States have, in part, contributed to these critiques.[60] Undoubtedly, this is a forceful narrative in the novel, signaled most obviously at the end when Jasmine leaves with Taylor, "greedy with wants and reckless from hope," following the "promise of America" over "old-world dutifulness," but I would argue that the Americanization narrative is marked as much by what leaks from it as what constitutes it (241). Jasmine leaves with Taylor and heads west in repetition of the classic American frontier narrative, assuming a freedom restricted at best for a single woman without a green card. On the other hand, this frontier narrative has itself been definitively changed through immigration and the politics of U.S. imperialism. While heading west is still mythologized in popular culture—automobile advertisements routinely rely on the driving-west-into-the-sunset image—as the paradigmatic American narrative of mobility, going west has vastly different valences for Asian Americans for whom Angel Island rather than Ellis Island constitutes cultural origins and cultural memory. Even South Asian Americans for whom New York might well be the first point of contact, have the legacy of California Sikhs who comprised one of the earliest Asian American communities in the United States. Likewise, the country's encounters first with Japan and then with Vietnam and Korea have transformed California as a Pacific rim zone. Mukherjee present us with both the hegemonic as well as the Asian version of California. Jasmine goes with Taylor, reiterating the trajectory of the westering male but with a difference because she clearly heads to Du, her adoptive son as well as potential lover who has himself gone to California to rejoin his family. Du, the orphan and legatee of empire, possesses Prakash's electronics skills and, like Jasmine, has survived the decimation of his family. "The smell of singed flesh is always with us" (240). Like Jasmine/Jane, his mobility into middle America is contingent on his restricted recognition—in his case as welfare immigrant and quick study. Thus, Jasmine's motivation to see Du in California also spells the marking out of solidarities and communities of those that are, in different ways, othered in the United States, and prefigures the beginning of a postcolonial community.

But this solidarity is also racially problematic. As pointed out earlier, the novel suggests that globalization has created a culture in which third world women in U.S. metropoles have now replaced black women as nannies and third world immigrants are latter-day versions of slaves. The imagery of middle passage mentioned earlier, as evoked for contemporary immigrants of color, intimates possibilities of a black United States analogous (although with obvious differences) to that of black Britain. Alternatively, one can argue that Mukherjee is postulating an underclass outside the black-white racial divide, albeit using the African American experience as shared political-cultural memory.[61] In either case, however, the relationship of African Americans to this new group is highly vexed because of the virtual absence, synchronically, of African Americans either as characters or within the cultural landscape of the novel. Kingsland, fellow passenger aboard *The Gulf Shuttle*, is Jamaican and possibly black; two other nannies Jasmine consorts with in Manhattan are similarly immigrants from Trinidad and Barbados and possibly black.[62] And while Mexicans appear on television and are the subject of immigration controversies, the sole black character in the novel is the clerk at the Flamingo Court motel where Jasmine is raped by Half-Face. The issue is not simply one of representation, although representation does become significant in a novel so focused on the urban underclass and the racialization of the underclass. Each new wave of immigration obviously changes the racial dynamics of the country, but simultaneously each successive wave must contend with the existing systemic forms of racial oppression of which the black-white binary still remains important. But instead of a relationship to African Americans that has, often in insidious ways as Noel Ignatiev points out, marked the subjectivity of all nonwhite immigrants, Jasmine posits a troubling correspondence and co-opting that all but erases the African American presence from this novel of transnationalism, migrancy, and Americanization.[63] This co-opting stands in stark contrast to forms of representation in a work like Mira Nair's movie, *Mississippi Masala*, in which similar claims to the legacy of slavery for South Asian diasporics are worked out through a large cast of African American characters and the tensions and contradictions of racial alliances are exposed.

Jasmine both appropriates and participates in a problematic erasure of African Americanness, while simultaneously offering a stringent critique of ideas of mobility, hybridity, and syncretism that are the staple of discourses of globalization. Unlike *Video Night* and *Fault Lines*, it points toward the power dynamics of racism and imperialism as central in constituting migrant subjectification, even as it gestures toward an easy performativity. And as a South Asian American narrative of migrancy, it speaks to and interrogates the assumptions of other such narratives, celebratory or otherwise, that presume Orientalist dichotomies.

CODA: GLOBALIZATION, ORIENTALISM, AND RACE

I have attempted to argue in this chapter that persistent forms of Orientalism, characteristic of imperialism, continue to circulate in U.S. narratives of globalization, migrancy, and transnationalism, limiting the cultural and social mobility of third world subjects. This does not mean that imperialist binaries are unchallenged—if they ever were—or unchanged, but that new forms of mobility and the global capitalism that engenders this mobility work very much via imperial power relations and consequently need to be examined through the framework of postcolonial critique. Further, this critique risks reproducing a neocolonial universalism if it does not contend with local forms of systemic racial oppression on which narratives of imperialism depend and facilitate.

A current example should make my arguments clear. I started the chapter by considering a recent advertisement; I will end by offering a provisional analysis of a contemporary labor practice predicated on flexible accumulation and cultural globalization. At the start of the new century, a few U.S. companies decided to accomplish the downsizing of their call centers by seizing on a cheaply found major asset in India—college education and the English language. The United States could now reap the benefits of British colonialism. Realizing that they could hire college graduates with fluent English to staff call centers at a tenth of the salaries of their U.S. counterparts, executives came up with a brilliant strategy. Capitalizing on cut-rate phone costs, Indians' command of the language, and the skills of the college graduates, executives concluded that with very little cost Indians could be "made" American and be equipped to handle the company's local call centers. A quick training program gave the Indians suitably generic American names such as Andy or Susie; employees were trained to cater to local callers by familiarizing themselves with essential apolitical cultural knowhow such as the status of Andy's football team in Tampa or the weather in Susie's Cleveland; above all, they were trained to speak with an "American" accent. And on no account were they to reveal that they were speaking from India.[64]

Now a globalization-enamored perspective would tout this practice as evidence of cultural mobility, the ability of people to partake of unrestricted identities, especially since locals "willingly" train in call center colleges and Indian companies happily participate in the system both in franchising and training. Some postmodern versions of performativity theory would similarly celebrate the ability of Indian phone operators (local versions of Jasmine who, as the novel suggests, murders one identity to take on another) to change identities at will. Perversely enough, editorials for India's chauvinistic nationalism are touting these jobs as signs of national strength, exemplifications of India's ability to beat America at its own game.[65] This scenario no doubt engenders all these perspectives. However, what this giddy excitement about such a transnational change of identities neglects are the restrictions and lack of access that the scenario depends on. Most obviously, Indians cannot hope to enter the ranks of U.S. phone operators speaking Indian-inflected English and must therefore pass the not-Indian cultural proficiency test. Virtual immigrants, they must be assimilated and "Americanized" to gain acceptance. They must change names as well as points of cultural reference, indeed undertake racial erasure, in order to be "recognized" by U.S. callers who, like Jasmine's benefactors, demand this restricted recognition. Further, what they must be assimilated to is not multicultural, immigrant America (in which case accents would not be a problem), but white America because the English taught to the operators is not black English or calo but what is perceived as bland, white, midwestern English. Global cultural space is thus both restricted and controlled by imperialism and racism at the same time as it partakes of mobilities and technologies that challenge earlier forms of colonialism. In a stark demonstration of the racism directed at the virtually unassimilated, Troi Terrain, Philadelphia radio show host of "Star and Buc Wild," phoned an Indian call center, pretending to order hair beads for his daughter and proceeded to heap invectives on the operator: "You're a filthy rat eater. I'm calling about my American 6-year-old white girl. How dare you outsource my call?" The host then encouraged his viewers to make at least one abusive call a day to Indian operators.[66] The raced dimensions of Terrain's vituperations, the likes of which are routinely received by Indian call center operators, could not be clearer.

I want to hold on to the term postcolonial, in its guise as a critique of neocolonial and imperial domination in reading different narratives of what is called global culture—whether emphasizing globalization, migrancy, or transnationalism—because, like Rey Chow, I believe that the "colonial" in the term "postcolonial" is operative within global capitalism and global culture.[69] Like U.S. narratives of freedom, mobility, and fluidity that operate by eliding state-sanctioned systemic racism, post-1965 South Asian American narratives of globalization and migrancy often rest on, even as they vigorously deny, racial hierarchies as well as the power dynamics of imperialism of which Orientalism still remains a major ideological tool.

CHAPTER FIVE

Claiming National Space and Postcolonial Critique

The Asian American Performances of Tseng Kwong Chi

> Rather than glorify the immigrant moment as a mode of perennial liminality, the diasporic self seeks to reterritorialize itself and thereby acquire a name.
>
> —R. Radhakrishnan, *Diasporic Mediations: Between Home and Location*

In their 1974 introduction to the landmark anthology of Asian American literature, *Aiiieeeee!*, editors Frank Chin, Jeffrey Paul Chan, Lawson Fusao Inada, and Shawn Hsu Wong argued forcefully for distinctively "American" conceptions of Chinese and Japanese American identity. They wrote:

> Chinese and Japanese Americans have been separated by geography, culture, and history from China and Japan for seven and four generations respectively. They have evolved cultures and sensibilities distinctly not Chinese or Japanese and distinctly not white American. Even the Asian languages as they exist today in America have been adjusted and developed to express a sensitivity created by a new experience. . . . Our anthology is exclusively Asian American. That means Filipino, Chinese, and Japanese Americans, Americans born and raised, who got their China and Japan from the radio, off the silver screen, from television, out of

> comic books. . . . Asian America, so long ignored and forcibly excluded from creative participation in American culture, is wounded, sad, angry, swearing, and wondering, and this is his AIIIEEEEE!!![1]

For the editors of *Aiiieeeee!*, making distinctions between the experiences of Asian Americans and Asians was politically crucial because Asian Americans had not been recognized as a significant constituency within the United States. Despite the fact that Asian immigrants had settled in large communities in the United States for a century, their claims to national identity, the particularity of their contributions and needs, were being denied, in part, by identifying them with their country of origin. Asian Americans were always "from" somewhere rather than inhabitants here, and therefore outside the sphere of nation as perpetual foreigners. In order to wrest an identity and claim rights for Asian Americans in the nation, Chin et al. felt it incumbent to emphasize the geopolitical and cultural differences between Asian Americans and Asians in ways that might seem purist. After all, given the fact that since the mid-1990s, the number of first-generation Asian Americans has outnumbered the U.S.-born, diasporic continuities need to be stressed. And in the age of the Internet, satellite television, and parachute children, prioritizing specifically Asian American experiences might seem retrograde both for the present moment and as a perspective for understanding Asian American culture.

Yet while the cultural continuities of first- and second-generation Asian Americans with their homelands are more immediate today, so are the disciplinary and interpellative prerogatives of the nation-state as it continues to racialize its citizens differently. Precisely because Asian Americans continue to be interpellated as Asian when their rights as citizens are at stake—as the cases of Wen Ho Lee, James Yee, and the racial profiling of South Asian Americans post 9/11 illustrate—the political necessity of consolidating an identity within the nation remains. Moreover, despite the global connections of Asian Americans, Arif Dirlik's point about the racial essentialism inherent in the diasporic privileging of points of origin is important. Such a privileging, that is, assumes that people are unaffected by the psychosocial and material realities of their places of residence, that they carry a certain unchanged identity derived from their places of origin.[2] For most Asian Americans, however, the changing, lived politics of everyday life, as affected by schools, the workplace, and the instruments of civil society, are central.

Yet in recent years, Asian American critics have declared the race and nation based perspective of Chin et al. outmoded. Thus, Viet Thanh Nguyen and Tina Chen, the editors of a 2000 special issue of *Jouvert* titled "Postcolonial Asian America," contend that a postcolonial perspective decenters the rhetoric of "claiming America" so integral to Chinese and Japanese American self-representation and introduces the contradictory concerns of homeland and diaspora as well as global capitalism that "creates the conditions of migrancy and resettlement for many postcolonial Asian populations."[3] Similar to the postcolonialists who theorize African American experience through a generalized immigration model, these scholars, while advocating a postcolonial approach to Asian American studies, conflate the postcolonial with migrancy and diaspora (collaborative postcolonialism) rather than with histories of race and struggle (resistance postcolonialism) that depend to an extent on the language of citizenship and the promise of rights within the nation-state, even as they are connected to revolutionary ties beyond the nation. In this chapter, I continue my interrogation of the politics of globalization and globalization-inspired postcoloniality in debates about Asian American studies and then examine the celebrated staged photographs of Tseng Kwong Chi. Tseng's photographs, I contend, illustrate the limits of a purely diasporic hermeneutic, and gesture instead toward the importance of a synergy of local interpellation and imperial subject constitution. Ultimately, they demonstrate the productiveness of linking the projects of critical race studies and resistance postcolonialism, of simultaneously situating racial politics and articulating a critique of imperialism.

Let us first examine some of the arguments of scholars who advocate the centrality of diaspora and mobility for Asian American studies. Most important, for these proponents, globalization rhetoric with its privileging of movement and porous borders is central. Thus, Susan Koshy, decrying the boundedness of located perspectives for Asian Americans, writes: "The emergence of the "borderless economy" has intensified linkages that defy containment within the nation state. . . . The effect of these changes on Asian Americans will be substantial. Asian Americans, who have historically disavowed their connections to Asia in order to challenge racist stereotypes as perpetual foreigners, will be able to renegotiate their links to Asia."[4] Refuting the arguments of those who critique migration-centered perspectives as elitist, Koshy rightly points to the preponderance of immigrant Asian Americans in sweatshops and restaurants. However, her own example of Tony Chan's film, *Combination Platter*, as illustrative of the unboundedness of communities is problematic because it is precisely the exploited, immigrant restaurant workers who do not have the luxury of constantly crossing borders. The restaurant workers in the movie might demonstrate the obvious—that migration isn't a cosmopolitan privilege—but the plight of Robert who constantly fears deportation isn't a narrative of migration as much as a narrative of desiring the safeguards of a citizenship. My point is not that analyzing Asian American culture requires the conceptual equivalent of closed borders but rather that when dealing with the dynamics of worker exploitation in *Combination Platter*, for instance, what is important is not so much the initial act of border crossing but rather the raced and imperial apparatuses including those of citizenship that disallow claims to space and coerce bodies to move.

Moreover, the very privileging of third world diasporas at metropolitan centers is a sorry comment on the politics of collaborative, globalism-inspired postcolonial studies given the fact that the most massive movements of population since decolonization have occurred among third world nations: Bangladesh to India, Afghanistan to Pakistan, Rwanda to Zaire, Zimbabwe to South Africa. More pertinent for Asian American studies, the very idea of these diasporic communities at the metropolitan center has acquired an essentialist core. It is presumed that these communities are inherently destabilizing and disruptive of modernity;[5] the idea that capitalism, the engine of modernity, thrives on and needs polymorphous groups, as world-systems theorists have cogently demonstrated, seems not to have been considered.[6] As a consequence of or as a precondition for the disruptive diaspora thesis is the idea of transnational diasporas as homogenous, a presumption critiqued by Jenny Sharpe who points out the problems in positing a similar diaspora for South Asians in Canada, the United States, and Britain;[7] similarly, R. Radhakrishnan suggests differences between diasporas of pain and hope, between the *jouissance* of metropolitan hybridity and the dislocation of postcolonial hybridity.[8] And as the particularities of Asian American literature reveal, not all such texts challenge modernity. Works like Jade Snow Wong's *Fifth Chinese Daughter*, Le Ly Hayslip's *When Heaven and Earth Changed Places*, and Meena Alexander's *Fault Lines*, for instance, affirm the binaries of Western rationality, logic, and progress, and Eastern irrationality, prejudice, and backwardness, binaries central to the narrative of capitalist modernity.

What is also problematic is that some of the calls for moving Asian American studies to a transnational rubric or postcolonial rubric are envisioned as moving into a space beyond race, thus echoing conservative colorblind adversaries of affirmative action and an attempt to challenge the radical rhetoric of race into safer forms of multiculturalism and ethnicity.[9] Calling for a postcolonial Asian America, Viet Thanh Nguyen and Tina Chen write: "Postcolonial identities . . . offer challenges to Asian America in terms of questioning the ability of racial identity to be an effective tool of mobilization and change. American identity is challenged in another, perhaps more surprising way through the histories of colonization themselves."[10] Sau-ling Cynthia Wong, in her critique of this developmentalist narrative beyond race and place eloquently points to its problems. "[T]o me it is not entirely coincidental," she writes, "that this self-critique echoes the trajectory of 'growth' prescribed for people of color in this country: that minorities need to liberate themselves from their outmoded, inward-looking preoccupations and participate in the more generous-spirited intellectual inquiries that 'everybody else' is engaged in."[11] Although I would not call histories of colonization, for instance, simply inquiries that everybody else is engaged in, and I would argue that attention to these histories is crucial, Wong's point that giving up concerns of nation and race is an acquiescence to model minority behavior is well taken. Giving up "claiming America" for Asian Americans would bring us back to what Frank Chin and Jeffrey Chan pointed out three decades ago, that "our present function as a minority is to be not black."[12]

Yet this perceived opposition between claiming America and transnational concerns, critiqued most eloquently by Wong, is itself of recent origin, coincident with the institutionalization of postcolonial studies by the late 1980s. As pointed out in chapter 1, just as postcolonial studies has moved from specific material analyses of domination and oppression to universalized, language-based negotiatory analyses of ambivalence and hybridity and has, in the process, tended to slight the writings of revolutionary anticolonial thinkers (embodying resistance postcolonialism) like Cabral, C. L. R. James, and Fanon (and thinkers such as Said) who wedded analyses of local colonial exploitation to critiques of Western colonization, so has the postcolonial debate within Asian American studies been premised on a forgetting of the latter's revolutionary origins. Leaders of the Asian American movement, such as Pat Sumi, were concerned with forging linkages among minorities in the United States, the colonized in the third world, and with formulating a resistance to the Vietnam War. Activists on the West Coast were influenced by the Black Panther Party, which had been founded in Oakland and which decisively traced the exploitation of minorities to U.S. imperialism. And, as William Wei forcefully reminds us, many revolutionary groups within the Asian American movement were inspired by Mao's party, which had managed to combine Marxism, Leninism, and Mao's thoughts with aspects of Chinese culture and created a country able to resist Western imperialism.[13] Notably, Wei Min She (WMS), which involved itself in unionization struggles of garment workers, described itself as an Asian American anti-imperialist organization.[14] Similarly, the Revolutionary Union (originally the Bay Area Revolutionary Union) had as its stated objectives the "development of a united front against imperialism."[15] Thus, the revolutionary beginnings of the Asian American movement were, in fact, postcolonial, and "claiming America" and transnational "postcolonial" concerns were not oppositions.

If Asian American studies are to be productively mapped as postcolonial, it is crucial that this mapping reflect the concerns of what I have called resistance postcolonialism; thus, a methodological linkage with the beginnings of the Asian American movement is critical. Postcolonial Asian American studies can then mark the points at which identities and spaces within the nation intersect with subjectifications produced through positionings of people's homelands with the United States through relations of neo-imperialism and neocolonialism. Wen Ho Lee, for instance, was considered a threat because he was interpellated as perpetual foreigner and because China was being positioned as the major economic rival to the United States. Indeed, the writings of many Asian-American scholars have, from the start, included national as well as transnational, postcolonial concerns—Elaine Kim's focus on immigration restrictions, Ronald Takaki's analyses of the racialization of each new immigrant labor force, and, more recently, Sucheng Chan's demonstrations of the linkages between imperialist relations of the United States and the homeland in the treatment of particular communities.[16] A fruitful linkage between postcolonial and critical race approaches would foreground the positionings of various homelands within relations of global capitalism, forge linkages with minorities and postcolonial oppression in other nations, and see how these relations intersect with the racial mappings within the United States. Thus, I am by no means suggesting that Asian American studies cultivate a curious xenophobia and duplicate earlier American studies narratives about American exceptionalism from empire. What I reject is the idea that racial specificities and particular positionings within the United States, resultant in part from the juridical and social constructions of racial formations in the country, need to be put aside in favor of a more enlightened globalized or postcolonial approach, postcolonial here being coded as a safe site providing the universalized language of hybridity and difference.[17]

The photographs of Tseng Kwong Chi illustrate my point that Asian American identity formulates itself by asserting ethnic space within the nation even as it evokes larger cultural histories of colonialism and Orientalism. I find Tseng's photographs particularly appropriate in demonstrating the importance of the narrative of claiming America because Tseng is ostensibly a quintessential diasporic subject whose work can arguably be read to evoke generalized tropes of liminality, hybridity, and border crossing.[18] Indeed, one could argue that given the migratory character of his own life and the global subjects of his work, interpellating him as Asian American is to circumscribe the reaches of his art. His short life might be described as one of many movements, multiple locations, and diverse affiliations. Tseng was, after all, raised as a child of recent immigrants to Hong Kong, born soon after his parents fled China in the aftermath of the Communist Revolution. While he was still a teenager, Tseng's family moved to Vancouver where he finished his schooling and attended the University of British Columbia and Sir George Williams University, Montreal. But Tseng's omnivorous education also included studying at *L'Academie Julien, L'Ecole Superior d'Arts Graphiques* in Paris. It was only in 1979 that Tseng settled in New York City, where he lived till his untimely death in 1990.

So perhaps it might be more accurate to think of Tseng, who grew up in Hong Kong and Canada, as Asian Canadian or to invoke the title of a recent collection of essays, "Asian North American." Indeed, both these appellations are useful in naming the subject, Tseng. But there is no reason to think that these identities displace the Tseng we think of as Asian American. If, as I have argued, racial identities are formed not simply by routes or movements but more important by where they find a roots/location, viewing Tseng also as Asian American is an acknowledgment of the continuing production of his racialized identity. Indeed, to delimit Asian Americanness by length of stay is also to restrict it in ways that have little connection to the manner in which Asian Americanness is constituted—through interpellation by the dominant culture, in the practice of everyday life as an Asian minority in the United States, and through self-identification. As Peter Wang's *A Great Wall* so adroitly demonstrates, both immigrants and second-generation Asian Americans might be equally foreigners when they return home. Tseng's photographs, particularly those taken at famous historical and recreational tourist sites in the United States, speak powerfully through all these forms of racial construction.

Tseng's pictures are famous for his signature Mao suit, his reflector dark glasses, as well as his military haircut and his photoidentification card. His primary oeuvre consists of approximately 150 black-and-white photographs taken between 1979 and 1983, with the artist posing in front of different American tourist attractions such as Niagara Falls, Golden Gate Bridge, and Cape Canaveral. After 1983, Tseng went international, posing in front of such well-known sites as the Eiffel Tower and Notre Dame, after which he entered a phase of nature photography from 1987 till his death from AIDS in 1990. Alongside his fine art photography, Tseng also made 50,000 documentary photographs of his friend Keith Haring at work on his famous subway drawings and murals.[19] Tseng's oeuvre took on different titles beginning with the implicit Orientalist critique signified by "East Meets West," to the appropriation of the American, masculinist westering rhetoric in the title "The Expeditionary Series" to the cosmopolitan subject of the posthumous exhibit, "Tseng Kwong Chi: Citizen of the World." Three features of Tseng's oeuvre are prominent here: his decision to begin his career by photographing national icons; the insertion of himself in each photograph, thus virtually creating a solo performance; and the constant marking of himself as racial outsider through the Mao suit. I will focus here mainly on Tseng's early period from 1979 to 1983 and demonstrate how these photographs of different monuments and tourist attractions in the United States cannot be understood without reference U.S. racial and gender formations, imperialist relations, and the racialized limits of mass culture. Tseng studies and comments on all these through a complex and parodic performance of his Chineseness.

Tseng's decision to use the Mao suit itself follows an interesting narrative of local interpellation and ethnic performance later recuperated in his photographs. In 1979, as the story goes, Tseng, the impoverished artist then living with his sister, was visited by his parents who wished to take the siblings to an uspscale Manhattan restaurant. In order to satisfy the restaurant's dress code of a gentleman's suit, Tseng came attired in the only suit he owned—a Mao suit recovered from a thrift store in Montreal.[20] Although his parents were aghast, the maitre d', taking Tseng to be a VIP, an emissary from China, was suitably deferential. From that day, Tseng chose to perform his Chineseness, completing his transformation from the quasi-western appellation signified by Joseph Tseng, to the more Chinese Kwong Chi Tseng, to the complete Chinese appellative Tseng Kwong Chi in keeping with the Chinese tradition in which the family name precedes the given name.[21]

Tseng's photography is undoubtedly performative, as Peggy Phelan reminds us that all portrait photography is, but it is a performative that recognizes the limits placed by race and colonialism.[22] For Judith Butler, performativity is mobile, shifting, and polymorphous, inherently destructive of hierarchical cultural and social binary categories, the main one being gender.[23] But although performativity has been effectively marshalled to question the permanence and ubiquity of gender and race categories, questions of access and power have often been overlooked. Therefore, while I do not wish to ascribe to racial performance the individualistic and asocial freedom Judith Butler bestows to gender performance (Tseng isn't free to perform the prototypical, unmarked white male), I want to suggest that the powerful, disruptive moments created in Tseng's photographs depend on a complex interplay of Chineseness, Americanness, outsider and insider identities as perceived in the United States. That is, Tseng performs a contemporary, Maoist Chineseness ironically. Between the charged political significance of his suit as a sign of revolution and its depoliticized exoticism (suggested by the obeisant maitre d'), Tseng plays to the ignorance and prejudices of his audience.

Tseng performs with a full awareness of the entrenched stereotypes of Orientalism such as mysteriousness, impassiveness, inscrutability, and alienness that transcend temporal differences and are attributed equally to a Mao suit as to chinoiserie.

Indeed, Tseng seems to have calculated the power and fixity of Chineseness as alterity in the United States when he crashed the opening reception for an exhibition of Ch'ing Dynasty costumes at the Metropolitan Museum. Dressed in his Mao suit, Tseng set up his camera, greeted guests as they came up the stairs, and invited them to pose with him. These celebrities, including Henry Kissinger, Andy Warhol, and Yves Saint Laurent, failed to notice the words "Visitor" and "Slutforart" printed on Tseng's photoidentification and treated him as the Chinese emissary he was ventriloquating rather than a postmodern photographer who was actively creating them as subjects for his art.[25] Tseng's performance at the Met was deliberately ironic. Whereas the celebrities, ready for an evening of Orientalist edification, had dressed in chinoiserie, absorbing the Other through racial cross-dressing, Tseng marked himself as insistently Other, yet not an exotic Other who could be dismissed. While the guests were participating in a collective Orientalist gaze, Tseng was self-consciously and ironically critiquing Orientalism as cultural exhibit, popularized most notoriously by P. T. Barnum who displayed Afong Moy, a woman with bound feet from 1834 to 1837.[25]

With this background of Tseng's artful staging of his persona, let us turn to some of his photographs in the East meets West series. Defamiliarizing the location by subjecting it through interrogation by an outsider is central to all.[25] In "Hollywood, California" (Fig. 5.1), Tseng obviously seeks to interrupt Hollywood's assumption of the California landscape by dwarfing the sign and towering over the hills. The photograph, shot from straight on, illuminates Tseng's face, his reflector glasses, and the press badge on his left breast pocket. The eye is immediately drawn to the two white objects in the photograph: the Hollywood sign and the badge. The one is a known entity, an industry producing faces and spaces that inhabit the American social imaginary; the other is a mysterious entity whose identity can be confirmed by close scrutiny of the badge and a comparison with the badge's wearer. Yet the comparison increases the mystery further because Tseng's reflector glasses hide part of his face. On the other hand, the rigid expression (which Tseng maintains in the "East Meets West" photographs but abandons in the photographs of his East Village friends in the series titled "The Gang's All Here"), the hidden eyes and the Mao suit produce a Chinese version of a well-known Orientalist stereotype: the inscrutable Orient.

Fig. 5.1. "Hollywood, California," 1979. Photograph by Tseng Kwong Chi, from the Expeditionary Self-Portrait Series. Copyright © 1979 Muna Tseng Dance Projects, Inc. New York

Versions of this stereotype had circulated in American popular culture ever since the entry of large number of Chinese laborers in the nineteenth century and infamously memorialized in Bret Harte's well-circulated poem, "The Heathen Chinee." Of course, the Hollywood dream factory was itself not exempt from perpetuating this stereotype. Through his own staging of it, Tseng critiques Orientalism and exploits it. But while this stereotype depends on what Johannes Fabian has described as a temporal distantiation of the Other, Tseng's invocation of it also involves an obvious presentness. Following Nixon's visit to China in 1972, China had emerged in the U.S. popular imagination, in its presentness, as open to American interests, yet unfamiliar in its revolutionary posture. Indeed, China as incendiary to social unrest was dramatized most vividly to middle America by the Black Panthers and left student organizations who circulated and propagated Mao's works. Tseng thus caricatures not simply the U.S. paranoia of the Yellow Peril, as Grady Turner suggests, but also the paranoia about the communist threat both within and without the country.[26] And Tseng plays up this threat by commingling the familiar and unfamiliar in the staging of his own body. The inscrutable Oriental, the menacing, Mao-like communist, wears the reflector glasses often worn by Hollywood celebrities and maintains the stiff, rigid posture that was also the hip look of new bands.[27]

While Tseng's own body puts into question the border between the known and the unknown, the past and the present, the remote shutter release in his right hand forces us to pay attention to the immediate present of the moment in which this very photograph is being taken. This might well mark what Homi Bhabha calls the Benjamanian present of astonishment through which writers of the diaspora, proceeding from conditions of interstitiality and unhomeliness, interrupt the narrative of modernity.[28] Yet, the relation between the figure and the landscape cannot be interpreted solely through ideas of global diaspora and transnationalism. The photograph specifically questions the raced narrative of nation and the exclusions on which it is predicated. What could be more quintessentially American than the Hollywood sign and what could be more foreign than the Chinese man in the Mao suit? At the same time, Tseng's act of photographing the scene suggests an appropriation of it, particularly as he stands tall above the scene. Is Tseng inside the narrative of nation constituted by the Hollywood sign or outside it? Can a person of Asian ancestry really be "inside" the nation or is she always interpellated, as Ronald Takaki suggests, as forever "foreign?"[29] And given the history of white actors playing yellowface, the photograph raises the pertinent question about whether a Chinese-America can ever be "inside" Hollywood.

Although Tseng's attire remains unchanged in every photograph, his affect, posture, and positioning interrogate the familiar in different ways. In "Mickey Mouse, Disneyland, California" (Fig. 5.2), as in "Hollywood, California," the drama derives from the apparent incongruity of oppositions brought together in the present moment: American and foreign, lighthearted and serious, freedom and restriction, known and unknown. Tseng poses as tourist (in a parody of the careless tourist photograph as suggested by the unbecoming pole in the middle of Mickey and Tseng), yet not a tourist next to Mickey; both subjects look away from the camera instead of toward it, disconnected from both the camera and each other. Yet the incongruity of the photograph, marked by the dissonance between the smiling face and Tseng's deadpan serious look, relates also to political differences and

Fig. 5.2. "Mickey Mouse, Disneyland, California," 1979. Photograph by Tseng Kwong Chi, from the Expeditionary Self-Portrait Series. Copyright © 1979 Muna Tseng Dance Projects, Inc. New York

political conformity. The intrusion of the communist figure into Disneyland undoubtedly signifies on the cold war origins of Disneyland as a propagandistic capitalist extravaganza inaugurated in 1956, replete with Tomorrowland's exhibit of the friendly atom and the atomic submarine ride, and into which Krushchev was denied entry in 1959. Nevertheless, Mickey's welcoming wave is less than unbounded.

In this supposedly clear picture, without heightened contrasts of light and dark, the oppositions between innocent gaiety and cold indoctrination seem firm. At yet another level, however, the photograph calls attention to the similarities between the two figures. If Tseng's expression is taut and forced, with a militaristic rigidity, Mickey's is supremely so. If Tseng is wearing a severe, forbidding mask, so obviously is Mickey. The mask/costume stages a persona so intent on being perceived as "real" that the identity of the human under the costume is completely hidden—for all we know it could be a diasporic Chinese-Hong-Kong, Canadian, American. The erasure under the costume that, as Henry Giroux has shown, is mandated by Disney (even if the performer is sick) is absolute, underscoring capitalism's production of a uniform subjectivity.[30] This similarity of performance is underscored by the visual similarity between Mickey's and Tseng's shining black shoes. And the wide eyes and the welcoming smile that make Mickey all-inclusive, and in popular mythology all-American, belie the fact that entry to this simulacra paradise of neatly trimmed hedges and spotless sidewalks is limited to those who can afford it.

The deliberate disconnect between viewer and subject, and between subjects deployed in the Disneyland photograph is exaggerated further in "Statue of Liberty, New York, New York" (Fig. 5.3) in which both racial and gender estrangements are emphasized. Although the "East Meets West" series most overtly announces cultural difference, it is important to remember that the very first image in the series was taken on the dunes of Provincetown, Massachusetts, an important destination for the gay community, as if emphasizing's Tseng's gay identity.[31] Indeed, one could argue that the cultural marginalization that Tseng so masterfully emphasizes in his "East Meets West" series is enabled by his simultaneous gender alienation as a gay male. As Richard Dyer argues with respect to gay films, although few texts announce themselves explicitly as such, gay authorship is important because of the authors' access to "sign systems which would have been like foreign languages to straight filmmakers" (188). But although Dyer discusses the difference of lesbian/gay authorship and sees African American critics as pursuing "equivalent issues," he does not consider how racial positioning might affect gender difference. I suggest that Tseng's "New York, New York" cannot be understood without considering Tseng's *double* alienation as gay and Asian American male.

In a parody of the "Man Against the Sky" shot used to claim the frontier for white males, Tseng stands, legs astride, almost as tall as the Statue of Liberty, looking into the distance, over New York. If the shot is, at one level, a clear mockery of frontier masculinity from the perspective of a gay male who with Whitmanesque casualty, with hand in his pocket, visually equates himself with Lady Liberty, this icon of American immigrant democracy, it is at another level, a different double interrogation: of the masculinizing imperative of Asian American cultural nationalists, and of the gendered imperatives of Western imperialism and Orientalism that have produced the stereotype of the effeminate Asian male. By visually

Fig. 5.3. "Statue of Liberty, New York, New York," 1979. Photograph by Tseng Kwong Chi, from the Expeditionary Self-Portrait Series. Copyright © 1979 Muna Tseng Dance Projects, Inc. New York

positioning himself in proximity to the white Lady Liberty, while nightmarish clouds hover over the horizon, Tseng defies the stereotype of weak effeminacy ascribed to Asian males as well as notes the paranoia about unassimilable aliens and miscegenation that have marked U.S. encounters with its "yellow hordes," its Asian male immigrants. At the same time, however, by portraying his "masculinist" takeover as dark and brooding, Tseng questions the injunction to claim yellow male masculinity which has been central to the writings of cultural nationalists such as Frank Chin.[32] Tseng's triple estrangement—from the dominant white culture, from its raced gender imperatives, and from the gender imperatives of the Asian American community—is further emphasized in the positioning of his line of vision. Tseng looks into the distance, away from the statue and the camera, thus emphasizing the schism between himself and the viewer, and with the welcoming nationalist icon. Thus, in every familiar tourist site, Tseng, the Asian American, is the outsider. The photograph simultaneously dramatizes Tseng's claiming of America and his raced and gendered foreignness from the imagined community of nation, creating a friction of encounter which calls for a transformation of the pedagogical narrative of nation which recognizes only assimilation, liberal multiculturalism, or multicultural tolerance.

At this point I would like to emphasize some crucial distinctions between Tseng's photographs and those of the postmodern portrait photographers whose techniques most obviously resemble his own. One of the best known photographers to focus on the restaging of her own body is Cindy Sherman. Some of Sherman's ironic self-portraits with her dressed as Caravaggio's *Bacchus* or Raphael's *Fornarina* forcibly remind us, as Barbara M. Stafford suggests, that the old masters do not fit her because gender constitutes the difference.[33] Similarly, in her "stars" series, Sherman emphasizes the stagedness of 1950s female types ranging from pinups to sweethearts by restaging the postures of women from Marilyn Monroe to Doris Day. Tseng's photographs are based on an obvious difference of his body from that of Mao. Clearly, Tseng with his reflector glasses and photoidentification is not the well-known Mao. Mao's Long March fascinated Tseng, particularly in the immediate transmogrification of Mao's photographs into mythic propaganda; he was particularly struck with an image of Mao standing on a mountain at sunrise, with a "faraway, determined" look on his face.[34] Yet, although the informed viewer might locate the drama of difference between Mao and Tseng in Tseng's own Long March, for the American viewer, there might, in fact, be little rupture in self-portraiture, little difference between Tseng the Chinese and Tseng the Mao-like Chinese. Tseng simply is the Chinese, the inscrutable Oriental. And this raced othering of the self, Tseng's photographs suggest, is central to being an outsider, the Asian American in the United States. And yet the very stagedness of the photographs is disturbing. As Dan Bacalzo suggests, "Tseng becomes an art object that is not himself, but neither is it completely an Other that can be exoticized and dismissed."[35]

In an analysis of Cindy Sherman's paintings, Cathy Davidson alerts us to the "coercions of a contemporary photocentrism so pervasive as to be virtually invisible," where we cannot even see that "we see ourselves primarily as seen, imaged."[36] But what Davidson sees as a defining feature of photocentrism has always been an ontological reality for the colonized and minority populations for whom being imaged is always a double imaging and for whom the raced imaging is central. The undifferentiated social mirror through which the subject experiences Otherness is, for minorities, always doubly othered through the difference of race. The experience of looked-at-ness, being othered and relegated to objecthood, memorialized so unforgettably by the DuBoisian "double-consciousness, this sense of always looking at one's self through the eyes of others," and later by Franz Fanon (in his incisive revision of Lacan), in the opening lines of "The Fact of Blackness"—"Dirty nigger!" Or simply, "Look, a Negro!" describes the subject constitution not only for blacks but for the alien Asian as well.[37] It is this experience of being othered, in Tseng's case through cliches of Orientalism such as mystery, inscrutability, unfamiliarity, and danger, that he exploits by constantly staging the drama between the familiar American tourist spot and the stranger inhabiting it. And in the United States, it is the Asian American, neither black nor white, whose foreignness no number of generations of immigrant lineage can erase.

As a final illustration of Tseng's complex negotiations with local interpellation, we can briefly look at "Lincoln Memorial, Washington, D.C." (Fig. 5.4). This is one of the few nonlandscape photographs in which Tseng turns his back on the camera and one that raises many disturbing questions. The photograph makes extensive use of light and dark to position Lincoln ambiguously as a godlike figure whose face and torso are aglow with light in contrast to the foreboding darkness above and the shadows below. Tseng stands once again with the remote shutter release in hand, in the shadow of the monument. His Mao suit is barely distinguishable and apparent only in synchronic connections we, as viewers of Tseng's photographs, make. Tseng stands as close to the monument as is probably legally allowed, but no closer. His pose is stiff and rigid, as if in militaristic respect to the patriarch. Yet the popular assimilative ethnic paradigm of national figure and immigrant obeisance is ambiguous here. Perhaps Lincoln's position as ambivalent architect of abolitionism (yet a supporter of African American colonization of Liberia and thus a conflicted icon of progressive racial policies) is underscored by the lighting. Lincoln's torso appears as if artificially lightened in comparison with the rest of the monument, indeed in relation to Tseng himself as well.

At another level, the almost luminous upper body of Lincoln, emerging from the shadows, in a composition replete with light and shadow, with Tseng looking at the monument but not up at Lincoln's face, his own body in shadow, marks the construction of what we can think of as postmodern mourning. That is, unlike traditional elegies that were refuges for nostalgia or modern elegies that, through melancholy, attempt to resist consolation, postmodern mourning puts into radical question what the object of the elegy is.[38] And this interrogative style is part of Tseng's post-

Fig. 5.4. "Lincoln Memorial, Washington, D.C.," 1982. Photograph by Tseng Kwong Chi, from the Expeditionary Self-Portrait Series. Copyright © 1979 Muna Tseng Dance Projects, Inc. New York

modern strategy of parody in which the object of parody is never singular. Just as his other tourist photographs parody, at once, conventional relations between the tourist and the attraction, as well as the cliches of Orientalism, this photograph raises a number of questions. Can Asian Americans be taken out of the shadows of U.S. racial oppression? Can they be enabled by the legacy of progressive racial movements? Are the nation's heroes the same for Asian Americans as for white America? All these questions are invoked, but not resolved in the photograph and lead us to concerns of race, immigration, citizenship, and freedom, all of which continue to be central to Asian American identity.

If Tseng's photographs of tourist sites present clear disruptions of race and space with Tseng as central, if not towering over the site, his photographs of the American West engage with American mythologies differently. The West as open frontier, as unpopulated land available for and beckoning settlers in the fulfillment of a unique manifest destiny, has long been part of the mythos of American exceptionalism. Jack Kerouac's *On the Road* is a classic paen to the liberating possibilities of the West absorbed, seen, and experienced by two white males. As a photographer of the American West, Tseng confronted a complex legacy. Nineteenth-century photographers presented panoramas of the West, but very often it was the West as it was being used, consumed, and possessed. William Henry Jackson's "Packtrain of the US Geological Survey," for instance, draws attention to the long line of horse-riding surveyors in the middle of the landscape while Timothy O'Sullivan's "American Nevada" pictures a snow-capped landscape with a small wagon with footprints leading up to it. Both photographers document westward expansion as part of the meaning of the West.

Ansel Adams's vast, panoramic, glorious images of the West, denuded of human contact on the other hand, conjure up the landscape as vast expanse, as uninhabited territory ready for settlement, belying the reality of both indigenous inhabitants and the poverty of laborers who helped the conquest. Tseng joins the tradition of activist photographers who, since the 1970s, have been battling the legacy of Adams and his misleading images of the West.[39] In his photographs of the Grand Canyon and of the Badlands National Park, South Dakota, Tseng is often at the edge of a photograph, sometimes a dimunitive presence in the landscape, and sometimes with his back to the camera. But in all of them he continues to wear the Maò suit and, in almost all, continues to stand rigidly. These photographs challenge both the magisterial gaze of the Adams photographs in which the vantage point inspires mastery and control and those of the nineteenth-century photographers who document the "settlement" of the West.[40] Tseng's photographs fracture the landscape by evoking different histories. They mark the unavailability of the expeditionary/conquest narrative for Chinese Americans who were brought into the West as cheap labor, and also question the rhetoric of manifest destiny by implicitly critiquing Mao's propaganda paintings of the Long March.

In ventriloquating Chineseness through the figure of Mao, Tseng obviously gestures to the Asian (i.e., transnational) aspect of Asian American, in this case, Chinese American identity. The Asian American as perpetual foreigner is, in a sense, simply the Asian foreigner in these photographs. Yet Tseng's photographs cannot be understood without reference to the collective social gaze that Fanon describes as the quintessential moment of racial interpellation and othering and which Said explains as Orientalism. It is as a subject of this gaze within the United States that Tseng's disruption of, and claim to, the icons of American culture makes sense. Tseng's case thus strongly suggests the need to foreground the idea of political visibility within the nation and the dialogues with narratives of the nation in the reading of Asian American texts. By playing out the politics of race and critiquing Orientalism, Tseng's photographs invite a progressive Post-Colonial critique of imperialism at the same time as they call attention to the systemic exclusion of Asians within the body politic.

Part Three

POSSIBILITIES FOR POST-COLONIAL CITIZENSHIP

CHAPTER SIX

Black Nationalism and Anti-Imperial Resistance in Assata Shakur's *Autobiography*

It might seem bizarrely counterintuitive to think about possibilities for Post-Colonial citizenship emanating from the retrospective autobiographical writings of an activist, incarcerated woman because both theorizations of neoliberal globalization and contemporary imperialism are invested in mobility, whether of peoples, cultures, or capital. Metropoles in the United States are seen as sites of heterogeneity and as recipients of an influx of migrants who move through urban spaces creating new and changing cultural mixes. Even though Subcomandante Marcos's term "wandering" is more appropriate than the glitzy term "mobility," it is movement that is seen to characterize the current landscape.[1] Yet, coextensive with this movement has been a steady increase in the level of incarceration in the United States. Indeed with the disappearance of the threat of the socialist bloc, the "war on crime" (followed by the "war on terror") has emerged as a major means of disciplining the population to the dictates of global capital. The combination of flexible production, corporate welfare, and attacks on the welfare state are producing the incarceration of Marx's industrial reserve army as an expedient means of social and economic control. At the same time, the corporatization of prisons, as evidenced by the growth of companies such as Corrections Corporation of America, and Wackenhut, what Angela Davis aptly dubbed the "prison-industrial complex," indicates the integration of the incarceration industry with global capitalism[2] as does the increasing use of prison labor contracted to private corporations. Indeed, the rising levels of incarceration in the United States in today's imperialist phase parallel uncannily the overcrowded prisons of England during its expansionist colonial phase. However, both arguments about universalized capitalism and comparative colonialisms need to be tempered with historical, racial particularity. While the prisons of England were filled with the industrial reserve army of the skilled, though unemployed who could potentially incite revolution, the prisons of the United States are disproportionately filled with people of color (who might well constitute this industrial reserve army). Incarceration in the United States, as Shakur's autobiography powerfully reminds us, is a site in which the technologies of racism and imperialism intersect.

Thus far, I have demonstrated the epistemological problems attendant on racial erasure or the deemphasizing of historically specific racialisms in the United States within some versions of postcolonial theory, feminist theory, and Asian American studies. I have also suggested a complicity between migration-and-exile centered narratives of globalization and ideologies of whiteness and imperialism. Mukherjee's novel, *Jasmine*, dramatizes the economic exploitation of the new underclass created by global capitalism and points toward the restricted and enforced racial-cultural recognition necessary for socioeconomic mobility. In the last part of this book, I want to examine trajectories of racial resistance in the United States and analyze the ways in which particular, antiracist resistances appeal to specific constituencies and forge larger, subaltern connections through this particularity. In chapters six and seven, I undertake this analysis through the works of Assata Shakur and Leslie Marmon Silko, both of whom see their writings as political interventions and who can be seen as organic intellectuals who identify with and speak on behalf of a community.[3] In the conclusion, I extend the analysis to contemporary activist organizations. Ultimately, I want to suggest ways in which these resistances articulate possibilities for a Post-Colonial citizenship that constitutes a globalization, as it were, from below. As stated in chapter 1, my use of capitalization for both post and colonial indicates the fact that the post for subaltern groups, such as Native Americans, can only be imagined because colonialism is a living reality for indigenous populations; and insofar as racial minorities function, as hurricane Katrina powerfully reminded us, as denizens of internal colonies, the "post" is still imaginary. On the other hand, I retain the use of the post because of the affective solidarities forged between racial minorities in the United States and nations that have overthrown or are engaged in overthrowing colonialism, and because of the possibilities inherent in imagining a Post-Colonial identity that includes, but goes beyond anticolonialism or anti-imperialism.[4]

The writings of political prisoners, whether produced in prison or subsequently thereafter, have always spoken both to specific constituencies as well as to an imagined community of the politically repressed worldwide. My intention in focusing on Shakur is not to invoke this general paradigm but rather to examine her autobiography as a political text negotiating the parameters of identity through systemic U.S. racism and imperialism at a specific historical moment of black nationalism. However, through Shakur, I also mean to explore the radical globalism of black nationalism and thus question the wholesale dismissal of black nationalism under the rubric of misogyny. This does not mean that a gender critique is not vital, but rather that such a critique should not result in a derecognition of black nationalism as an anticolonial movement. The politics of the Black Panther Party, particularly its emphasis on the self-empowerment of African Americans, and its forging of linkages with nationalist movement against colonialism and imperialism are central to understanding Shakur's politics. Although the Black Panther Party was not a homogenous movement, it is interesting that while a majority of black nationalist leaders espoused and participated in anti-imperial and anticolonial politics, the far-reaching scope of black nationalism has generally been neglected.[5] Despite, for instance, her allegiance to the Communist Party, in her autobiography, Angela Davis, like Shakur, forges connections between black liberation and anticolonial struggles.

Connecting black nationalism to struggles worldwide was a significant component of the Black Panther Party, the major organization for the black liberation struggle, and to which Shakur was connected. Founded by Bobby Seale and Huey Newton in 1966 in the aftermath of the Watts riots, the disaffection with Martin Luther King's pacifism given the violence inflicted on black people, and the daily police harassment of blacks in the streets of California, the party grew to become a major national and international presence. It is in its role as militant black protector that the party is popularly known as reflected in its full title, "the Black Panther Party for Self-Defense." In accordance with California law that permitted the carrying of registered firearms, party members, fully armed, wearing black leather jackets began patrolling the streets of Oakland and, in what is widely recognized as a precedent for the Miranda rights, began reading African Americans being intimidated by the police, their rights. Yet this very local performance of self-empowerment, necessitated as it was by the particularities of unwarranted police intimidation of African Americans, was simultaneously an enactment of the party's platform on self-determination, couched in the language of third world decolonization. It was a refusal to recognize the state as legitimate and to substitute themselves as alternatives to state power.[6] Indeed, the ten-point program of the Black Panther Party included the demand for a "United-Nations supervised plebiscite to be held throughout the Black colony in which only Black colonial subjects will be allowed to participate."[7] The writings of Frantz Fanon, Mao Tse Tung, and the liberation of Algeria as well as the Cuban revolution remained central inspirations for even the most polarized figures of the party.

Yet it was, to a great extent, the different visions of the party's connections to other revolutionary and protest movements that tore it apart. Although most party members, for instance, joined antiwar groups in denouncing the war in Vietnam as a racist one and urged African Americans not to fight in the war, the party's coalition with the predominantly white Peace and Freedom Party drew the ire of Stokely Carmichael, who resigned as the party's Prime Minister in 1969.[8] Similarly, an enraged Roy Wilkins condemned Huey Newton's offer to send African Americans to fight for the National Liberation Front in Vietnam as a disengagement with racial repression at home.[9] While Eldridge Cleaver and other Black Panther Party members in Algeria continued to think of themselves as emissaries of a nation and sought (and often received) international recognition from revolutionary governments, Newton, after his release from jail, theorized a postnational political order derived from a critique of imperialism. He argued that the combination of U.S. imperialism and the power of mass media to serve the ends of imperialism meant that the cultural, political, and economic self-determination necessary for nationalism had been undermined. Newton consequently deemed the Panthers "intercommunalists" "because nations have been transformed into communities of the world"[10] and later proceeded to prioritize community programs such as the breakfast programs for children over armed militancy. Newton's expulsion of the international section of the Black Panther Party under the leadership of Eldridge Cleaver completed the division of the party. The Black Liberation Army, composed of former Panthers committed to revolutionary armed struggle, was formed under such internecine battles. The Black Liberation Army thus manifested an even more radical version of the subversion of the nation-state than the Black Panther Party.

When Shakur was falsely arrested on charges of having shot a policeman at a New Jersey turnpike in 1973, she was a member of the Black Liberation Army, having left the Black Panther Party earlier. I mention Shakur's political affiliations not to pigeonhole her autobiography within a movement presided by Newton, but to map the varied, sometimes contradictory, genealogies of her political articulations. A Black Panther who critiqued party hierarchy, the arrogance of many of its members, the rigidity of the party line that even required her to tear down a poster with the word "international" in it because the party was "intercommunal," the machismo of party members who routinely derided women, and the party's stifling of criticism, she remained at the same time committed to armed struggle, arguably a visible sign of power, long after the party abandoned it.[11] Shakur saw the importance of the liberatory goals of the Black Panther Party, even as she questioned its methods.

I use Shakur's text as a particularly apt model for resistance and Post-Colonial citizenship for several reasons. First, through its close attention to the politics of race within incarceration as well as to the continuities between racial and imperial systems, it articulates a political identity formed through an ongoing and productive dialectic between the raced particular and a Post-Colonial, anti-imperial solidarity. At times, pan-Africanism provides an emotional subjectification for Shakur as an African American woman; at other times, her position as a member of the Black Liberation Army links her politically and structurally to anticolonial movements that are not necessarily African. Second, as I will discuss later, although the activism adumbrated by Shakur stridently resists hierarchical organizational modes and stresses the importance of the relationships among race, capitalism, and imperialism, its strong rootedness within the history of slavery, figured through maternal tropes, and thus its commitment to systemic analysis, offers liberating alternatives to postmodern political models such as Deleuze and Guattari's that stress relationship alone and risk the danger of becoming immaterial. It thus interrogates the rooted versus relational binary posited by postmodern political thought. Instead, Shakur invites us to think through different kinds of relatedness, all ensuing from the "root" of racial oppression: that between the raced local and state engineered racial power; between systemic racism and imperialism; between subjective racial identity and systemic racial hierarchies; and between private, familial space and racialized public space. In addition, Shakur's autobiography is written as political activism, a process rather than an end product, one that articulates and opens possibilities in the very manner of its construction.

Shakur's text draws attention to the structural continuities between the technologies of incarceration and those of the surveillance of different Black Liberation groups and blacks in general, thus pointing to the criminalization and disciplining of blackness on which U.S. civil society rests. It also posits an integral relationship between the disciplinary technologies of the U.S. nation-state directed toward its minorities and those of U.S. imperialism. Here it is important to consider the dynamics of contemporary incarceration in the United States. From 1997 to 2008, the prison population jumped from 1.8 million to 2.3 million, giving the United States the dubious distinction of having the largest prison population in the world (far more than China) as well as, what some would argue, the highest rates of incarceration (over 1 percent).[12] Not surprisingly, African Americans and people of color constitute a disproportionate percentage of those incarcerated, impacted from the 1980s by a racialization of drug laws and more recently by terrorist racial profiling. As the Human Rights Watch statement to the United Nations Commission on Human Rights pointed out in 2000, although African Americans constitute 13 percent of the U.S. population, they compose almost 50 percent of the prison population, having an eight times greater chance of being incarcerated than whites.[13] If we add Hispanics to the picture, the percentage of people of color in incarceration jumps to almost 70 percent. Cynical manipulations of these already skewed numbers are well known. George H. Bush's infamous Willie Horton advertisement, which used the image of an African-American man going through a revolving door to make an argument about stiffer prison sentences, appealed to the racism of whites by insinuating that African American men were dangerous and needed to be locked up. The prison thus continues to function as a means of disciplining the African American population.

This racialization of incarceration has been seen by many as a manifestation of capitalism's historical requirement of inequality, and which, according to Wallerstein, thrives on a constantly changing ethnicization.[14] Angela Davis's connections between the global restructuring programs of the 1980s, the criminalization of single women of color, the exploitation of third world women, and the expansion of the prison industry are also apropos here.[15] More recently, with the virtual free rein given the FBI under the hastily passed Patriot Act, increasing numbers of people of color are being incarcerated without charges being brought against them and with many, like Sami Al-Arian (held in jail without bail for three years and forced to plea bargain and agree to be deported in exchange for his release), becoming scapegoats. Just as the security and well-being of the nation are currently being presented as dependant on the increased surveillance of Arab Americans and other Muslims, as well as on the detention without charges of over six hundred prisoners in Guantanamo Bay, the security of the nation in the early 1970s was shown to depend on the containment and repression of black liberation movements of which the Black Panther Party was perhaps the most visible. In fact, FBI director J. Edgar Hoover labeled the Black Panther Party as the greatest internal threat to the security of the nation and gave the FBI carte blanche to suppress its activities. It is ultimately her belonging to the Black Liberation Army that led to the incarceration of Assata Shakur despite the smokescreen of her attack on a police officer.

I have chosen to focus here particularly on the autobiography of Assata Shakur from a host of other autobiographies from the black power movement such as Elaine Brown's *A Taste of Power*, Malcolm X's *The Autobiography of Malcolm X*, Huey Newton's *Revolutionary Suicide*, Angela

Davis's *Autobiography*, George Jackson's *Soledad Brother*, and Bobby Seale's *Seize the Time* because Shakur constructs her narrative as a process in which the relationship between the "I" and "we" (both African American and transnational) is constantly being reconfigured even though the two are conceived as mutually constitutive. The aesthetic, that is, insistently asks to be read as a politics in the making at the same time as Shakur sees her writing as political intervention. In addition, in Shakur's autobiography, the local, raced particular and global dialectic is present as productive of knowledge from the very beginning. International solidarity is not the teleological end as with Malcolm X, but rather a beginning epistemological framework through which the local can be revolutionizing and revolutionized. Just as significantly, Shakur actively questions and critiques hierarchical party structures, exemplified, for instance, by Newton's taking on the title of Supreme Commander.[16] And in contrast to Elaine Brown's more personal and clearly retrospective account of her involvement with leaders of the Black Panther Party, Shakur strives to write as a dissident intellectual for whom the personal is part of an imagined political community of both blacks at home and the colonized abroad.

It is significant that Shakur's autobiography, like Davis's, begins by describing experiences of incarceration and surveillance that are personal but which metaphorically demonstrate the technologies of disciplining colonized black bodies because these representations specify the particular ways in which both the disciplinary apparatus and civil society depend on the criminalization of blackness. Foucault's insights on the nature of modern disciplining are useful here in explicating the ideological necessity of criminalization, even as they reveal the limits of an unraced theory of disciplining. Foucault argues that the end of the eighteenth century spells a new technology of power based on a theory of contract in which the citizen is presumed to have accepted the laws of society. The criminal, having broken with the pact, "is therefore the enemy of society as a whole" and his offense "opposes an individual to the entire social body."[17] Modern incarceration techniques are premised on this notion of the social deviant whom the state must normalize; however, Foucault's theory does not take into account the fact that the colonized and raced subject does not enter into citizenship through a Hobbesian theory of contract in which she gives up certain personal rights in order to gain the protection of the state. In fact, the contractual citizenship of the dominant group is dialectically related to the denial of rights of raced and colonized others who are criminalized in order to be set apart from the social body.[18] The modern regime of power, premised on the biopolitical control of all, was always challenged in the colonial situation where race fractured it, and it is similarly fractured by race in the United States.[19] It is such an account of incarceration and surveillance that Shakur presents. That is, it is not simply disciplining or generalized surveillance that she is subject to, the forms that Foucault argues constitute aspects of modern social control, but forms of exceptional disciplining that Foucault deems as having disappeared but that have always regulated African American lives in the United States.[20]

Shakur wrote her autobiography in Cuba where she arrived in 1984, five years after her dramatic escape from the New Jersey prison where she had spent six and a half years, two of them in solitary confinement. The autobiography was published in 1987. Strictly speaking, it is a work of exile or, as the title of Edward Said's memoir suggests, being "out of place"; but the major focus of the book is on being forced to be "in place"—in the prison and as a black woman. Shakur opens her autobiography with a narrative of the state marking her as deviant Other. The book begins with the hallucinatory memory of her arrest along with that of Sundiata Acolia after she has been shot by state troopers on the New Jersey Turnpike. The loud imprecations of police officers during her arrest point to the need of the state to interpellate her as abjected: "Bitch, you'd better open your goddamn mouth or I'll blow your goddamn head off"; "We oughta finish her off." "Let'er lay in the gutter where she belongs" and later, "Is your mother a nigger whore like you?"[21] Shakur is envisioned as animalistic, scum, trash, sexual excess, that which needs to be expelled from the social body. And as the use of "nigger whore" clearly suggests, the abjected body is also the racialized body, one that recalls here the tortured history of the sexualization of African American women as justification for rape. More important, Shakur dramatizes her incarceration as a contemporary version of the sexual and political control over black women's bodies since slavery. Hounded by the police after her arrest, Shakur is imprisoned under inhuman conditions. Even so, she manages to conceive while in prison, and gives birth while shackled to a daughter who is immediately taken away from her, thus repeating the forced separation of mother and child during slavery. The contemporary United States is thus also represented as a slave society, replicating the familial conditions of slavery.

Shakur represents her experience of interrogation, when taken to the hospital, in terms of colonial trauma where the native is stripped of all identity. Severely injured during her apprehension, Shakur's recollection of doctors and policemen questioning her recalls the classic story of the limits imposed on black identity in Ellison's *Invisible Man*. Just as the narrator of Ellison's novel sits in a "cold, white rigid chair," wearing white overalls and sees women in white looking at him as he struggles to remember his name,[22] Shakur describes the hospital as an extension of white social power: "The hospital is glaring white. Everybody i see is white" (4). Shakur is constantly asked her name and address, but her repetitions of her name remain willfully unrecognized till she gives the nurse her "slave name," JoAnne Chesimard. Shakur's representation of her experience as a narrative of colonial dominance is made painfully clear as she describes the Nazi salutes of her police guards and the diatribe of one who revels in white supremacy. "He went on to say that the white race had invented everything because they were smart and worked hard, that other races wanted to riot and use terrorism to take everything the white race had worked so hard to get. . . . He talked about empires, the Roman, the Greek, the Spanish, the British. He told me white people had created empires because they were more civilized than the rest of the world" (10). In personifying white supremacy through the raced logic of imperialism and colonialism, Shakur is tracing a well-documented history of white American imaginative continuity with European colonialism.[23] She is also articulating a fundamental premise of black revolutionary nationalism—that of the United States as a raced empire.[24] However, for Shakur, these connections are not theoretical abstractions but rather premises arising from historical specificities. The guard is, as Shakur herself points out, a representation of the long-standing Nazi sympathies of New Jersey Germans who, as scholars have pointed out, helped repatriate Nazi soldiers.[25] Thus, from the beginning, Shakur uses a specific site—here the hospital/prison—as lived space or space subjectively experienced (in contrast to the prison as conceived space) to demonstrate the continuities of racism and imperialism.[26]

Writing in 1978, H. Bruce Franklin theorized that although contemporary U.S. prison literature thematized "America, prison house of the Black nation," this consciousness had transcended the experience of African-Americans. "[I]t perceives itself and is seen around the world as part of a global revolution of Third World peoples."[27] Although Franklin attributes the consciousness of social incarceration, and hence the revolutionary global potential of prison writing to the actual experience of incarceration going back to slavery, many African American liberation movements, whether nationalistic or otherwise, have drawn inspiration from or posited a collectivity with other oppressed groups. For instance, the Declaration of Rights of the Negro Peoples of the World produced at the first of the Univeral Negro Improvement Association's (UNIA) annual conventions in 1920 included a clause that stated, "We believe in the freedom of Africa for the Negro people of the world, and by principle of Europe for the Europeans and Asia for the Asiatics; we also demand Africa for the Africans at home and abroad."[28] Although many African American activists challenged the legitimacy and ruthlessness of apartheid laws in the United States by appealing to Pan Africanism or racial alliances within regions, a recognition of the importance of anticolonial resistance was not lost to even ardent supporters of race patriotism such as Cyril V. Briggs, who exhorted African Americans: "Make the cause of other oppressed peoples your cause, that they may respond in kind, and so make possible effective co-ordination in one big blow against tyranny."[29] W. E. B. DuBois in his manifesto of the second Pan-African Congress, published in *Crisis* in 1921, preceded his demands for blacks in the United States by demonstrating the systematic underdevelopment of native communities in British, Belgian, Portugese, and Spanish colonialism and finally of blacks in the United States.[30] These activists, like Silko and William Apess speaking for Native Americans, did not erase the historical particularities of African American experience but instead argued for the need to make alliances among different forms of systemic racial oppression in order to appeal to a world community, while crucially recognizing the importance of local struggles. Yet coalitions around the issue of racial brutality remained central. As Stokely Carmichael would write years later, "all non-white peoples who have been colonized can join hands, understanding of course that our fights remain entirely different."[31]

In Shakur's autobiography, transnational alliances are premised on a strong engagement with issues of racial oppression nationally. At one level, Shakur is interested in demonstrating the representativeness of her life as a black woman as she encounters the realities of segregation, racism, sexism, and black poverty. Such conditions, it is implied, are prime for the fomenting of a larger revolutionary consciousness. Margo Perkins suggests that both Shakur's and Davis' autobiographies are teleologically driven, with the writers attempting to read the early years of their lives to illuminate how they arrived at the present.[32] However, such a reading presumes a causality and logic that the very structure of Shakur's texts repudiates and that Davis's text also belies. Neither autobiography follows a simple birth to present chronology (although there is a rough chronological movement in both). Indeed, I would argue that both, along with Silko in *Almanac of the Dead*, illustrate what to Benjamin is a characteristic of revolutionary historical writing—that of establishing connections between what has been and now by blasting open the continuum of history.[33] Shakur deliberately labels her work as autobiography, thus entering the domain of post-Enlightenment, individualized, privatized, and universalized subject formation and the teleological narratives it habitually uses, in order to contest these assumptions, these regimes of representation, through her insistence on a sublation of the self into different forms of collective identities.[34] The very overt structure of the autobiography lays bare the racialized structures of oppression that connect the personal, familial Shakur and the political, incarcerated Shakur. Shakur chooses to structure her autobiography as a deliberate and insistent alternation between chapters detailing her imprisonment and public trial and those recreating her childhood and adolescence. As we move from the intimate space of the home to the disciplinary space of the prison and the courtroom, we are constantly made aware of how the intermediary organs of civil society are denied African Americans. The opening chapter recounting her arrest is followed by an account of her childhood; this chapter is succeeded by one detailing her torturous treatment in the prison hospital, which is then followed by a narrative of her years in junior high. The final section, the "Postscript," finds her reunited with her daughter in Cuba. Far from simply being symptomatic of a postmodern antilinearity, however, the chapters about her childhood and youth are, in the Gramscian sense, attempts to inventory the traces of raced dominance on her as she lives as an African American subject in the nation-space of the United States.[35]

The importance of being rooted in and formed through the historical legacy of African American slavery is made clear through the formal strategies of the text itself. The text shuttles back and forth in a hallucinatory manner between the space of the prison and the narrative of her childhood and adolescence, thus attesting to the unreasonable continuity of the carceral in black persons' lives. The social injunction in school to speak "properly" like white people, in order to prove herself as good as a white person, is mirrored in the prison where Mrs. Butterworth, the white warden, patronizingly instructs the "girls" to "behave like ladies."[36] In an early chapter, Shakur writes that although her grandparents instill black pride in her and teach her never to be subservient to whites, they remain imprisoned within an ideology that evaluates success in terms of white equivalence and beauty through white standards. Shakur, like Toni Morrison's Pecola, grows up valuing light skin and desiring Shirley Temple curls. This chapter is immediately followed by one in which Shakur, in her letter "To My People," details the systemic nexus of imperialism and racism that determines the incarceration of blacks and people of color at the same time as it forms her as a public intellectual.

However, although Shakur clearly wishes to mark the ideological apparatuses that school her in a white racial hierarchy, she also attempts to write herself as an agent in the representation of her subjectivity by contesting both the regimes of representation that govern dominant images of African Americans as well as established ideologies of the autobiographical self. The text is shot through with linguistic experimentations that signal its affective, imaginative interventions. Shakur's autobiography calls attention to its juxtapositions of poetry and prose, italics and regular print, thus emphasizing her construction of her life story beyond linear causality and the singular self. While the prose sections demonstrate the marking of Shakur's subjectivity as child, adolescent, and incarcerated woman, through the twinned imperatives of racial oppression and resistance, the lyrical poems, written in the oral tradition and urging defiance, are rhetorically addressed to African American women or, additionally, to a larger community of African Americans and other people of color. The harsh, violent conditions of her imprisonment and the brutality engendered therein are affectively understated in the prose sections; in the poetry sections, all bringing together moments of African American history and women's resilience in the time of the now, emotions are let loose. Thus, her poem for Eva, a fellow prisoner incarcerated for over a decade, is addressed to and inspirational for all African American women and registers the pain of simultaneously having to be strong and resistant while oppressed: Rhinocerous woman/Who nobody wants/and everybody used./They say you're crazy/ cause you not crazy enough/to kneel when told to kneel."[37]

Throughout the text, Shakur's spellings also attest to the attempt to write resistance into language. In the tradition of e e cummings and preceding bell hooks, Shakur replaces the egocentric "I" of patriarchal capitalism with the collective, lowercase "i;" "amerika" is similarly lowercased, designified as proper noun assuming imperial nationhood and rewritten phonetically with a "k." Indeed, following the tradition of the black power movement, Shakur too makes the word "america" operate as a signifier of racial terror when, reporting on the disproportionate incarceration of African Americans, she spells the adjective with a kkk as "amerikkkan."[38] Throughout the text, Shakur also writes the U.S. as the lowercase "u.s.," which typographically resembles "us," the collectivity that is metaphorically split or a reclaiming of the national space by the people written out of the national imaginary. This conscious construction of her narrative simultaneously as an aesthetic, cultural, and political artifact creates a space that challenges both disciplinary regimes of knowledge and the disciplining of the state that views incarcerated radicals as terrorists. It calls attention to what Marx pointed out as the difference between *vertreten* or representation in the political sense of speaking for and *darstellen* or semiotic representation. For Spivak, this distinction is central to what she sees as Marx's nascent critique of both individual and collective agency and his articulation of the discontinuities within and between individual and collective agency.[39] However, for Shakur, whose major optic is race rather than class, political and semiotic representation, individual and collective agency, are not necessarily discontinuous with each other. The semiotic gestures toward the political although in multiple and irreducible ways.

Shakur juxtaposes the experiences of racial-social incarceration, the incarceration of minorities within the prison, and the imperialist oppression of people of color to emphasize that imperialism and racism are vitally connected and crystallize in the power of the prison-industrial complex. Let us examine a few examples of the numerous moments when Shakur links the experiences of black and third world peoples in the United States:

> They call us murderers, but we do not control or enforce a system of racism and oppression that systematically murders Black and Third World people. (51)

> Ninety percent of the prison population in this country are Black and Third World people who can afford neither bail nor lawyers. (51)

> Prisons are part of this governments's genocidal war against Black and Third World people. (65)

> They [the all white jury] had bought the amerikan dream lock, stock, and barrel and seemed unaware that, for the majority of Black and Third World people, the amerikan dream is the amerikan nightmare. (119)

> Because ninety percent of the men and women in this country's prisons are Black and Third World. (169)

Such frequent invocations of interconnectedness might, as with Bhabha in his problematic metaphoric equation of the middle passage with diasporic experience (discussed in chapter two), or Haraway's analogizing of women of color and the cyborg (discussed in chapter three), risk appearing purely discursive. However, unlike these language-based connections, Shakur's linkage is part of an epistemology crucially tied to material practices. The context of the first two quotes, for instance, is Shakur's prison address "To My People," which attempts to counter media representations of the Black Liberation Army as senseless and violent with an analysis of the systemic violence of both racism at home and the violence of the Vietnam War. The phrase "Black and Third World" invites different kinds of readings, particularly as it is invoked through the site of the U.S. prison system that is disproportionately filled with African Americans and Hispanics. At one level, it points to the workings of power with Hispanic subjects, most of them Mexican American, arguably third world, who are subject to imperial control. Yet, in the context of the Vietnam War, the term "third world" also insistently gestures beyond Mexico and Puerto Rico (a colony) to a larger constituency with which Shakur attempts to link African Americans. The connective "and" between "Black" and "Third World" suggests that the two constituencies are not identical or reducible to each other; yet both are subject to U.S. oppression and control.

Most importantly, the phrase demonstrates Shakur's use of her own experiences in the prison as lived space to construct possibilities and solidarities by turning her incarceration as a site for alliances that transcend the physical space of the prison.[40] Such a use of the carceral to open up a space in which black liberation and anticolonial struggle extend their identities through each other is also evident in Angela Davis's *Autobiography*. On her way from the jail to the courthouse, Davis notes with sadness, the "Black maids on their way to work for the Palo Alto rich. But always there was the stark and obscene Moffett Airfield, the coven from which planes were sent to kill Laotians, Vietnamese and Cambodians" (334). Davis not only marks the conjuncture of racialized and imperial power in the same geographical space, but, by doing so from a police car, calls attention to the carceral too as part of the material and ideological component of the space, thus marking an alliance between black resistance and third world liberation struggles. That Shakur does not spell out a specific program for black and third world solidarities suggests perhaps an inchoateness, but also, possibly, an openness to mapping a liberatory politics. What Shakur clearly wants to stress is the importance of the third world, both subject to and resisting imperialism, a crucial component in the imperialism-racism network. In an interview with Paul Davidson, Shakur commended Cuban intellectuals for theorizing imperialism and race: "Cuba is not only talking about racism in abstract terms, but connecting it with imperialism, which is the underlying motor of racism today. . . . I think anybody who is honestly struggling against racism must struggle against imperialism and vice versa."[41]

Shakur's message, "To My People," which she recorded in 1973 and includes in her autobiography, includes a similar theorizing. Shakur begins her message by identifying herself clearly as a black revolutionary against the systemic violence of racism in the United States. "Like all other Black revolutionaries," she writes, "amerika is trying to lynch me" (50). Clearly, her position as revolutionary is linked to the continual violence inflicted on African Americans in post-Reconstruction United States and the present. Yet what Shakur goes on to insist is that the oppression of African Americans and the forces of imperialism are different manifestations of a machinery of violence in which ideologies of racism and imperialism are embedded. Shakur continues in her address to argue for an affective empathy with activists resisting colonialism and imperialism. The real criminals, she argues, are "Nixon and his crime partners [who] have murdered hundreds of Third World brothers and sisters in Vietnam, Cambodia, Mozambique, Angola and South Africa" (50). And Shakur persistently charts a genealogy of imperialism that connects slavery and the counterrevolutionary maneuvers in South America. Shakur ends the address by exhorting her listeners to fight for black liberation and invoking Malcolm X's credo: "We must gain our liberation by any mean necessary" (52).

Interestingly, despite her specific affiliation to the Black Liberation Army, Shakur dates the beginnings of her political consciousness to 1964 when, having befriended African students from Columbia University, she is asked her opinion about the Vietnam War and is shocked at her own ignorance and internalization of media justifications for war. Thus begins her knowledge of imperialism. Yet it is important for Shakur to point out that her understanding of imperialism is crucially tied to an affective cognition of her systemic position as an African American, even as she recognizes the heterogeneity of roles that individual African Americans choose. Thus, to her disbelief about U.S. atrocities in Vietnam, her friend Bonnie asks, "What do you mean, you don't believe it?" "Just take a look at what they're doing to you."[42] However, Shakur follows this racially constituted "you" with a narrative of disjuncture, delineating her distance from the hip and "upward-bound" African Americans that she as a young woman has been associating with. What Shakur suggests is that there is no unproblematic passage from a raced "I" to a raced "we" to a collectivity of the subjects of imperialism, at the same time that it is vitally necessary to recognize such solidarities politically. Similarly, Shakur describes how at Manhattan Community College she is hurled into activism by the black and third world students who constitute a large percentage of the college population. It is here that she relearns the active role of African American resistance in U.S. history and encounters groups such as the Garveyites, Malcolm X's Organization of Afro-American Unity, and Black Muslims. And although the Republic of New Afrika (under the auspices of which she changes her name), an organization she is enamored of, thrives on a problematic cultural nationalism, one that Huey Newton derided as "pork-chop nationalism," what becomes important for Shakur is a methodology for theorizing the nexus of racism, capitalism, and colonialism.[43] It is a quest that immediately alienates her from her earlier group of friends—African Americans enamored with consumerism and a bourgeois lifestyle—and articulates a form of Post-Colonial citizenship. Thus, the understanding of the interconnectedness of systemic racism within the nation and imperialism without coexists with the knowledge of irreducible lived differences of class within.

But if class fractures race, race importantly fractures class. The critique of capitalism helps Shakur, in chapter twelve, to articulate the link between the machinery of capitalism and its need for spatiotemporal fixes via support of fascist regimes that keep open their markets to finance capital. Shakur writes, "Both the democratic party and the republican party are controlled by millionaires. . . . They were interested in supporting fascist dictatorships in South and Central America, while i wanted to see them overthrown. They were interested in supporting racist, fascist regimes in Africa while i was interested in seeing them overthrown" (190). In a similar fashion, Shakur theorizes the links between capitalism and the Vietnam War, and between capitalism and the continued colonization of Puerto Rico. And yet, as Shakur realizes, capitalism alone (when problematically seen as universal, rather than as Eurocentric as Wallerstein and others have amply demonstrated)[44] does not suffice as an explanation for either internal or external colonialism. Indeed, racism operates within the structures of progressive white socialist groups to which Shakur feels she ultimately does not belong. White members in these groups pay little attention to race as they position themselves as the privileged theoreticians of black liberation and routinely downgrade the contributions of third world revolutionaries such as Castro and Ho Chi Minh. Theorizing the nexus of race and class in colonialism, Fanon had postulated that "the cause is the consequence; you are rich because you are white, you are white because you are rich. That is why Marxist analysis should always be slightly stretched every time we have to do with the colonial problem."[45] Fanon was, of course, well aware of the contradictory position of the native bourgeoisie and their propensity for neocolonialism. What he wanted to emphasize, however, was the importance of racial oppression within colonialism. Shakur delineates a racial hierarchy within socialist organizations that hearkens to colonialism when she recalls being told by a white male socialist to quit college and work in a factory in order to mobilize workers, although he himself needs to stay in college to organize students.

It is important to emphasize that major figures of black liberation in the late 1960s and early 1970s negotiated disparate, yet in many ways similar, relationships to Marxism. Whereas Shakur frames her connection to Marxism within the context of racial oppression, Davis in her autobiography foregrounds the intellectual grounds of Marxism that consequently enable her to place black racial struggle in the United States within the context of worldwide struggle. Her introduction to the works of Marx and Lenin while a high school student in New York are formative for Davis. Unlike Shakur, Davis does not address the conflictual relationship of Marxism to questions of race; rather she critiques Stokely Carmichael's dismissal of Marxism as white ideology. Yet despite Davis' frequent attempts to present Marxism as an unraced horizon, thus omitting discussion of the contradiction between capitalism's demand for abstract labor and its workings through systemic racism for racially differentiated labor,[46] her specific participation within the Communist Party is racially marked. Her induction to the Communist Party is made through its black cell. As Davis writes a few decades later, "I probably would not have joined the Communist Party at that time if I had not been able to enter the Party through an all-black collective in Los Angeles called the Che-Lumumba Club."[47] For Huey Newton, on the other hand, it is the particular manifestations and workings of classlessness in specific locations that are important. Thus, although China seems exemplary of socialism, Newton's visit there confirms for him the dictum of "making a concrete analysis of concrete conditions,"[48] a principle that was operative in the formation of the Black Panther Party for Self-Defense.

The intersecting yet separate concerns of class and race are central to chapters twelve and thirteen of the autobiography that are pivotal in understanding Shakur's articulation of black liberation as a model for Post-Colonial citizenship. Shakur follows chapter twelve, the chapter delineating the beginnings of her political consciousness of imperialism, racism, and class while at college, with a poem titled "To My Momma" that uses the maternal as a figure for political filiation. However, this maternal is not a pre-Oedipal figure outside the Symbolic, attractive in its inarticulateness, but rather one through which the structures of the raced Symbolic are both transmitted and resisted. Indeed, in what might be taken as an answer to Kristeva's calls for a new theorization of motherhood beyond Christianity and science, Shakur presents having a child as the most radical of her political acts—not just symbolically but materially. Thus, while the Momma of the poem is both victim of the American dream of accumulation and an ideology of whiteness that stunts African American self-recognition, she is also the "butchfem momma,/who has always/taken care of business" (194). As a figure for a collective racial identity, the mother confirms a shared history of African American oppression that Shakur suggests is foundational in marking her political self: "We have all been infected/with a sickness/that can be traced back/to the auction block" (194). The poem ends with a confirmation of the importance of being nurtured through the raced maternal: "My roots run deep./ I have been nourished well" (194).

The very next chapter, however, introduces a different theorizing. It begins with a hallucinatory, affective representation of the assassination of Martin Luther King written as manichean colonial dynamic, "*The tanks are coming. The natives are restless. The tanks will quiet the natives. The tanks are coming. . . . The grim reapers are abuzz. Reports about the natives. They are excited. . . . I am thinking about revolution. . . . I want bullets*" (195–196). The aftermath of the assassination of Dr. King, narrated not through African American history, but through the language of colonial dominance and resistance, suggests the imperative to read African American history within a larger framework of colonialism and imperialism. Thus, though the assassination foments ideas of revolution, the "revolutions" Shakur gets involved in are not simply those of black liberation but those of the American Indian Movement, members of which had taken over Alcatraz; those of the Chicano Brown Berets; as well as those of South and Central America, trying to fight U.S. imperialism. Shakur here marks her understanding of revolution through the workings of the Black Panther Party whose members at once challenge the surveillance and state violence directed against African Americans by marching to the California senate floor armed, and also envision their struggle as part of a transnational revolution: "They took the Black liberation struggle out of a national context and put it in an international context. The Party supported revolutionary struggles and governments all over the world and insisted the u.s. get out of Africa, out of Asia, out of Latin America, and out of the ghetto too" (203). The chapter ends, however, with a focus on the brutalization of African Americans—the death of Jonathan Jackson and the police pursuit of Angela Davis, thus emphasizing the importance of particular racial oppressions to the formation of revolutionary consciousness and the imagining of a Post-Colonial citizenship.

In these pivotal chapters of her autobiography, Shakur demonstrates the importance of recognizing and valorizing a specific genealogy of racial oppression that forms the roots of her activism, and through which she formulates links with other colonized spaces. Shakur's articulation of the problematic of African American racial oppression as connected with the particular history of North American slavery and insistently figured through tropes of motherhood and the family, and with U.S. imperialism abroad, questions the validity of postmodern models of activism as well as the binaries such models rely on. For instance, Laclau and Mouffe's inspiring articulation of a radical democratic imaginary that includes the postulation of utopia as well as the construction of positive programs is predicated on the rejection, historically, of "privileged points of rupture."[49] For Shakur, however, privileging slavery as a point of rupture in the discourse of black liberation is central, but it does not mean buying into master narratives of Euro-American reason or modernity. Rather, it is a recognition and indictment of the systemic imperatives of modernity through which African Americans have been and continue to be oppressed. As Howard Winant points out, "the racialization of the world is both the cause and consequence of modernity."[50]

Shakur's delineation of a radical political practice also breaks down Deleuze and Guattari's widely influential distinctions between rooted and rhizomatic knowledge, and between Said's binaries of filiation and alliance (although I would argue that Said's lifelong commitment to the Palestinian struggle is undoubtedly and productively filiative).[51] Shakur in effect demonstrates the oppositions between filiation and affiliation to be false because, for her, revolutionary political consciousness includes an intense recognition of the "roots" of African American oppression as well as the connectedness of the black struggle with that of others. Models such as Shakur's also expose the problems of constructing oppositions such as filiation and alliance that are based on the premise that filiation is simply a matter of accepting and buying into genealogies, whereas alliance involves a healthy affirmation of difference and choice. Post-race, ethnicity theorists such as Werner Sollors, attempting to replace the concept of race as systemic oppression with the benign idea of ethnicity as choice, similarly distinguish between filiation (read: unprogressive) and alliance (read: progressive).[52] But African Americans cannot disaffiliate themselves from slavery any more than postcolonial natives can disaffiliate themselves from colonialism. The voluntarism implicit in these binaries meets a dead end in the face of systemic oppressions.

It is not accidental, therefore, that Shakur ends her autobiography by continually pointing to the need to remember U.S. racism and slavery as integral to African American experience. Implicitly, such acts of rememory, to use Toni Morrison's term, contest the idea of nation as a free space of individuated becoming. At the same time, Shakur also celebrates a solidarity of black resistance throughout the world. Speaking from outside the temporality of the narrative and within a politicized present, Shakur writes, "Every day out in the streets now, i remind myself that Black people in amerika are oppressed. . . . The less you think about your oppression, the more your tolerance for it grows. . . . But to become free, you have to be acutely aware of being a slave."[53] This nation-based articulation of African American oppression, which is simultaneously a critique of the United States as raced national space, engenders an imagined Post-Colonial community beyond and including the nation, as figured in the poem, "Tradition." Here, U.S. black liberation is envisioned as part of global black resistance beginning with slavery. Using the cadences and repetitions of an oral tradition, Shakur urges the reader to "Carry it on now/Carry it on."[54] Thus, in the final chapter of the autobiography, Shakur's reunion with her daughter in Cuba is represented through a continuum of ongoing slave resistances. As she sees her daughter, mother, and aunt deplaning, she thinks, "How much we had all gone through. Our fight had started on a slave ship years before we were born."[55]

This sublation of the personal into national and transnational forms of solidarity through the mutually implicated vectors of race and imperialism marks much of black nationalist thought and figures in the autobiographies of many activist intellectuals. Huey Newton situates his autobiography, *Revolutionary Suicide*, as a text within the trajectory of black culture and radicalism by including epigraphs from a gamut of figures such as Paul Robeson, James Baldwin, Bobby Seale, W. E. B. DuBois, George Jackson, and Margaret Walker. Like Shakur, and in contrast to autobiography's traditional exposition and valorization of the singular self, Newton derives his title, "revolutionary suicide," from an embrace of a communal self adumbrated in an old African saying, "I am we." In its attempt to interpellate the personal within the racial by narrating her going underground as a latter-day version of a slave narrative, Angela Davis's autobiography also sublates the personal within the racial. Yet Newton's and Davis's autobiographies also intimate a rupture between an individualized heroic self and the communal, sharper than that of Shakur's. Newton's paens to black leaders and his theorization of a communal self stand in contrast to the iconic portrait photographs of Newton as leader and to the movement of the autobiography that, in linear fashion, charts his rise as a public figure. Similarly, Angela Davis's highly individualized plotting of courtroom suspense with which her autobiography ends invites attention to the cautionary critique of neoslave narratives that John Edgar Wideman provides: "Vicarious identification with the narrator's harrowing adventures, particularly if the tale is told in the first person "I," permits the reader to have their cake and eat it too. They experience the chill and thrill of being an outsider. . . . The fate of one black individual is foregrounded, removed from the network of systemic relationships connecting, defining, determining, undermining all American lives."[56]

But while Shakur eschews the personal as heroic, she also insists that her political exile in Cuba be recognized in its particularity as part of a history of slavery. In other words, her exile cannot be read through the generalized discourses of liminality or border crossing. On her election as governor of New Jersey, Christie Whitman vowed to double the reward for Shakur's capture and in 1995 sought to match a $25,000 appropriation for her capture. The demands for Shakur's return to prison culminated in a Christmas eve broadcast by the New Jersey State Police in

1997 to announce that they had written to Pope John Paul II to intervene during his upcoming trip to Cuba.[57] New Jersey's actions effectively illuminated the role of the state as fugitive hunter, a reality with racial undertones not lost on Shakur. Rather than defining herself through generalized tropes of exile, Shakur, in her open letter in March 1998, described herself as "a 20th century escaped slave" and the machinations of the New Jersey State Police as "the reincarnations of the Fugitive Slave Act. All I represent is just another slave that they want to bring back to the plantation."[58] By suggesting that it is the nation-state that has interpellated her as fugitive slave, Shakur redefines the United States as plantation or white space that demands structural overthrow. So while Governor Christie Whitman attempted to use the discourse of international law and order necessary to situate the country as civilized member, Shakur used the terrain of nation to write herself as an African American whose role has been scripted by the history of systemic racism.

If Shakur's theorizations about the black liberation movement in the 1970s provides us with possibilities for imagining a model of Post-Colonial citizenship from within the United States today, Shakur's and Angela Davis's current analyses of the prison-industrial complex suggest newer ways of theorizing the relationship between filiative and affiliative, located and global. Interestingly, Davis uses the antebellum term "abolition" to argue for a radical rethinking of the prison system. Angela Davis suggests that the predominance of people of color in the prison population, combined with the reliance on companies using prison labor by multinational corporations such as IBM, Motorola, and Honeywell, point to the role of racialization in global capitalism in which black bodies are dispensable in the "free world" and a source of profit in the prison.[59] However, Davis's attempts to theorize raced incarceration through the capitalist imperatives of the prison-industrial complex alone point only to an intersection that fails to explain the preponderance of people of color in the prison population.[60] On the other hand, if one sees capitalism itself as a raced enterprise beginning with slavery, continuing today with the labor of the South, the dynamics of raced incarceration are compelling.[61] Shakur concurs that the U.S. prison-industrial complex is an essential component of modern global capitalism, but, in keeping with her focus on a located, raced continuity, describes it in the language of slavery. She argues that the prison-industrial complex aims to "sustain a system of super-exploitation, where mainly black and Latino captives are imprisoned in white, rural, overseer communities."[62] Today, in the aftermath of September 11, the Patriot Act has only added other communities of color to prisons that must now support the military-petroleum complex and the might of what is increasingly seen unapologetically as the American Empire.

CODA: RACE, NATIONAL CONSCIOUSNESS, RESISTANCE

> National consciousness, which is not nationalism, is the only thing that will give us an international dimension.
>
> —Frantz Fanon, *The Wretched of the Earth*

> We could never afford to forget the lessons we had learned from COINTELPRO. As far as i was concerned, building a sense of national consciousness was one of the most important tasks that lay ahead of us. I couldn't see how we could seriously struggle without a strong sense of collectivity, without being responsible for each other and to each other. It was also clear to me that without a truly internationalist component nationalism was reactionary.
>
> —Assata Shakur, *An Autobiography*

I conclude this chapter with Shakur's re-rerouting of Fanon for black nationalism in order to speculate on ways in which the solidarities generated by this nationalism can offer Post-Colonial possibilities. Formed through sites of struggle such as prisons, national consciousness for Fanon was to be sharply distinguished from nationalism that was premised on the exclusion of the masses and on the power of the native elite. Shakur's insistence on the importance of a black national consciousness is not based on a racial essentialism or a mythologizing of blackness and Africanness, but on the strategic necessity of such a consciousness in the face of violent state repression; it is a condition for what Shakur sees as a precursor to a war of maneuver; on the other hand, this consciousness, located in the nation, both needs and abets worldwide resistances to racism, colonialism, and imperialism.

Fanon's vision of local struggle, and furthermore a struggle constantly changing, as the basis of internationalism, is particularly appropriate when we think about siting Shakur's autobiography. Both Angela Davis's and Shakur's autobiographies were written in Cuba, Shakur's because of her exile there and Davis's at Castro's invitation. In the 1970s, Cuba had provided safe haven to black liberation activists such as Huey Newton, Robert Williams, and Eldridge Cleaver, as it did for Shakur in the 1980s. For Shakur, Cuba functions as a revolutionary space from which, and through which, the black liberation struggle is seen as part of, and *as* anti-imperial struggle. Mediating the representation of Cuba through her status as fugitive black liberation activist on the run from the repressive state, Shakur writes Cuba as free territory or safe haven for African Americans. That Shakur romanticizes the openness of Cuba is less a sign of her unwillingness to engage in Cuban politics than her desire to write Cuba as an oppositional space that challenges the exclusions of the nation, similar to Michael Moore's representation of Cuba in *Sicko*. And her open letter to the nation, where she describes Cuba as a resistant palenque or Maroon camp of escaped slaves, demands that the nation-state acknowledge not only its contemporary racism but also its othering of Cuba as a challenge to capitalist racism.[63]

Just as the Cuban revolution serves as an inspiration for Shakur's black nationalism, minority groups throughout the world, racially oppressed, economically disenfranchised, and denied participation in the public sphere, have sought to emulate the combative demeanor of the Black Panther Party and appropriated its name for their particular ends. The early 1970s, for instance, witnessed the formation of the Polynesian Panther Party in Auckland, New Zealand, the Israeli Panther Party created by Sefardis, and the Dalit Panther Party constituted by untouchables in India. The actions of the Dalit Panther Party offer an interesting example of the resistances abetted through affective solidarities. The quirky relationship of Dalit (untouchables) activists and U.S. black nationalists raises questions about location and resistance that are briefly worth considering. The Dalit Panther Party formed in Mumbai in 1972 was clearly based on a recognition of alliances based on oppression. However, the question of Dalit oppression as a racial issue has always been a vexed one. Although Ambedkar, the founder of the Dalit movement, rejected racial readings of caste in his book *Revolution and Counter-Revolution* and emphasized its religious and social aspects instead, the struggle of recent activists to have caste read as race has generated heated debates that have opened up interesting questions about nation, resistance, national consciousness, and internationalism.

Spurred on by the continuing oppression of Dalits despite government aid programs, Dalit activists and NGOs saw the 2001 Durban Conference on Race as an important international arena through which to shame the Indian government via an appeal to a global discourse on human rights. Arguing forcefully to have caste read as race, and therefore included in the conference, Dalit activists drew parallels between the effects of U.S. racism and the Indian caste system.[64] This strategic and, in many ways, intuitive connection is not meant as a substitute for what I have discussed earlier as the place-based politics expounded by Dirlik and others, but rather a means of challenging the repressive nationalism of the state with a Fanonian sense of revolutionary national consciousness that Shakur also proposes.[65] Not surprisingly, conservative intellectuals as well as officials in the Indian government not only denounced the race-caste argument, declaring caste to be an issue internal to the confines of the nation-state, but also declared the Dalits' arguments as inviting threats to national sovereignty. Caste was subsequently dropped from the agenda of the conference. As R. Upadhyay wrote, "why should caste discrimination be discussed in an international forum? . . . In the name of global solidarity, India cannot place its sovereignty in [sic] international forum for scrutiny."[66] What the contours of the argument demonstrate is how different forms of located resistances can connect together to challenge the disciplinary structures that perpetuate oppression.

CHAPTER SEVEN

Recognition and Decolonization in Silko's *Almanac of the Dead*

Inside the front cover of *Almanac of the Dead*, preceding the title page, Silko both charts out the complex trajectories of her novel and reconfigures the maps of Euro-American conquest by shattering the time-space trajectories of conventional mapping. In one of her four explanatory statements on the map, she writes: "Sixty Million Native Americans died between 1500 and 1600. The defiance and resistance to things European continue unabated. The Indian Wars have never ended in the Americas. Native Americans acknowledge no borders; they seek nothing less than the return of all tribal lands."

Polemical, militant, revolutionary, and prophetic, these lines declare a radical indigeneity manifesto for North America and anticipate the rhetorical, temporal, and spatial structuration of Silko's novel. Published to coincide with the celebrations of the Columbus quincentennary, Silko's novel insists on subalternity as perspective and demands that her readers acknowledge the genocide of Native Americans consequent on European colonialism. Silko insistently defines Native American identity as one of resistance to European domination, emphasizing Native Americans as historical beings rather than essentialized beings of nature, engaged in a continuous struggle against occupation and the emblems of colonial authority (European devised borders), defiantly demanding the rights to their lands. Furthermore, by interpellating Native Americans as a group of disinherited, indigenous peoples asserting their common claims to land instead of different nations pursuing redress only through the very legal channels that have served as means of dispossession (treaties), Silko asserts her commitment to a pan-tribal Native American identity.

Leslie Marmon Silko's *Almanac of the Dead* challenges the technologies of colonial domination by postulating different imagined Post-Colonial communities outside the recognizable racial parameters of the colonial nation-state and emphasizing the centrality of rebellions, thus placing the indigenous subalterns as subjects of their own histories.[1] Like Walter Benjamin, who repeatedly emphasizes the importance of claiming and seizing moments of the past in their revolutionary potential, Silko not only invests past moments with resistance but also envisions a revolutionary Post-Colonial solidarity for the present and future.[2] Contemporary capitalist globalization is presented not as something radically new but a continuation of the process of settler colonialism and disinheritance of the Natives that began five centuries ago. Like Shakur, who traces the continuities between chattel slavery, the creation of a black underclass, and the disproportionate incarceration of African Americans, Silko constantly brings past and present together in a continuous history of colonization. As organic intellectual, Shakur chooses a figure resonant with the history of the community—that of a fugitive slave—as a means of self-identification and as a catalyst for change; Silko as intellectual writes resistance to occupation as central to Native American as well as all tribal identities, and as the motor of revolution in the Americas.

> For every image of the past that is not recognized by the present as one of its own concerns threatens to disappear irretrievably.
>
> —Benjamin, Thesis V, *Illuminations*

In the spirit of *Almanac of the Dead*, a novel set insistently in a violent, decadent, yet revolutionary present, and also one in which five hundred years of European colonization of North America are ever-present, I want to suggest that the envisioning of a Post-Colonial future through pan-tribal and transracial solidarities has a history in Native American thinking, one that needs to be invoked so that a past of revolutionary, Post-Colonial possibilities can be related to the present and the future. The writings of William Apess, a Pequot, a baptized Christian, a missionary, an ordained Methodist minister, and later architect of the 1833 Mashpee revolt offer an early instance of such possibilities.[3]

Apess's short, polemical concluding section of *The Experiences of Five Christian Indians of the Pequot Tribe* (1833) titled "An Indian's Looking-Glass for the White Man" and his "Eulogy on King Philip" both envision imagined Post-Colonial communities that foreshadow the alliances that Silko delineates. In *Experiences*, Apess turns the conventions of colonial discourse on themselves. Conversion narratives typically detailed the process of a person's life before religious awareness, recounted the steps toward awareness, the temptations and doubts that beset the follower, and a final overcoming of doubt. The pattern was one of "assurance, decline, and reassurance."[4] Apess, however, not only details religious doubts but argues that the suffering of sinners are the results of colonial depredation: "My sufferings certainly were through the white man's measure; for they most certainly brought spiritous liquors first among my people" (121). It is at the conclusion to five such narratives that "An Indian's Looking-Glass for the White Man" is appended. Here Apess makes clear that the schooling of natives in the ideology of the dominant culture is backed by a machinery of violence. Native women are seduced by white men and left to prostitution, communities are invaded and destroyed by alcohol, and land is ruthlessly expropriated.

In North America, colonial power over Native Americans was exercised through a series of binaristic relationships between the whites and natives conceptualized through modes of filiality, dependency, and extinction. Apess, however, throws the very terms of the binaries into chaos. The white overseers of the Mashpee township were operating under the terms of a binaristic racial opposition between whites and Native Americans when they prevented free blacks from being adopted within the community. Apess's strategy for refusing the opposition and creating a space of anticolonial disruption is to posit a discursive identification with a category hitherto unimagined both by the dominant culture or by Native Americans: "man of color," an interpellation that, in certain ways, resembles the contemporary term, "people of color." Apess begins by provincializing whiteness and then rewriting it as the color of crime.

> Assemble all nations together in your imagination, and then let the whites be seated among them, and then let us look for the whites, and I doubt not it would be hard finding them; for to the rest of the nations, they are still but a handful. Now suppose these skins were put together, and each skin had its national crimes written upon it—which skin do you think would have the greatest? . . . Can you charge the Indians with robbing a nation almost of their whole continent, and murdering their women and children. . . . And to cap the climax, rob another nation to till their grounds and welter out their days under the lash with hunger and fatigue under the scorching rays of a burning sun? (157)

In "An Indian's Looking-Glass," whiteness emerges as a signifier for the history of brutal colonization and slavery. Against this posited transnational category of white colonialism emerges the imaginative solidarity of those of color that provides a site of discursive identification across national and regional boundaries and temporal markers. Such a reformulation of the binaries beyond recognizable national or juridical parameters is, in effect, a discursive and political moment of imagining a Post-Colonial disruption against the regulatory racial categories of the nation-state. It is a moment of becoming because it transgresses the racial demarcations of the dominant culture to posit a solidarity of purpose. Apess's essay repeatedly evokes this community: "why is not a *man of color* respected?" "Is it not the case that *everybody that is not white* is treated with contempt" (158, emphasis mine); "Let me ask why the *men of a different skin* are so despised" (159, emphasis mine).

By the time Apess delivered his lecture, "Eulogy on King Philip" at the Boston Odeon in January 1836, his discursive identification with a community of color as well as with a pan-Indian community were well established. Apess's glorification of Metacom (known to the English and Apess as "King Philip"), earlier identified as the king of the Pequots, is a carefully orchestrated attempt at rewriting Native American history to project a cross-tribal identity. What might be considered identity positions at odds with each other—the assertion of a particularized racial identity, cross-tribal affiliation, and an identification with a cross racial community—instead intersect to articulate a resistance to the dominant order. This intersection should not, however, be confused with a resistance against all conceptions of racial solidarity, but rather viewed as a strategy for resisting the racialized order of the nation-state and one that, moreover, needs the specificity of Native American resistance to articulate broader alliances.

Apess is aware that challenging white dominance and undermining white social recognition in the early nineteenth century, when colonial difference was being brutally legitimized through different "Indian" removal acts, requires additional forms of social solidarity—a pan-tribal identity and an affiliative identity of people of color imagined through subaltern knowledge. But these new solidarities are not meant to replace a radical particularist identity, only to work through and with it. It is significant that the excoriating rhetoric of "An Indian's Looking Glass," which bespeaks a pan-tribal identity, comes as a conclusion to *The Experiences of Five Christian Indians of the Pequot Tribe*. The particular difficulties and depredations faced by the Pequot tribe become the basis of an "Indian" identity through which Apess can more effectively critique white power. In "Eulogy on King Philip," Apess's biography of Metacomet, Apess's fashioning of a cross-tribal identity is well established. Apess minimizes the intertribal hostilities of the period in order to fashion for all Native Americans of his own time a hero whose strategies in the war rival and exceed that of Washington crossing the Delaware and who Apess declares to be "the greatest man that ever lived upon the American shores" (290). Apess not only seizes hold of the past for Native solidarity but also imagines future possibilities for revolutionary alliances. He writes:

> Let every friend of the Indians now seize the mantle of Liberty and throw it over those burning elements that have spread with such fearful rapidity, and at once extinguish them forever. . . . We want trumpets that sound like thunder, and men to act as though they were going to war with those corrupt and degrading principles that robs one of all rights, merely because he is of a little different color. (307)

Almost two centuries later, Silko uses the historical novel to prophesy a massive insurrection that seems superficially disconnected from Apess's call for resistance to racial oppression. El Feo, who along with his twin brother, Tacho, has led an uprising of Indians in the Mexican mountains, muses on the nature of this new insurgency:

> The government wanted groups because they hoped for leaders to crush or buy off. But this time the story was going to be different because the people no longer believed in leaders. People had begun to gather spontaneously and moved as a mob or swarm follows instinct, then suddenly disperses. Ths masses of people in Asia and in Africa, and the Americas too, no longer believed in so-called "elected leaders"; they were listening to strange voices inside themselves.[5]

El Feo's cogitations almost read like a blueprint for what are being touted as contemporary resistances concretized in the battle of Seattle and the decentered structure of the World Social Forum. Such movements are seen as radical breaks with older revolutionary forms, whether class-based, racial, anticolonial or national. El Feo's masses of the disenfranchised, moving without centralized structures, attack sources of power and domination. They are simultaneously disconnected from each other, yet connected in their very lack of structure. The diverse array of characters and groups fomenting revolution in *Almanac of the Dead* also suggest a postmodern form of resistance in which singularities of oppression cannot be reduced to a common cause.[6] Tacho and El Feo, spiritual leaders who communicate with spirit macaws, head a movement of Indians; Vietnam veterans Rambo Roy and Clinton attempt to organize an Army of the Homeless in the alleys of Tuscon; Awa Gee, the techno-savvy Korean American hacker, plans blackouts all over the United States; Green Vengeance eco-warriors plan suicide bombings of dams; Angelita aka Escapia—"the Meat Hook"—

espouses a revolutionary Marxism, oversees the execution of Indian-betrayers and supports the more pacifist projects of Tach and El Feo; ex-con Native American Barefoot Hopi not only fundraises and lobbies for the return of Indian lands but also plans nationwide jail and prison uprisings. At the end of the novel, many of these groups, including busloads of European New Agers, converge at the International Holistic Healers Convention where, in room 1212, Barefoot Hopi explains his vision of a multiracial coalition of the have-nots plotting revolution.

In contrast are an equally motley group of vampire capitalists: the unscrupulous, paraplegic organ harvester of the unsuspecting homeless, Trigg; eco-destructive developer Leah Blue whose plan for the gated community, Venice, Arizona, includes siphoning off the area's water supply; Beaufrey who makes a lucrative business out of pornographic torture videos, including those of rape and strangulation; Serlo, the white supremacist whose plan to combat the brown and black hordes overtaking the earth encompasses supporting research on a designer HIV virus for specially targeted groups; the corrupt Judge Arne of Phoenix; Max Blue, killer for contract and friend of numerous entrepreneurs and officials in Tuscon. The novel itself is structured as a disordered and disconnected order. Jumbling synchronies of time and space, its 763 pages include over seventy characters including the living and the dead. Fashioned, according to Silko, like an almanac in which entries are not connected, plot lines converge in the most bizarre manner. The past of the last five hundred years jockeys for attention with the present and visions for the future.

In one sense, *Almanac of the Dead* envisions a postmodern resistance of the multitude. Environmentalists, prison resisters, spiritualist healers, Native Americans groups supporting guerrilla warfare, activists for the homeless—all come together at the Holistic Healers Convention under a section Silko titles, "One World, Many Tribes." Here these singular groups communicate to each other their common desires. And, as if in a self-conscious ironic awareness that resistance can also be subject to the dictates of vampire capitalism, the convention attracts a busload of New Age Europeans ready to consume Native American resistance. Furthermore, this resistance rests on a putatively postmodern epistemology that resists reified notions of race and identity. Yoeme, whose name is the word Sonoran Yaquis used to refer to themselves, marries the white Guzman and her mixed race grandchildren, Lecha and Zeta, become central to preserving Native American history.[7] Yet the lost almanac that the Demerol and codeine-addicted Lecha is entrusted with translating is not Yaqui but Mayan, and is typed by the white woman, Seese. Seese maintains a bond with Lecha whose psychic powers she has witnessed in a talk show. As Eva

Cherniavsky suggests, "In contrast to ethnonationalisms, and their sustaining rhetoric of cultural purity, tribal knowledges in *Almanac of the Dead* are avowedly impure, non-organic, and non-innocent, and their subjects are media-savvy talk-show queens, computer hackers, high-tech smugglers, and smart shoppers."[8]

Yet I would argue that the present and future insurgencies represented in *Almanac of the Dead* cannot simply be subsumed under the rubric of new postmodern, global resistances without a center. And although the novel eschews hypostatized notions of tribal, even racial identity, race as a signifier of colonial dispossession, domination, and expropriation is as central in *Almanac of the Dead* as it is in Apess's "An Indian's Looking-Glass." As I have explained earlier, the usefulness of thinking about race through Omi and Winant's conception of it as "an unstable and 'decentered' complex of social meanings constantly being transformed by political struggle" is that race is at once mobile and a central node of power and resistance.[9] To think of Native Americans as a racialized group, however, is not to equate their particular oppressions with those of other minority groups in the United States or to weaken the status of tribes (by subsuming them under a "race") questioning the legitimacy of the U.S. government's takeover of tribal lands. Rather, it is to recognize that despite the complex negotiations and alliances of different tribes with white settlers and later the U.S. government, the calls for pan-tribal alliances from the seventeenth century onward, and the unremitting oppressions meted out to Native Americans, suggest a racialization of Indian tribes. It is in this sense that race becomes a central axis in *Almanac of the Dead.*

At the heart of the novel is colonialism and the genocide of Native Americans that begins the process of disinheritance, the occupation of Indian lands and their loss of self-determination, and continues in the colonialist, capitalist globalization of the present. If postmodernity might be seen in Lyotardian terms as the end of grand narratives, Silko's novel is not postmodern because it insists that the grand narrative of colonialism and decolonization be privileged. And even if colonialism has involved ambivalent strategies and native collusions, Silko's novel argues that the brutality of colonialism for Native Americans must be recognized and the subalterns placed at center stage. In the tradition of Ogala Sioux, Nicholas Black Elk, who spoke about Indians in general even as he related specific battles, and whose book, in Vine Deloria's words, became "a North American bible of all tribes," Silko constructs a pan-tribal, Native American identity, one that includes but is not limited to achieving cultural recognition.[10] Silko insists that recognition restage or to use Toni Morrison's term "rememory" past and present injustices and put under question the terms of U.S. nationalism and citizenship. Through the process of this recognition, Silko charts alliances with other oppressed groups and portends a revolutionary decolonization of North America.

THE TERMS OF SUBALTERN RECOGNITION

Of the hundreds of Maya codices or Mesoamerican handwritten books extant before the Spanish conquest, only four major ones are known to have survived the wholesale burnings carried out by Spanish clerics in the sixteenth century. In true colonial fashion, three of the four codices, souvenirs of Spanish loot, are called the Dresden, the Madrid, and Paris Codices, named for the cities in which they are kept and exhibited; the fourth, the Grolier codex, discovered in the 1960s in the Chiapas, is named after the Grolier Club in New York where it was first exhibited in the early 1970s. The codices present information either through the Maya Long Count calendar or according to the 260-day ritual calendar used for divination and prophecy.[11] Silko writes that in *Almanac of the Dead* she conceived of a fictional counterpart to the three Mayan codices.[12] Yoeme passes down to Lecha an ancient almanac that has survived colonial destruction and has been circulating among Native Americans. *Almanac of the Dead* is interspersed with quotations from the almanac that had prophesied the exact time of the appearance of Cortes and which also predicts the "conflict with, and eventual disappearance of things European. . . . Without the almanacs, the people would not be able to recognize the days and months yet to come, days and months that would see the people retake the land" (270).

The survival of the almanac becomes central to the novel because the almanac is not simply past, but living history. As their tribe is being relentlessly wiped out by invaders, the elders divide the almanac into parts and entrust four children to carry different portions of the almanac north to survivors. While the children endure fatigue and hunger on their journey, they literally consume parts of the almanac after they memorize the pages. The almanac nourishes their bodies while they carry its message in their memories. Only one of the four parts of the almanac survives and is passed on through generations of people who, in turn, continue adding to it. The arduous journey of the four children and Yoeme's annotations to it become part of the almanac.

If the almanac in Silko's novel is a fictional counterpart to the three Mayan codices (the only ones Silko thought were extant), Silko makes it clear that the almanac in the novel draws its prophecies from extant subaltern histories. The almanac explicitly relies on the Aztec story of Aztlan, the mythical homeland to be reclaimed by the indigenous. Predominantly, it relies on *The Books of Chilam Balam*, the sacred books of the Maya, named after the apocryphal Mayan prophet of the late fifteenth and early sixteenth centuries, who supposedly foretold the Spanish invasion.[13] In her analysis of the different kinds of histories used in *Almanac of the Dead*, Daria Donnelly explains Silko's seemingly idiosyncratic combination of a supernatural and Gramscian-Marxist one as a technique by which Silko undermines hegemony by foregrounding stories of the oppressed and unsettling "predominant consciousness by placing it within a much larger cosmic narrative, one quite foreign to the dominant culture."[14] Donnelly, that is, sees Silko using two very different kinds of narratives—the materialist one of history as a narrative of domination and exploitation and a larger, presumably pan-Indian narrative of life, destruction and rebirth. The deployment of two different epistemologies in *Almanac of the Dead*, noted by many critics, is not one I'm disputing. Rather, I suggest that it is the nature of these differences that must be questioned.

Most critics, for instance, see Silko introducing contrasts between Western linear time and Indian sacred/absolute time;[15] Western solipsism and avarice and the transcendent story of the almanac;[16] Western androcentrism and an ideal of Indian harmony with the earth.[17] The effect of these oppositions is to reify the familiar binaries of materialism and spirituality, modernity and tradition, that have been central to the Euro-American colonial project. "Indianness" in these different manifestations becomes a condition outside of history and struggle while Native American resistance to oppression takes place within a vicious world of class and race clashes. Native American recognition would thus involve a splitting, a recognition of a redemptive world of "Indian" values such as oneness with the land, harmony, and so on, outside of Natives working with the machinery of colonial domination—in negotiations with treaties and alliances with/against settlers.

However, Silko's project in *Almanac of the Dead* is precisely to rewrite the history of North American settler colonialism from the point of view of Native Americans without essentialized material-spiritual binaries. Whereas current philosophical debates on the left, particularly after the collapse of the Soviet Union, have been stymied by the polarization between the struggles for cultural recognition epitomized by multiculturalists like Charles Taylor and those of the Marxists for redistributive justice, Silko's novel forces a different kind of recognition. It involves not simply the Fanonian cognizance of a static misrecognition at the heart of the colonial encounter epitomized by the cry, "Dirty nigger!" or "Look, a Negro," but also a more positive injunction that cultural recognition for Native Americans include a recognition of colonial destruction and anticolonial resistance.[18] Indeed, it is significant that Silko chooses the Pueblos,

Mayans, and the Yaqui as the major characters for her novel because all of these tribes had won important battles against the Europeans.[19]

As mentioned earlier, the almanac that serves as the moral center of the novel and prophesies the eventual destruction of Euro-American influence on the continent draws heavily from *The Book of Chilam Balam of Chumayel* in which the spiritual and quotidian, the sacred and material, thoroughly intersect. The Mayan books not only illustrate the attributes of different deities but also record, in excruciating fashion, the consequences of the Spanish invasion. In her almanac, Silko combines direct transcriptions of *Chilam Balam* with productive revisions emphasizing colonial destruction. For instance, a part of XVIII (A Series of Katun Prophecies) reads: "The face [of the lord of Katun] is covered; his face is dead. There is mourning for water; there is mourning for bread. . . . Blood vomit is the charge [of the Katun]."[20] Section XIX (The First Chronicle) includes the sentence, "The 11 Ahau was when the mighty men arrived from the East."[21] In Silko's almanac, these portions are rewritten as follows: "The face of the Lord of Katunsi is covered; he is dead. There is mourning for water, there is mourning for bread/ Bloody vomit of yellow fever. . . . Eleven Ahau is the Katun when the aliens arrived" (575).

Silko's rewriting of "mighty men" as "aliens" is significant here. Although *The Book of Chilam Balam* continues to list the diseases introduced as a result of Spanish conquest, the characterization of the Spanish as "mighty men" is consistent with the post-conquest attribution of Native prophecies of incoming godlike men that supposedly led to the Spanish being welcomed. Notwithstanding Silko's problematic acceptance of the idea of Natives prophesying Spanish arrival, her term "alien" emphasizes the Indians' rightful belonging and the illegitimacy and outsidership of the Europeans (here Spaniards). Simultaneously, the term alien signifies on and ironically inverts the contemporary terminology used in the United States to refer to (among others) migrant workers from Mexico. Sacred books, with concepts of absolute and linear time, Silko demonstrates, are highly political and part of the historical being of Native Americans. Thus, the cultural recognition of Native Americans must necessarily include bringing into the present, in a charged and disruptive manner, both the genocides perpetrated against them as well as Native Americans' sustained resistance to colonialism.

Walter Benjamin's angel of history has his face "turned toward the past" because he recognizes that "*even the dead* will not be safe from the enemy if he wins," and that the enemy "has not ceased to be victorious."[22] Silko's revolutionary heroine, Angelita, similarly knows that narrating the history of Native American resistances is itself part of the struggle both on the behalf of previous generations and for historical memory to reinvigorate the present.[23] When Bartolomeo, the Marxist who is contemptuous of tribalism (and has advertised the accidental killing of Menardo by his Indian chauffeur, Tacho, as a deliberate anti-capitalist act), is being tried by the people's assembly, Angelita presents as evidence a history of indigenous revolts that Bartolomeo doesn't acknowledge. Angelita's list includes Native American revolts from the sixteenth century to the present in Cuba, Colombia, the United States, Peru, and Bolivia:

> 1536—Peru—Incas ries up against Pizarro and lay siege to Cuzco and set it afire. Rebellion spreads down Rimac Valley where Incas say siege to Lima. . . .
> 1622—U.S.A.—Indian uprising at James River, 347 Europeans dead. . . .
> 1911—Mexico—Zapata leads the Indians, who demand "land and liberty." (530)

Spanning over five centuries and crossing national borders, the timeline of Native American resistance and revolution presents history as rife with the continual possibility of anticolonial uprisings and rebellions, the counterpart to the continuity of colonial domination.[24] As Angelita grimly reminds her audience, such a conception of history is essential precisely because the enemy has been victorious. Stark figures of the "Native American holocaust" make this amply clear: in 1500, seventy-two million people lived in North, Central, and South America; by 1600 this population is reduced to ten million.

Yet Silko does not present this history as a transcendent narrative, the recognition of which will provide a stable and fixed anticolonial identity for Native Americans. Indeed the problem with the verdict reached by the people's committee is the idea that Native American dispossession or crimes against Native American history can be so clearly and easily compensated for. The summary execution of Bartolomeo, in a ruthless dispensation of community justice, suggests the need for an agonistic (rather than antagonistic) notion of subaltern recognition. Such a recognition would not mean giving up an agential narrative of revolution but rather not using this narrative as a violent foreclosure of identities yet to be negotiated. Thus, Silko concludes Bartolomeo's execution with commentaries and ruminations that challenge the verdict of the revolution-inspired crowd. El Feo holds out the possibility that "once the people got their land back the killing would be stopped" while another spectator jokes, "So, sadly, they have been forced to terminate their relationship with dear comrade Bartolomeo" (532).

TRIBAL INTERNATIONALISTS OR SUBALTERN COALITIONS

The aspect of *Almanac of the Dead* that has generated the most controversy among scholars of Native American literature is Silko's espousal of pan-tribal and cross-racial affiliations. Elizabeth Cook-Lynn, for instance, while commending Silko's nationalistic approach to historical events, finds this nationalism ultimately unworkable because of the simultaneous commitment to pan-Indian connections that disallow specific tribal histories.[25] For Cook-Lynn, "the very origins of a people are specifically tribal (nationalistic) and rooted in a specific geography (place), that mythology (soul) and geography (land) are inseparable, that even language is rooted in a specific place."[26] Cook-Lynn's insistence on the specificity of tribal histories and their connections to a particular place is undoubtedly important. Indeed, as I have argued thus far, we need to be vigilant of globalizing epistemologies that are insensitive to the concerns of particular communities. However, the problem of locating identity in origins conceived in static terms (rather than, as in Silko's case, a reconstruction of origins for political purposes in the present) is that it cannot deal with the massive dislocations and dispossessions that Native Americans, in particular, have endured. How, for instance, can tribal identity be articulated for those who were moved from their lands two centuries ago? How long would it take for forcibly moved tribes to claim an affiliation with another geopolitical history? Should they?

A thorough discussion of the juridical politics of tribal nationalism or the costs of claiming a pan-tribal Native identity is outside the scope of this chapter, although one cannot uncritically accept Silko's own position that thinking in terms of specific tribal identities is simply a denial of "the Indian way" that requires one to see how a person is "inside their heart."[27] It can be argued, however, that a legal tribal identity needed for pressing Indian claims through juridical channels, on the basis of sovereignty, need not be divorced from a political, Native American identity that allows one to make strong inroads in the public sphere on behalf of the North American indigenous. William Apess's role as leader of the Mashpee rebellion, his creative changes to Metacomet's biography, as well as his use of a pan-tribal identity should make clear the possibility of working through both legal and political identities. Similarly, as Nicholas Black Elk's recollections suggest, the affective and political symbology of the ghost dance at Wounded Knee in 1890 was possible because of the participation, among others by Brules, Lakotas, and Ogala Sioux. And although Silko has criticized the American Indian Movement (AIM) for its secular (read: non-Native American) politics, AIM activists such as Mary

Crow Dog lay simultaneous affective and legal claim to both tribal and pan-tribal identities. For instance, Mary Crow Dog notes differences between Plains tribes and Pueblos and is impatient with the apparent pacifism of the latter;[28] she participates in the occupation of Wounded Knee in 1973 as it is declared an independent Ogala nation in accordance with the Fort Laramie Treaty of 1868, but does so as part of a larger community of Native Americans;[29] Mary Crow Dog's husband, Leonard, is a Sioux medicine man, but finds it affectively and politically crucial to participate in ceremonies to feel the "rebirth of Indian unity."[30] Similar conceptions of tribal and pan-tribal, indigenous identities have been offered by Hopi-Miwok Wendy Rose and Ward Churchill.[31]

In *Almanac of the Dead*, Silko attempts to wrest a revolutionary past for, and write an alternative present and future on behalf of, the indigenous peoples of the Americas, particularly those of the Southwest.[32] It is no accident that Silko's formulation of this revolutionary movement of the indigenous, poised to take over the state, was important for the Zapatistas. In the summer of 1993, several revolutionaries read *Almanac of the Dead*; on January 1, 1994, the Zapatista National Liberation Army (EZLN), comprising the indigenous and peasants from Chiapas, declared war on the Mexican government, kidnapped the former governor of Chiapas, freed prison inmates, and demanded food, housing, and redistribution of land stolen from the natives. While it would obviously be far-fetched to attribute complete causality linking the *Almanac of the Dead* and the Zapatista uprising, it is clear that the revolutionaries were obviously fascinated with Silko's vision of an indigenous, pan-tribal uprising. Subcomandante Marcos subsequently quoted Silko on the back cover of his *Shadows of Tender Fury*[33] and Silko heralded the uprising as a war with a five-hundred-year-old history of resistance by the indigenous people of the Americas.[34] On the other hand, whereas the Zapatistas have reached out to many different constituencies and embraced an agenda critical of capitalist globalization, the particularities of Mayan culture and resistance in the Chiapas have been essential to the movement and remain pivotal to it.[35] (It is only through a complete disregard for their history and the specifics of their takeover of towns in the Chiapas that the Zapatistas can be viewed as simply a leftist movement of the multitude, although, no doubt, it has leftist agendas.)[36]

In *Almanac of the Dead*, in addition to a revolutionary view of indigenous subalterns, derived in part from foregrounding histories of resistance, Silko also suggests possibilities of coalitions with other oppressed groups, notably African Americans. Clinton, the black Vietnam veteran, finds common cause in the oppression of the indigenous across continents. Clinton's Radio Broadcast #2 on the first successful slave revolution in the

Americas begins, "Slavery joined forever the histories of the tribal people of the Americas with the histories of the tribal people of Africa. On La Isla de Hispaniola escaped African slaves called maroons fled to the remote mountains where the remaining bands of Arawak Indians took them in" (428). Further energized by his talks with Weasel Tail and Barefoot Hopi at the Holistic Healers Convention, Clinton pledges to undo the racial exclusivity he sees in African Americans by constantly revealing to African Americans their shared causes and histories. Like Angelita, who makes a timeline of Native American rebellions, Clinton sketches in his notebooks a history of slave revolts in the United States from the sixteenth century up to the Civil War. But interspersed within this narrative of revolts, which includes prominent ones such as Nat Turner's and Gabriel Prosser's, are numerous resistances engineered by African American and Native American alliances. Thus, Clinton's timeline begins in South Carolina in 1526 when "Negro slaves rise up, flee to live with the Indians" and includes numerous examples of alliances such as the New York city uprising of 1712 when Indian and black slaves conspired together or Sancousy's 1727 discovery of Natanapalle, a village of runaway Indian and black slaves (742–743).

In an examination of the cross-cultural coalitions envisioned in *Almanac of the Dead*, Romero Channette suggests that these coalitions attempt to contain the tension between Silko's material revolutionary tendencies and the spiritual resistance promoted in ancient Indian prophetic texts. Channette writes, "A movement led by a multiplicity of ancestor spirits, who do not recognize racial divisions between people, attempts to avoid the limitations of a politics based on race and ethnicity by privileging spiritual affiliation. This privileging allows Silko to envision resistance as not simply reactionary but as based on ancient alliances and beliefs."[37] Channette argues that this privileging of the spiritual, promoted by Silko herself in interviews, ultimately downplays the political power of the book, which fosters cross-cultural social justice networks.[38] Channette's analysis highlights the two important issues that have been repeatedly addressed in relation to *Almanac of the Dead*: a politics beyond race and new forms of social justice organizations.

First, I want to argue that *Alamanac of the Dead* does not augur a post-race politics; instead, the particularity of different racial politics is important in forging cross-racial networks. If racial politics are reactive in challenging forms of systemic oppression, such reactivity needs to be nurtured to activate racial justice and therefore social justice. The *Almanac of the Dead* derives its counterhegemonic energy, for instance, from a resistance to the continuing colonialism faced by Native Americans. It is this specific anticolonial politics that links together blacks and the indigenous in the Americas and African Americans and Native Americans in the United States. Silko's transracial alliances are not simply spiritual (i.e., beyond race and history) but derive their energy from the specific history of maroon communities of runaway slaves and Indians that Clinton ponders on and broadcasts.[39] While Barefoot Hopi connects the Americas and Africa through indigenous religions with the spirits of Damballah and Quetzalcoatl appearing to people in both continents, the prophetic message of the spirits is the political one of armies marching north, following Tacho and El Feo (735). Indeed, through Weasel Tail, Silko spells out the coalitional politics as explicitly anticolonial, committed to a postcolonial future: "Sixty million dead souls howl for justice in the Americas! They howl to retake the land as the black Africans have retaken their land!" (733).

Even in fragments of the almanac that are almost direct transcriptions from *The Book of Chilam Balam*, one of the sacred books of the Mayas, Silko has subtly revised the original lines in order to repoliticize the work for transracial political affiliations. While the lines in *The Book of Chilam Balam* read, "The rope shall descend; the poison of the serpent shall descend, pestilence and three piles of skulls," Silko's almanac reads "The rope shall descend,/The poison of the serpent shall descend,/Pestilence and *four* piles of skulls" (emphasis mine) (575).[40] The three piles of skulls mentioned here and elsewhere in *The Book of Chilam Balam* refer to those of the Spaniards, the mestizos, and the Indians. Silko rewrites the sacred book and spells out her revised history: "Four piles of skulls: Spaniards, mestizos, Indian slaves, Africans" (575). Silko's pointed changes express both an empathy for African slaves as well as a need to create coalitional histories with other races that have been similarly oppressed.

Second, the subaltern alliances envisioned by Silko differ from a network of heterogeneous social justice movements in that they depend on specific affective, material, and political histories. Silko's Native American and African American alliances are premised on the specific histories of dispossession that drew them together earlier in parts of the American South. As I have previously argued, John Brown Child's concept of transcommunality is particularly useful in thinking about the idea of Post-Colonial citizenship postulated by Silko, black nationalists such as Assata Shakur, and different race-based contemporary resistances in the United States today. The construction of a coalition of African Americans and Native Americans in *Almanac of the Dead* depends on what Childs calls "emplacements of affiliation," an emplacement being "a site of collective life shared by a group of people that provides them with a rooted and demarcated sense of shared perspective and affiliation."[41] Emplacements may be geographical or spiritually located in a geographical setting or based on sites that are ideological. It is precisely Silko's emphasis on Native American emplacements of affiliation that energizes her construction of an alliance with African Americans. And the ideological site privileged by Silko is the narrative of colonialism and decolonization. As Angelita muses, "They had watched the tribes of Africa retake the land from Europeans; in the Americas they might have another fifty years or even one hundred, but time was running out" (471).

INDIGENEITY AND REVOLUTION

Silko concludes her sprawling novel with a chapter titled "Home" in which Sterling, the boarding-school educated, alienated Laguna Indian, exiled by the Tribal Council for allowing a Hollywood film crew to see the sacred stone snake, returns "home." Hiking alone across Laguna territory, far from the commercial world, sleeping three days and awakening to a rebirth followed by a cleansing bath in the Laguna River, impelled by a desire to see the stone snake, Sterling is the Odysseus struggling to reach home and find himself. Yet the highly scripted chapter, coming at the end of the novel, also invites us to read through Sterling questions about the politics of Native American identity and resistance in the present.

As many critics have pointed out, the chapter de-essentializes the idea of an unproblematic Native American identity that can be regained by a return to home or nature.[42] The Tribal Council that had exiled Sterling neither forgives Sterling nor welcomes him back, but simply ignores him, and his extended family holds him at bay. (Of course, as Silko reminds us elsewhere, the Tribal Council itself "is an alien form of government that was forced upon the Indian people by the U.S. government in 1941 by the Indian Reorganization Act.")[43] Sterling distances himself from the accoutrements of pop culture and his life at Tuscon, but his is far from a simple return to nature, outside of history. Even though Sterling attempts to banish from his mind the melange of militant organizations and people he has encountered in Tuscon, dismissing them as a bad dream and thus problematically disavowing his connection with present-day revolutionary imaginings, he is haunted by visions of old spirits speaking to people in Africa and "armies of indigenous people to retake the land" (762). The novel ends with Sterling's belief that "The snake was looking south, in the direction from which the twin brothers and the people would come" (763). Tuscon's revolutionary underside reaches the Laguna.

Silko thus ends the novel in an imagined and prophetic future, expressing belief in a dialectical view of history from a Native American point of view. And this dialectic involves alliances with other groups resisting colonialism. If the continued settler colonialism of the Americas has been enabled through a double process of brutal domination and hegemony through wars of maneuver, Silko suggests that the imagining of a full frontal assault is now necessary to forge the workings of a Post-Colonial identity. Hegemonic adjustments through the organs of civil society, Silko suggests, are not viable in face of colonialism and racism. Such an imagining transforms both ideas of home and citizenship. Sterling returns home to Laguna, but it is a home that, in Sterling's mind, has been reconfigured as a site of revolutionary possibilities. The stone snake at the uranium pit stands not only as an indictment of the government and of Laguna Pueblos' complicity and greed but also portends uprisings in tandem with those in Africa. Schooled in a prescriptive citizenship through white boarding school teachers who are "required by law" to produce contented Indians, Sterling had earlier identified with white outlaw Robin Hoods—Pretty Boy Floyd and Dillinger's gang—who challenged the status quo and were on the run from the law. By the end of the novel, Sterling has decided to root himself as a Laguna Pueblo but this identity—temporally, spatially, and affectively—is shot through with antiracist, anticolonial struggles that invigorate a limited idea of citizenship and community with the imagining of an unlimited community.

Paradoxically, it is a similar *un*limited imagined community that is often invoked by indigenous groups fighting for a limited sovereignty. Amar Kanwar's documentary, *A Night of Prophecy* (2002), which focuses on marginalized groups in modern India, offers a particularly good example of this unlimited imagined community. The film records the mourning of various indigenous Naga tribes for their lost homeland as well as the monuments that memorialize freedom fighters for Nagaland; yet, at a poignant moment of historical retelling, a Naga woman reads aloud the statements made by Native Americans during their takeover of Wounded Knee in 1971. The imagined community being invoked is that of indigenous peoples worldwide and the film itself, while scrupulously specific about the history of Naga dispossession, also forges links to other marginalized groups in India and beyond. It is a perspective Apess had anticipated and Silko would approve.

CONCLUSION

Rethinking Keywords and Notes on Located Resistances Today

> The dispute over the reality or non-reality of thinking that is isolated from practice is a purely scholastic question.
>
> —Karl Marx, Second Thesis on Feuerbach

I choose to conclude this book with a reflection on the keywords I have engaged and been in dialogue with, because, like Raymond Williams, I believe that the cultural semiotics with which we live are deeply ideological and the result of complex social processes. Williams's project in *Culture and Society* was to trace the workings of certain keywords such as "industry," "democracy," "class," "art," and "culture" in literary works from the Romantics to Orwell. In his *Keywords*, he demonstrated the social and political values beneath the veneer of objectivity and authority of the OED, even as he relied on the latter.[1] Williams's keywords are the product of a particular historical moment as well as of his working-class and regional origins—two factors that would become central to British cultural studies. Missing from Williams's keywords is the term that has been definitive to the lives and experiences of the West and the rest—"colonialism," just as the blind spot in *Culture and Society* was its complete neglect of the effects of colonization during the period of the industrial revolution.

Today, a quarter century after Williams's revised edition of *Keywords* in 1983, a new vocabulary has emerged to explain both the workings of culture and society and it has its own blind spots. I have suggested that keywords such as "race," "postcolonialism," "colonialism," "imperialism," "locatedness," and "oppression" are central to understanding cultural productions and social processes in the contemporary United States. Indeed, the undue emphasis on and the rhetoric of inevitability that surrounds popular keywords such as "globalization," "flows," "migration," "transnationalism," "postnationalism" and "hybridity" glosses over both the effects of racism and colonialism in our lives and underestimates the liberatory possibilities of specific, located movements for racial justice. A particular concern in the book has been to rescue postcolonial critique and race theorizing from their subsumption under language-based, poststructuralist models that privilege a celebration of liminality and difference and instead to emphasize structures that produce economic and sociopolitical oppression. Of necessity, many, though obviously not all, of these structures are those of the nation-state.

As universities, particularly the humanities and social sciences, change their curricula to ostensibly "reflect" the realities of globalization, it is crucial that these curricula not become the structural equivalents of U.S. neoliberalism that uses the language of globalization to push imperialist, economically punishing programs for the world's South, as well as to its own citizens, whom it continues to racially segment even as it abrogates the state's role as the provider of social welfare. A quick glance at conference topics and course syllabi in cultural studies today (and the humanities in general) will reveal the preponderance of the terms "transnational" and "global" in their titles. My argument has been that these more neutral terms very often jettison or make secondary more politically charged terms such as colonialism, imperialism, and racism, all of which are "global" but emphasize a world structured in inequality and dominance. Furthermore, I have suggested that the impetus to develop paradigms of theory that are global, even if to energize us with possibilities for resistance, are problematic because they are, in the tradition of colonial knowledge production, universalizing and need to be critiqued. Indeed, scholars have argued that the contemporary moment calls for a resurgence of universal theorizing.[2] I have pointed out the problems of this universalizing impetus in some versions of postcolonial and feminist theory. Thus, if postcolonial theory, for instance, speaks in a universalized language of globalization by celebrating all minority identities as similar challenges to the center, it misses the effects of differential racial oppressions that mark particular racialized groups, just as does the valorization of a historically unmoored liminality and difference in feminist theory.

Similarly, as we continue to privilege border crossing, migration, and cosmopolitanism in order to challenge fixed identities and a hegemonic nationhood, there is a danger that the disciplinary imperatives of the racialized nation-state will be minimized. Tseng Kwong Chi's photographs powerfully remind us that the need for Asian Americans to "claim America" is as important as focusing on the porous border between Asian and Asian American. The work of critical race studies scholars, central in furthering the examination of particular racial formations, helps us understand the importance of such an imperative, for instance, for Asian Americans. Interestingly, in the *New Keywords* (2005), the entry on race makes no mention of the works of any of the critical race studies scholars; terms like "imperialism" and "hegemony" are simply missing from the collection as are Williams's terms signifying his local interests such as "dialect," "folk," "peasant," and "regional."[3] Of course the term "local" is missing as well.

I have used the term "Post-Colonial citizenship" to point to the liberatory possibilities of movements working toward racial justice because they continue to envision their struggles as both national and part of resistances to colonialism and imperialism worldwide; spokespersons for these struggles, using their writings as political interventions, have imagined a "post" of different possibilities that hinges on a politicized, rights-based differentiated citizenship that addresses the needs of racialized groups and an activist citizenship that participates in undermining structures of colonialism and imperialism. Today, when the United States is once again at its most racist and imperialist moment, it is vital that the legacies of black nationalism, the Asian American movement, and the anticolonial nationalism of Native Americans not be dismissed as racial essentialim or parochialism, but rather mined for their antiracist and anti-imperialist possibilities as part of an activist pedagogy. Cultural productions, as mediators and creators of value, are central in understanding these possibilities.

In the rest of this chapter, I want to briefly consider the workings of a number of contemporary racial justice movements as embodiments of Post-Colonial citizenship. I make this move not to position cultural production (including theory) and activism as oppositions but rather to trace a particular set of continuities between the two. The black power movement of the 1970s, of which Shakur saw herself as a spokesperson, coalesced around a series of specific historical conjunctures including continued racial disenfranchisement, discontent with civil rights pacifism, and the Vietnam War, all of which contributed to productive solidarities between radical African American and anti-imperialist struggles. Native American struggles for rights, which inspired Silko, continue in myriad forms to be heard in national and global forums. At present, racial oppression continues to intersect with imperialism in new and powerful ways. The hypermodern machinery of violence, the prison-industrial complex, for instance, has become central to the disciplining of both minorities and the colonized abroad. Prisons in the United States house over two million people, 70 percent of them people of color, including 50 percent African Americans.[4] As mentioned in chapter six, today's incarceration levels uncannily evoke the overcrowded prisons of England during its period of colonial expansion. Abu Ghraib, infamous for the lurid tortures carried out by grinning U.S. soldiers, was refurbished under the direction of torture-condoning Lane McCotter, director of a large Utah-based private prison company, forced to resign from the Utah Department of Corrections in 1997.[5] And in what is surely a harnessing of internal colonialism to imperial ends, federal prisoners were made to work overtime for companies such as UNICOR to accelerate the production of war machinery during the Gulf War.[6]

Yet despite the continuity of racial oppression and imperialism, longstanding indigenous as well as newer local resistances, particularly those organized around issues of race and colonialism, get short shrift in left circles where it is suggested that globalization has changed the very nature of struggle today. However, arguments that most new resistances are against the privatization of the global commons, for instance, fail to recognize that indigenous peoples have had their commons taken over a long time ago, both by private profiteers and settler nation states.[7] Indeed, an organization like the World Social Forum, which claims to be a nonhierarchical, global entity, pitted against a rapacious neoliberal agenda, has seen fit to remain remarkably indifferent to concerns of race and has not given any prominence to the black question in global resistance.[8] And, ironically, groups like the Zapatistas have been excluded from the forum because they are involved in armed combat. As third world critics have charged, concepts like self-determination, neocolonialism, and racism too often get subsumed under critiques of neoliberalism and calls for civil society.[9]

Thus, although contemporary struggles in the United States that are simply nonsystemic, nonlocal, and antiprivatization are significant, it is important to recognize that many resistances coalesce around specific facets or material practices of U.S. imperialism and are organized by longstanding groups and dedicated cadres of workers who have a specific agenda and have evolved particular strategies of protest. As with the Black Nationalist Movement of the 1970s, it is the ability of these groups to forge Post-Colonial solidarities with other groups through protesting local/national practices that marks these resistances as contemporary heirs of anticolonial struggles. These groups, that is, consistently critique the nation as empire in its consolidation of capitalist racism and forge activist connections with other anti-imperial groups, thus marking a Post-Colonial solidarity through local struggles. In this chapter, I will use specific examples to map various types of resistances in order to chart different kinds of possibilities for Post-Colonial citizenship emanating from them. I will also examine the contours of a very local, New York–based struggle in order to tease out the conjunctures between the raced particular and anti-imperial solidarity within it.

In January 1998, Congressman John Conyers (D-Michigan) presented a bill, H.R. 40, a "Commission to Study Reparations for African-Americans Act," before the House of Representatives. Using the number 40 as a symbol of the forty acres and a mule that the United States had initially promised the freed slaves, Conyers exhorted Congress to establish a commission to study the impact of slavery and subsequent *de jure* and *de facto* racial and economic discrimination on African Americans and to make appropriate recommendations to Congress to take corrective measures. Although only twenty-eight members of Congress, eighteen of whom were black, approved the measure and the bill never made it out of special committees, the importance of bringing the issue of reparations to the national stage cannot be overstated. The current political climate in which affirmative actions programs are being blocked by being perversely labeled racist, in which African American incarceration has reached alarming proportions, and in which the specter of the Muslim/Arab terrorist menace can be used to co-opt any progressive, antiracist initiatives, is one that demands concerted efforts toward racial justice.

The arguments generated around the issue of reparations reveal the continued importance of antiracist struggle in attempting to claim national space culturally, psychically, and economically, at the same time as they reveal the limits of hegemonic capitalist and imperialist nationalism. Foremost for all who have argued the case for reparations is the importance of a national acknowledgment of slavery as a crime against African American people and with consequences which continue till today. It is an issue of recognition, one demanded by William Apess and David Walker over a century ago, a racial recognition at once absolutely necessary and necessarily incomplete insofar as the process of Othering needs to be constantly critiqued; it is also a call for redistributive justice in the present, continuing the agenda of black nationalists of the 1970s and Native Americans today. Randall Robinson's *The Debt: What America Owes to Blacks*, powerfully links the material, psychic, and cultural disenfranchisement of African Americans to the economic benefits generated for white America and implores African Americans to see reparations not as charity but as debt owed to them.[10] Yet it is interesting that Robinson brings up the issue of reparations at the end of the book after repeatedly demonstrating how African Americans have been cast outside the bounds of a nation that has always been imagined white: "African Americans had never been allowed to own the idea of America. Had never been allowed to glimpse in its mirror the complex whole of the ancient self they had presented to it."[11] The nation-state can reflect back to the African American only a shattered Fanonian political, economic, and sexual identity. It is this sense of outsideness to the nation in terms of rights and yet insideness in being the source of the nation's wealth that has allowed proponents of reparations to articulate an expansive notion of African American activism by forging Post-Colonial solidarities with other groups.

Thus, the New Panther Vanguard Movement, following Huey Newton's postulation of an intercommunal (rather than international) order consequent upon U.S. imperialism, proposed in 2001 an "Intercommunal Reparations Campaign" based on an "organizational unity" among the African American community through which, and based on which, there could be a strategic alliance among "Africans on the Continent, Africans living in the Americas, and Indigenous People."[12] Applying a Post-Colonial logic, similar to that of Silko's, to the situation of African Americans and Native Americans, the New Panther Vanguard Movement further argued the inseparability of both racial struggles because the economic might of the United States has been made possible by the "stolen labor and land, from our African ancestors and indigenous people."[13] The case for African American reparations, while particular to African American slavery, thus has the potential for creating the political groundwork for solidarity possibilities between African Americans and indigenous peoples, as envisioned in *Almanac of the Dead*, both in the United States and the world as well as with the descendants of trans-Atlantic slavery.

I describe the potential for the reparations movement as future possibilities because, at present, mainstream African American organizations such as the NAACP and faith-based groups have not actively pursued the issue as have black nationalist organizations such as the Republic of New Africa (RNA) and the National Coalition of Blacks for Reparations in America (NCOBRA). However, just as the Black Panther Party imagined and created coalitions with other colonized and subaltern groups, so has the reparations movement; and just as the Panthers were deemed unnational, and therefore a threat to be suppressed, so have the proponents of reparations. At the 2001 World Conference Against Racism in Durban, reparations became the key issue uniting African Americans with African and Caribbean nations and against official U.S. nationalism. The official position of the United States that slavery was not "a crime against humanity" revealed both the raced limits of bourgeois nationalism as well as the limits necessary to absolve the nation-state from participation in global justice. On the other hand, Dudley Thompson, the foreign minister of Jamaica, stressed reparations as key to Post-Colonial justice: "Reparations is not about asking for money. You can't pay me for raping my grandmother. . . . What we demand is the restitution of our human dignity, the restoration of full equality, politically, socially and economically, between the oppressors and the oppressed."[14] It is because the issue of reparations invites a reading against sanctioned versions of official nationalism that it has attracted the ire of right-wing commentators such as David Horowitz who have labeled the reparations movement "anti-American" and its proponents racists; however, Horowitz's own characterization of Robinson's book as "anti-white, anti-American" tellingly reveals the racism that drives contemporary nationalism.[15]

While the reparations movement combines issues of cultural and material dispossession with a specific agenda that is nonetheless utopian, an organization like La Raza Unida has sought to use the mythical signifier of Aztlan to foreground a history of colonial oppression as a basis for both pragmatic and revolutionary utopian demands. Drafted as "El Plan Espiritual de Aztlan" in March 1969 for the Chicano Youth Conference in Denver, Colorado, the idea of Aztlan as a homeland, usurped by colonialism, has been used as a means of self-affirmation by various Chicano/a organizations. Although, as critics have suggested, Aztlan has contradictory cultural and political resonances, some of them problematically biological, Aztlan as a starting point for an anti-imperialist agenda within the Partido Nacional La Raza Unida (PNLRU) has important liberatory potential that is useful today.[16]

Central to the conception of PNLRU as a revolutionary organization, rather than a Hispanic version of the Democratic Party, is an assertion of the necessity of decolonization and anti-imperialist struggle. Thus, the platform of PNLRU combines quotidian agendas of better employment conditions and education opportunities with platforms on sovereignty, land restitution, and a wholesale repudiation of the official idea of immigration. As the PNLRU states, "We see no human being as 'illegal.' Those who have arrived to the U.S. with heritage indigenous to the Americas, and specifically those crossing the southern border, are migrants on their own continent."[17] Based on conceptions of right to land, the identity espoused by PNLRU works to encompass the heterogeneous people in the southwest, affected by U.S. colonialism. As Xenaro G. Ayala recently stated, "our identity as Chicanos is open to all Raza and indigenous people who live in Aztlan and struggle on a daily basis for a better life. . . . This position does not mean that we are pushing aside our Mexicano Cultural Identity, but that we are making our movement stronger with the active participation of our brothers and sisters from all over "America." Chicano is the identity that can embrace all Raza from America."[18]

But because PNLRU views itself as an anticolonial and anti-imperial organization, it is able to articulate and forcefully bring to light the continuities of colonialism and neocolonialism that animate the world today. While being mindful of the divergences among different struggles, the PNLRU posits a similarity with the movements for self-determination in Ireland and Palestine, citing as evidence the facts of colonization, invasion, occupation, the forfeiture of land, the marginalization of the natives, and the subjection of the native to the systemic racial inequality of the nation-state.[19] In the face of an overwhelming acceptance of the rhetoric of globalization as an explanation of contemporary sociopolitical formations and of the importance given to globalized forums funded largely by the West, anticolonial struggles being relegated to another temporal realm or simply marginalized in the left imaginary, PNLRU's emphasis on the status of colonized populations is an important political intervention. As Aziz Choudry puts it, "Many struggles against globalization taking place in the South are connected to anti-imperialist, anti-colonial mass movements with long histories. However, the voices heard most loudly . . . are rarely those of grassroots community activists from the South, let alone indigenous Peoples of the global North."[20] Indeed, many NGOs and activists from the United States function from "a state of colonial denial and refuse to make links between human rights abuses overseas, economic (in)justice, and the colonization of the lands and peoples where they live."[21] The local and global efforts of PNLRU—to revolutionize its local population and to address international organizations such as the United Nations through a forum such as human rights—speak to its attempts to challenge the legitimacy of U.S. colonialism and a raced neoliberalism normalized as democratic nationalism. Just as important, PNLRU's endeavors to make alliances with other activist organizations in order to foreground the links between imperialism abroad and colonialism at home fills an important gap in contemporary thinking about activism. As a recent document states, "When people see that nuclear weapons, for example, are related to an agenda of global imperialism, it will be easier to pull in people for anti-colonial work."[22] At the same time, PNLRU recognizes the continual policing of racial resistance organizations by the nation-state from the COINTELPRO of the 1970s to the Patriot Act of the twenty-first century.[23]

But whereas PNLRU continues to attract some members, its ability to mobilize people has waned considerably since the 1970s when leaders such as Corky Gonzalez formulated ideas of a revolutionary nationalism based on Aztlan. More important, a utopian organization like PNLRU, which has the potential, like all utopias, to shake up current colonial and imperial modes of thought, needs to link itself to groups like Coalition for Justice in the Maquiladoras (CJM), which are spatially defined and particularly concerned with the rights of Mexican workers who are often migrants on their own continent as they shuttle between Mexico and the United States. Indeed, CJM has been instrumental in pressuring companies like Levi Strauss, which have outsourced their manufacturing to maquiladoras such as Lajat, to allow workers the right to form their independent unions.

The contemporary reparations movement in the United States, stemming from the specific disenfranchisement of African Americans and organizations like PNLRU, focused on the exploitation of Latinas, have forged solidarities against necolonialism and imperialism that are particularly important in light of the nation's unilateral military style imperialism as well as attempts to legislate a dogmatic nationalism centered on the need for "security." In addition to resistances stemming from racial activism, there are important long-standing movements that challenge specific aspects of U.S. imperialism that intersect with racism. Leti Volpp contends that September 11 facilitated the consolidation of a new racial category of people who appeared to be "Middle Eastern, Arab, or Muslim," who were identified as terrorists and cast outside the bounds of nation.[24] Although Volpp is right about the hyperracialization of the Middle Eastern/Arab/Muslim category post-September 11, the racialization of Arabs through old Orientalist tropes has been long-standing in U.S. culture and was particularly intensified since 1967. Any attempt to support the Palestinian cause, to see Zionism from the viewpoint of its victims, as Edward Said powerfully and poignantly demonstrated, has been deemed both anti-Semitic and unnational through the ubiquitous association of the Palestinian with the "terrorist" in the national imaginary—a process of Othering similar to that accorded black nationalists in the 1970s. Yet despite this racialization and the government's massive funding of Israel's military structure that almost makes the country "an offshore US military base," the Palestinian struggle has attracted activists who attempt to interrupt the U.S.'s proxy support for colonialism.[25]

I want to examine here the representations surrounding the death of Rachel Corrie on March 16, 2003, caused by an Israeli bulldozer operator in Rafah in the Gaza Strip. Rachel Corrie was a member of the International Solidarity Movement (ISM), a group dedicated to using nonviolent and risky methods to challenge Israeli occupation. The most dangerous of these methods is using their bodies as human shields to deter demolition operations or violence against Palestinians. ISM members have often been successful in protecting Palestinians such as when they managed to enter Arafat's headquarters when the compound was surrounded by Israeli troops ready to force Arafat out. Often, they attempt to place themselves between Israeli bulldozers and the Palestinian homes facing demolition in the belief that Israeli forces will retreat rather than attack unarmed Europeans and Americans. Thus performatively, these activists challenge occupation by emphasizing Palestinian right to specific space/land through a paradoxical display of their own strategically (mis)placed bodies. Most of the times, activists have been able to deter Israeli forces. However, on March 16 as Rachel Corrie, dressed in a bright-orange jacket and megaphone in hand, stood imploringly in front of the house of a pharmacist, Samir Nasrallah, the bulldozer operator knocked her over and, without lifting the blade, reversed the machine, fatally injuring her. Minutes later, her dead body was delivered to a nearby hospital.

What emerges most interestingly from the responses to her death is how critics of Corrie in the United States have employed the manichean strictures of dogmatic nationalism and Orientalist racism separating Us from Them to designate Corrie as un-American, deluded, and in cohorts with "terrorists." In turn, the label "terrorist" (often indiscriminately applied to all Palestinians), like the label "criminal" applied to black liberation activists of the 1970s, is based on a severance of the terrorist from the body of the nation/civilized world and a paradoxical insistence that the terrorist constitutes a threat to this national/civilized body. In the reconfigured geopolitics of the post-Cold War period, the nation, as leader of the "civilized" world is constituted through an absolute separation from an Arab terrorist Other of which the Palestinian is an adequate metonym. Samuel Huntington's thesis about immutable and irreconcilable cultural differences between the West and the rest, primarily between the Christianity and Islam as constituting post-Cold War polity clearly pervades the demonology evident in popular media representation of Palestinians and activists engaged in the cause of a Palestinian homeland.[26]

Corrie's motivation for working with the Solidarity Movement stemmed, on the other hand, from a conviction that anticolonial alliances could be forged between communities, across perceived cultural differences. One of Corrie's goals, for instance, was to initiate a momentum for her hometown, Olympia, and Rafah in Palestine, to become sister cities.[27] In an e-mail to her mother, Corrie similarly attempted to explain the motivation for violent resistance by eliciting an empathy for Palestinian loss of livelihood. She also evinced an acute political and ethical awareness about her own participation, as a US citizen, in the genocide of Palestinians. "I am in the midst of a genocide which I am also indirectly supporting, and for which my government is largely responsible."[28]

Although Corrie's death received minimal media attention, being buried on page A15 of the *Washington Post*, for instance, her politics were the object of heated disputation and vituperation. Critics sought to discredit Corrie by marking her as Other and by separating her from Us/Nation. The most striking illustration of this severance was the controversial cartoon in the March 18 issue of the University of Maryland student newspaper, *The Diamondback*, which strove to represent Corrie as misguided, immature, and without a constituency. The cartoon depicts the terror-stricken, baffled face of a young girl as she sits ready to get up from a cross-legged position

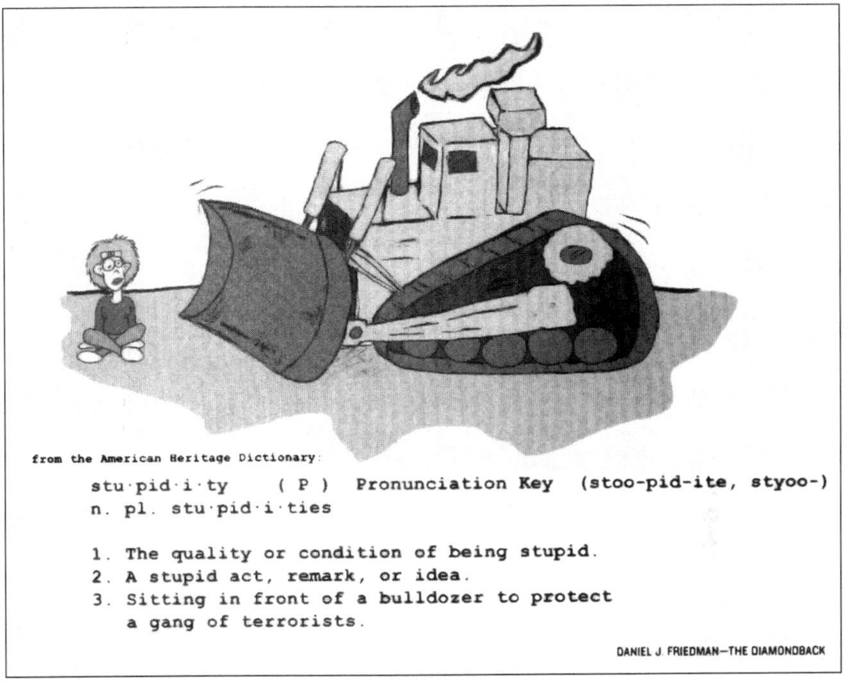

Fig. C.1. Editorial cartoon from *The Diamondback*. Reprinted by permission, *The Diamondback*, University of Maryland.

while a moving bulldozer inches perilously close to her. It defines Corrie as "stupid," thus depoliticizing her activism and interruption of American-Israeli colonial-racial policies; yet it simultaneously others her politically by associating her with "a gang of terrorists" (read: Arab/Muslim), those who putatively threaten American/Western democratic institutions. Most interestingly, however, Corrie is visually othered through a complete lack of human contact, thus suggesting that her actions merit no empathy. The bulldozer moves, inexorably, seemingly of its own volition, with no visible human operator, and therefore no culpable agent. Corrie herself sits alone, without any of the Solidarity members or any of the terrorists mentioned in the caption in sight in the cartoon. At the same time, however, as in the dynamics of colonial discourse where the stereotype needs incessant repetition, the cartoon warns against ambivalence or any possible sympathy for Corrie by telling us how to interpret the actions of a lone young woman facing the bulldozer.

While the *Diamondback* cartoon elicited numerous protests in the Maryland campus and on Web sites, many hostile to Corrie's actions continued to mark her as outside the body of the nation. A student wrote to *The Diamondback*, "I'd say that in order to be an American hero, one important criterion is that the hero must support America."[29] Similarly, Joshua Hammer, Jerusalem bureau chief for *Newsweek*, attributed Corrie's misplaced politics to her unnational education at Evergreen State College in Olympia, Washington. For evidence, he cited the college's 1999 commencement address by Mumia Abu Jamal via audiotape from death row. "A distrust of authority and a passion for unpopular causes permeate the politics of both students and faculty."[30] It is this isolation of Corrie as outside of the national body politic that Naomi Klein excoriated when she contrasted the glorification of Jessica Lynch, the soldier "rescued" from the Iraqis, with the forgetting of Rachel Corrie.[31] The iconic status accorded Jessica Lynch in the national media, just two weeks after the virtual neglect of Rachel Corrie, reveals the extent to which collective racial fantasies define the nation. While the rescue of Jessica Lynch harmonized perfectly with the captivity narrative genre that hinges on differences between an imperiled whiteness and a threatening savagery variously coded as Native American, African American, or, now, Arab/Arab American, Rachel Corrie's activism called into question these very binaries. In an act of political miscegenation, Corrie had given up white privilege and crossed over to become part of a Palestinian family and indeed identified with a family who had "adopted" her.[32] She was therefore marginalized as unthinking, immature and misguided, without a viable politics.

In the archives of resistance, however, Corrie has been lionized precisely through her role as participant in a larger movement of anticolonialism and anti-imperialism. Antiwar protesters in New York and New Jersey on March 29, 2003, for instance, linked their cause with that of Palestinians by protesting both the Iraq war and U.S. support for Israeli occupation. In the middle of the protest, the crowd observed a moment of silence in honor of Rachel Corrie.[33] Perhaps the most interesting tribute to Corrie was in the form of a mural in the Mission District of San Francisco where her face appeared on an axle, a symbol of workers' struggle, in between the images of Che Guevera and Mumia Abu Jamal, thus linking the Palestinian struggle with that of the Cuban revolution and African American oppression. This is an imagined Post-Colonial community beyond the boundaries of nation, but one that emanates from resistance to a particular racial policy of the nation-state and functions through a performance of race and place specificity.

These resistances to racist imperialism all draw on different constituencies at the national level and form progressive coalitions with different groups to form transnational, Post-Colonial solidarities. The International Solidarity Movement also involves varying degrees of physical danger and personal sacrifice that are often beyond the pale of ordinary people who want to act in a socially responsible manner or who wish to imagine and, to an extent, enact Post-Colonial solidarities. However, there are also more local resistances, what one can think of as resistances of the everyday, that are equally noteworthy and that should be promoted because not to do so would (a) write off resistances as peripheral to the business of ordinary living and (b) deny the political will of many who see themselves as enacting politically significant choices in their everyday lives.

Accordingly, the everyday type of resistances I want to focus on are those that offer opportunities to register opposition through the politicizing of one's professional or ethnic identity. As an example, I will examine the workings of Workers' Awaaz, a New York–based group focused exclusively on the exploitation of domestic workers from South Asia. Workers' Awaaz was founded by Nahar Alam, an immigrant from Bangladesh, fleeing an abusive husband. Resettled in Brooklyn, New York, Alam, unable to speak English, found the only employment she could—as a domestic worker. Forced to work up to twelve hours a day for as little as $50 a week, Alam discovered she was one among many intimidated South Asian workers being similarly abused. Alam took refuge with SAKHI, a nonprofit domestic violence prevention program for South Asian women in New York City and subsequently worked to include fair working conditions as part of SAKHI's agenda. In 1997, Alam founded Workers' Awaaz, an organization devoted solely to fighting the abuse of South Asian domestic workers. The case of middle-aged Ms. Kaur, an immigrant from Punjab, is typical of the ones handled by Workers' Awaaz. Ms. Kaur's work for an Indian immigrant doctor couple in Long Island included getting up at 4:30 A.M. to serve tea, preparing and cooking fresh meals several times a day to different family members, and cleaning grout in large tiled areas with a toothbrush. All told, she worked sixteen-hour days, six or seven days a week without overtime pay. When she finally refused to cook additional food for twenty-five guests, Ms. Kaur was fired on the spot and told to move out in the middle of the night.[34] Workers' Awaaz came to Ms. Kaur's aid, enabling her to file a federal lawsuit; the doctor couple decided to settle out of court for $50,000.

At first glance, a highly local, ethnically specific labor organization like Workers' Awaaz might seem an unlikely site for Post-Colonial citizenship. I would argue, however, that it is the simultaneous insistence on particularity and the forging of alliances across ethnic groups that is important about a group such as Workers' Awaaz. Although the organization was formed to specifically aid South Asian domestic workers rendered vulnerable because of their poor English language skills and cultural norms that, to an extent, militate against workers' rights (domestic workers in India routinely work ten- or twelve-hour shifts, six to seven days a week, and are not protected by worker laws), it has often worked in conjunction with other groups not specific to South Asian Americans. As a minority labor organization, Workers' Awaaz shares concerns with other labor groups that experience raced capitalist exploitation. Degrading worker conditions, particularly in metropoles, are part of capitalist imperialism's alliance with racism through which the uneven geographic development necessary for capitalism, as demonstrated by world systems theorists, can be maintained internally through sweatshop and other industries that rely heavily on third world immigrant labor. This labor resolves the basic contradiction of capitalism—its simultaneous need for theoretical equality and practical inequality.[35] Indeed, Coco Fusco has called these workplaces a manifestation of "late feudalism" rather than late capitalism.[36]

Thus, Workers' Awaaz has sponsored the Campaign Against Workplace Servitude, a group that exposes the exploitative nature of workplaces, particularly those that employ immigrant women. It also initiated an Ain't I a Woman!? Campaign demanding respect for women's work, based on the National Ain't I a Woman organization that challenges sweatshop conditions of women's work in the United States. Recognizing the neo-slavery conditions of such metropolitan labor, both organizations hearken back to Sojourner Truth's 1851 speech in Akron, Ohio, in which she repeatedly asked "Ain't I a Woman?" to challenge the white patriarchal race and class-based constructions of womanhood in the nineteenth century. In October 2002, Workers' Awaaz urged its members to unite with other labor groups in marching on Albany to denounce Governor George Pataki's dismal record on delivering workers' compensation benefits. In turn, Workers' Awaaz has been supported in its efforts by several immigrant labor organizations. A common strategy of Workers' Awaaz for shaming abusive domestic employers and procuring compensations for their victims is to stage demonstrations outside the home and/workplaces of recalcitrant employers. In their demonstration outside the home of an exploitative domestic employer, Bill Sawhney, for instance, Workers' Awaaz was joined by members of the Chinese Staff and Workers' Association, the Latin American Workers' Project, the New York Taxi Workers' Alliance (the majority of New York cabdrivers are third world immigrants), as well as the National Mobilization Against Sweatshops.[37]

An organization like Workers' Awaaz thrives on its connections with local ethnic groups. For instance, its success in procuring remuneration for unjustly treated domestic workers has depended, in part, on the public protests and letter writing campaigns by members of the South Asian community in New York who recognize the particularities of their living conditions in the metropole. At a broader level, the campaigns and the publicity generated by Workers' Awaaz call attention to the domestic living practices of wealthy South Asian immigrants and thus to the practices of this community not only in the United States but also to the treatment of domestic workers in South Asia. Many domestic workers, for instance, are hired in their home countries and come to the United States with the arrangement that their salaries will be paid to family members at home.[38] Exploitative salaries in the home country ensure that even doubling a domestic helper's home salary keeps it well below the poverty level in the United States.

Everyday activism can also involve an intervention into the political through activities often considered outside politics: our professional lives, living arrangements, and buying practices. In the United States, where the shift from producer to consumer capitalism has been long-standing, interventions in consumer practices are important. As sweatshop activism has demonstrated, the choice of whether or not to buy a Nike sweatshirt is not politically inconsequential. Concerted efforts to redirect consumer choice and protest degrading labor practices do produce results. Overwhelming technological changes have also made possible for protest to be incorporated into everyday life. The turn of the century finds half of the country's households with Internet access and thus theoretically an instantaneous connection to incipient movements that are unable to find voice through traditional channels such as newspapers, magazines, and television. Although the utopian vision of the Internet as an information highway connecting the world through a World Wide Web needs to be tempered with the sobering fact that access to safe drinking water remains a major concern to a fourth of the world's population and that only .5 percent of households in India, for instance, have computers, the qualitative changes in communication in the United States remain undeniable.

While the very form of the Internet—unbounded and in virtual space—might make the idea of the local suspect, I would argue that net activism might enable the local to find a larger voice and can productively engage the local in a radical globalism: witness a recent faculty petition—The Campaign to Stop Funding Hate—directed at South Asian faculty in the United States. In March 2002, Gujarat, India, witnessed bloody riots when the burning of a train compartment carrying fifty to sixty Hindu fundamentalists, committed to rebuilding Hindu temples over existing Islamic mosques, triggered a misguided revenge rampage in which over two thousand Muslims were murdered with the tacit support of local police and politicians. In the aftermath of the riots, concerned Indians in the United Kingdom and United States found each other through the Internet and formed the

Campaign to Stop Funding Hate (SFH). In the United States, the campaign launched Project Saffron Dollar, the purpose of which was to stop organizations parading as charities to collect funds from individuals and corporations for fundamentalist networks in India. Notable among these organizations was the India Development Relief Fund (IDRF), which was disbursing over 80 percent of its funds to Sangh Parivar, a Hindu fundamentalist group in India. Because corporations like CISCO, Sun, and AOL Time Warner were matching employee contributions to IDRF, Saffron Dollar sought to influence the corporations by launching a campaign to enlist the support of South Asian faculty and South Asian Studies scholars in the United States. When over three hundred signatures were received in the span of a few days, several corporations withdrew their contributions, thus signaling a victory for the campaign.

This campaign reveals several interesting features about the intersection of the located and the global. At first glance, the Saffron Dollar Campaign, impelled by events halfway across the world, seems to answer more to a politics of diaspora that stresses the point of origin rather than the place of habitation. However, despite the undoubted significance of diasporic origins, the focus of the campaign's energies is on the particular intersection of the raced religious with the workings of multinational capitalism in the United States. The campaign seeks to enlist support by linking people's everyday professional roles as academics with their racial identification as South Asians and their political affiliation with progressivist, antifundamentalist politics in order to disrupt the unholy alliance of capitalism and fundamentalism.

These faculty were hailed to politicize their roles as possessors of ethnic intellectual capital in the United States in order to persuade corporations to discontinue their contributions to IDRF. In their petition to corporations, faculty emphasized their roles as educators of South Asian American youth.[39] The campaign interrupted fundamentalist diaspora with location, disrupting the unholy alliance of capitalism and fundamentalism to press for a reconfigured globalism. However, this reconfigured globalism has to take into account the geopolitics of knowledge. Part of activism's agenda is to disclose and make available located subaltern knowledges to a global community in order to enable new forms of resistance. However, we need to part company with activists that seek to politicize particular resistances to imperialism within a model of liberal multiculturalism that has followed the Civil Rights era in the United States. Such a model bases itself on an acceptance of cultural difference (and economic inequality) paradoxically ensuing from the idea that difference is easily understood, easily translatable. Hence, the complexities of Tibet's colonization, for instance, are transmuted to the ubiquitous "Save Tibet" bumper stickers. Such stickers implicitly suggests that a voluntaristic act of empathy/seeing will make it simple for people to imagine living in Tibet and sharing the plight of the victims.

What needs to be emphasized, however, are the complexities and difficulties of a recognition based on a politics of Post-Colonial citizenship. Such a politics, as Fanon reminds us in *The Wretched of the Earth*, cannot be based on an obliteration of differences. In the case of making saving Tibet a bumper sticker, we need to recognize that the politics of uneven development that guide the geopolitics of knowledge are also the part of the politics from which we as immigrants or citizens of the United States benefit from. New resistances thus need to be sensitive to the particularities and pains of subaltern knowledge production and cognizant of the complexities involved in campaigning for the Other. I will end by suggesting, as an alternative to easy identification, an advertisement for Campaign to Stop Killer Coke. In the powerful disadvertising indictment of Coke, a giant Coke glass standing on Colombia in the map of South America is filled with a liquid on which float bodies of three men riddled with bullets, their faces submerged in the liquid. The overt political message is obviously clear: Coke's politics are deadly and intolerable, although its media images are seductive. The picture calls on us to boycott Coke, but ambiguities abound. The liquid in the glass might well be blood, but we don't know. But we cannot ever *know* the victims of Coke's union-busting policies. As the picture suggests, the float is "unthinkable"; it defies known categories of recognition and urges us to act from a position where our categories of the known are thrown into question. The best of activist thinking in the United States solicits us in ways that challenge our modes of comprehension and call for new modes of action.

Notes

CHAPTER ONE

1. Lisa de Moraes, "Kanye West's Torrent of Criticism, Live on NBC," Saturday, September 3, 2005; C01. http://www.washingtonpost.com/wp-dyn/content/article/2005/09/03.

2. "Fearful Southerners buy firearms at torrid pace," *Chicago Tribune*, September 8, 2005. http://www.chicagotribune.com/news/nationworld/chi-0509080205sep08,1,2178742.story?coll=chi-news-hed.

3. "Troops told 'shoot to kill' in New Orleans" ABC Online, September 2, 2005.

4. See Harilos Stecopoulos's analysis of the photo in *Reconstructing the World: Race, Region and Empire in the American Century, 1898–1976* (Ithaca: Cornell University Press, 2008), p. 1.

5. See Jonathan Dancy, "The Particularist's Progress," in Brad Hooker and Margaret Olivia Little, Eds., *Moral Particularism* (Oxford: Oxford University Press, 2000), pp. 130–155.

6. For a short discussion on the dialectical relationship between the descriptive and theoretical, see Etienne Balibar, *We, the People of Europe?: Reflections on Transnational Citizenship* (Princeton: Princeton University Press, 2004), p. viii.

7. Here I part company with Paul Gilroy, who argues that because of the circulation of African culture via diaspora, racial hierarchies aren't of major significance today. Of course, one cannot help being sympathetic to his call for an ethical culture beyond color. See Paul Gilroy, *Against Race: Imagining Political Culture beyond the Color Line* (Cambridge: Belknap, Harvard University Press, 2000).

8. I see my project as a broader version of what Nikhil Pal Singh maps out in his compelling book, *Black Is a Country* (Cambridge: Harvard University Press, 2004).

9. Dipesh Chakrabarty, *Provincializing Europe: Postcolonial Thought and Historical Difference* (Princeton: Princeton University Press, 2000), p. 217.

10. Lynn Dobson, *Supranational Citizenship* (Manchester: Manchester University Press, 2006), p. 4.

11. Karl Marx, "On the Jewish Question," in *Marx-Engels Reader*, Ed. Robert Tucker (New York: Norton, 1972), p. 32. Cited and analyzed in Lisa Lowe, *Immigrant Acts: On Asian American Cultural Politics* (Durham: Duke University Press, 1996), p. 32.

12. T. H. Marshall, "Citizenship and Social Class," in *Citizenship and Social Development*, Ed. T. H. Marshall, pp. 71–134 (New York: Anchor, 1967); John Rawls, *A Theory of Justice* (Cambridge: Harvard University Press, 1971).

13. David Scobey, "The Specter of Citizenship," *Citizenship Studies* 5: 1 (2001), pp. 11–26.

14. Iris Marion Young, "Polity and Group Difference: A Critique of the Ideal of Universal Citizenship," *Ethics* 99 (1989), p. 251.

15. Dobson, *Supranatural Citizenship*, p. 26.

16. Inderpal Grewal, *Transnational America: Feminisms, Diasporas, Neoliberalisms* (Durham: Duke University Press, 2005), p. 11.

17. Martha C. Nussbaum, "Patriotism and Cosmopolitanism," in Ed. Joshua Cohen, *For Love of Country: Debating the Limits of Patriotism* (Boston, Beacon Press, 1996), p. 7.

18. Michel S. Laguerre, *Diasporic Citizenship: Haitian Americans in Transnational America*(New York: St. Martin's Press, 1998), pp. 8–13.

19. Andrew Dobson, *Citizenship and the Environment* (New York: Oxford University Press, 2003), p. 47. See Lynn Dobson's critique of Andrew Dobson's concept in *Supranational Citizenship*, pp. 35–38.

20. I am indebted to an anonymous reader for SUNY Press for this insight.

21. Robert Young, *Postcolonialism: An Historical Introduction* (New York: Blackwell, 2001), p. 57.

22. Young, *Postcolonialism*, p. 58.

23. This refers to Edward Said's explanation of the "Orient," seen to signify passivity, fatality, and degeneracy, as a Western construct designed to justify or prefigure colonialism. See Edward Said, *Orientalism* (New York: Vintage, 1978), pp. 52–57.

24. Johannes Fabian uses the idea of chronopolitics as central in his analysis of Western anthropologists' colonial relationship to their African subjects. The Western anthropologist interacts with the African at a particular moment, but when the anthropologist writes about or represents the

African subject, the subject always inhabits the past, while the Westerner inhabits the present. This problem of not inhabiting the same time frame is the colonial problem of coevalness. See Johannes Fabian, *Time and the Other: How Anthropology Makes Its Object* (New York: Columbia University Press, 1983).

25. See John Ralston Saul, "The Collapse of Globalism and the Rebirth of Nationalism," *Harper's Magazine*, March 2004, pp. 34–35.

26. "Editors' Comments," *Public Culture* 1 i (Fall 1988), p. 1. Acknowledging that their inattention to the asymmetrical flows and the shift to the term "transnational" from "neocolonial" might elide problems of inequality, they nevertheless maintained that the shift "does allow us to analyze cultural processes, traffic and flows" that the term neocolonialism doesn't (p. 2).

27. Arjun Appadurai, *Modernity at Large: Cultural Dimensions of Globalization* (Minneapolis: University of Minnesota Press, 1996), pp. 32–33.

28. *Modernity at Large*, pp. 2–3, 19. Appadurai makes the distinction between cellular and vertebrate structures to name the new global moment in *Fear of Small Numbers: An Essay on the Geography of Anger* (Durham: Duke University Press, 2006), pp. 25–27. Responding to critiques of *Modernity at Large*, he focuses in this book on the darker aspects of globalization.

29. Manuel Castells, *The Information Age: Economy, Society and Culture Vol II: The Power of Identity* (Malden, MA: Blackwell, 1997), p. 351.

30. *The Power of Identity*, p. 359.

31. Michael Hardt and Antonio Negri, *Empire* (Cambridge: Harvard University Press, 2000), pp. 134, xiv, 247.

32. *Empire*, p. 127.

33. *Empire*, pp. 212–213; 280.

34. *Empire*, p. 43.

35. *Empire*, p. 180.

36. Anthony Appiah, *Cosmopolitanism: Ethics in a World of Strangers* (New York: Norton, 2006), p. 108.

37. Appiah, *Cosmopolitanism*, pp. 78–80. Even though Appiah claims that cosmopolitanism includes universality and difference, he tends to cast any critique of imperialism or multinational capitalism as nostalgic for cultural authenticity. He argues, for instance, that attempting to protect the American family farm stems only from an outdated sense of cultural authenticity and homogeneity that makes no economic sense. There is no consideration, however, of the ecological and labor costs of agribusinesses that might have little to do with authenticity (104).

38. For a critique of James Clifford's discrepant cosmopolitanism and Homi Bhabha's hybrid cosmopolitanism, see Pheng Cheah, "Given Culture: Rethinking Cosmopolitical Freedom in Transnationalism," *boundary* 2 24 ii (Summer 1997), pp. 157–197.

39. Rohit Saran, "How We Live," *India Today International*, July 28, 2003, p. 14.

40. See Kwame Anthony Appiah, "Cosmopolitan Patriots," in *Cosmopolitics: Thinking and Feeling Beyond the Nation*, Eds. Pheng Cheah and Bruce Robbins (Minneapolis: University of Minnesota Press, 1998), pp. 91–113.

41. *World Development Report 1995, Workers in an Integrating World* (Washington, D.C.: World Bank), p. 53.

42. Castells, *The Power of Identity*, p. 66.

43. *Empire*, pp. 44–46.

44. David Harvey, *Spaces of Hope* (Berkeley: University of California Press, 2000), p. 13. For the problems in accepting cosmopolitanism as visionary in face of a market-driven globalism, see Richard Falk, "Revisioning Cosmopolitanism," in Martha C. Nussbaum, Ed., *For Love of Country* (Boston: Beacon Press, 1996). Doug Henwood sees the term "globalization" as a euphemistic and problematic substitute for imperialism, one that falsely poses globalization as the enemy rather than capitalist and imperialist exploitation. See Doug Henwood, "What Is Globalization Anyway?" in *World Bank Literature*, pp. 60, 62.

45. The political aesthetic of the Brazilian "Anthropophagist Manifesto" of 1921, centering on the cannibal as a figure for Brazilian identity, would be an example of an anti-imperial, located aesthetic. Lisa Lowe and David Lloyd also argue for the importance of connecting subjugated practices, but they emphasize that their collection focuses on connections not prediacted on cosmopolitanism but rather those that emphasize "diversely localized projects and struggles." See Lisa Lowe and David Lloyd, *The Politics of Culture in the Shadow of Capital* (Durham: Duke University Press, 1997), pp. 5–6.

46. John W. Blassingame, *The Slave Community: Plantation Life in the Antebellum South* (New York: Oxford University Press, 1972). Similarly, focusing on the late 1990s in India, Ashis Nandy demonstrates how indigenous traditions, often seen as archaic by the elite but which are actually open ended and democratic, have the potential to challenge the technologized language of the colonized nation-state and its machinery of violence. See Ashis Nandy, *The Savage Freud and Other Essays on Possible and Retrievable Selves* (Princeton: Princeton University Press, 1995).

47. Singh, *Black Is a Country*, pp. 192–193.

48. Cited in Rob Wilson, "Becoming Global and Local in the U.S. Transnational Imaginary of the Pacific" in his *Reimagining the American Pacific: From South Pacific to Bamboo Ridge and Beyond* (Durham: Duke University Press, 2000), pp. 251, 253. See also Naomi Klein's discussions of Nike's use of the creative expressions of inner city African American youth in *No Logo* (New York: Picador, 2000), p. 73.

49. *Empire,* p. 195.

50. *The Power of Identity*, p. 59.

51. Lenin, *Imperialism*, p. 10.

52. Cited in Howard Winant, *The World Is a Ghetto: Race and Democracy since World War II* (New York: Basic Books, 2001), p. 126.

53. This is the view that underdeveloped countries are like the "developed" ones at an earlier stage of their development. World systems theorists like Samir Amin argue on the other hand that underdeveloped countries form part of a world system and that their integration into the world system created their particular structure, which has nothing in common with what prevailed prior to their integration. See Samir Amin, *Accumulation on a World Scale: A Critique of the Theory of Underdevelopment,* 2 vols., Trans. Brian Pearce (New York: Monthly Review Press, 1974), p. 8.

54. Immanuel Wallerstein, *The Capitalist World-Economy* (New York: Cambridge University Press, 1979), p. 61.

55. *The Capitalist World Economy*, p. 71. Despite Wallerstein's recent ruminations about the current transitional phase in which the world system might be collapsing, he still sees neocolonialism as rampant at the end of the twentieth century, exercised through U.S. control of international regulatory bodies. See Wallerstien, *The Decline of American Power: The U.S. in a Chaotic World* (New York: New Press, 2003), p. 39.

56. Amin, *Accumulation on a World Scale*, pp. 3, 19.

57. Fatemah Farag, "Empire of Chaos Challenged," *Al-Ahram* 609, October 24–30. p. 3.

58. Samir Amin, *The Liberal Virus: Permanent War and the Americanization of the World*, trans. James H. Membrez (New York: Monthly Review Press, 2004), p. 23.

59. See also Noam Chomsky's indictment of contemporary U.S. unilateralism in *Hegemony or Survival* (New York: Metropolitan Books, 2003).

60. In late modernity, Giddens argues that emancipatory politics that operate from "freedom from" need to be linked to a more urgent politics of self-actualization that operate from a "freedom to" in which there are no Others. See Anthony Giddens, *The Consequences of Modernity* (Stanford: Stanford University Press, 1990), pp. 71, 156.

61. Walter D. Mignolo, *Local Histories/Global Designs: Coloniality, Subaltern Knowledges, and Border Thinking* (Princeton: Princeton University Press, 2000), p. 337.

62. Mignolo, p. 338.

63. See Amin's *The Liberal Virus: Permanent War and Americanization of the World* (New York: Monthly Review Press, 2004); similarly, Mignolo talks about the global colonialism managed by TNCs in *Local Histories/Global Designs*, p. ix.

64. See also Carl Eblen's *The First and Second American Empires* (1967), and Richard Drinnon's *Facing West: The Metaphysics of Indian-Hating and Empire Building* (1980). My book, *U.S. Orientalisms* (1998) mapped the significance of the "Orient" as a site of political and cultural intervention in the nineteenth century; John Carlos Rowe's *Literary Culture and U.S. Imperialism* (2000) demonstrated the centrality of imperialism to U.S. culture.

65. The emphasis for the "postmodern hybridite," as Rey Chow puts it, shifted from the "colonial" to the "post," enabling an equivalence of the postcolonial with "cosmopolitan" or "international." See Rey Chow, "Between Colonizers: Hong Kong's Postcolonial Self-Writing in the 1990s," *Diaspora* 2: 12 (1992), p. 157.

66. Benita Parry, "The Postcolonial: Conceptual Category or Chimera?," *Yearbook of English Studies* 27 (1997), pp. 19, 3, 13.

67. Edward Said, "Globalizing Literary Study," *PMLA* 116 i (January 2001), p. 66.

68. Aijaz Ahmad, *In Theory: Classes, Nations, Literatures* (New York: Verso, 1992), p. 3. For a critique of the "euphoric valorization of difference," the "difference revolution" in postcolonial theory, see Rey Chow, *The Protestant Ethic and the Spirit of Capitalism* (New York: Columbia University Press, 2002), pp. 129–131.

69. Arif Dirlik, "The Postcolonial Aura: Third World Criticism in the Age of Global Capitalism" in Anne McClintock et als., Eds., *Dangerous Liaisons: Gender, Race, and Postcolonial Perspectives* (Minneapolis: University of Minnesota Press, 1997), p. 503. Bruce Robbins sees the "ultraleft paranoid" criticism of postcolonial theory as misguided, like the Communist attacks on the progressive French university on the eve of the Nazi invasion. See Robbins, *Feeling Global: Internationalism in Distress* (New York: New York University Press, 1999), p. 116.

70. Robert J. C. Young, *Postcolonialism: An Historical Introduction* (New York: Blackwell, 2001), pp. 67–68.

71. Vijay Mishra and Bob Hodge, "What Is Post(-)colonialism?" in Patrick Williams and Laura Chrisman, Eds., *Colonial Discourse and*

Post-Colonial Theory: A Reader (New York: Columbia University Press, 1994), p. 282.

72. Ranajit Guha, "Dominance Without Hegemony and Its Historiography," in Ranajit Guha, Ed., *Subaltern Studies VI: Writings on South Asian History and Society* (New Delhi: Oxford University Press, 1989), p. 229.

73. For a critique of Minh-ha's turning of "woman" and "race" in Woman/Native/Other into metaphors alone, see Sara Suleri, "Woman Skin Deep: Feminism and the Postcolonial Condition" in Patrick Williams and Laura Chrisman, Eds., *Colonial Discourse and Post-Colonial Theory* (New York: Columbia University Press, 1994), p. 249.

74. Sau-ling C. Wong, "Denationalization Reconsidered: Asian American Cultural Criticism at a Theoretical Crossroads," *Postcolonial Theory and the United States: Race, Ethnicity, and Literature*, Eds. Amritjit Singh and Peter Schmidt (Jackson: University of Mississippi Press, 2000), p. 139.

75. Significant titles in the area include works such as Patricia Williams, *The Alchemy of Race and Rights*, Michael Omi and Howard Winant, *Racial Formation in the United States*, Noel Ignatiev, *How the Irish Became White*, Cornel West, *Race Matters*, Mike Dyson, *Race Rules*, and David Roediger, *The Wages of Whiteness.*

76. Richard Delgado, "Introduction," *Critical Race Theory: The Cutting Edge* (Temple: University of Philadelphia Press, 1995), p. xv.

77. Jean Francois Lyotard, *The Postmodern Condition: A Report on Knowledge*, Trans. Geoff Bennington and Brian Massumi (Minneapolis: University of Minnesota Press, 1984; orig. pub., 1979), p. 60.

78. Lisa Lowe, *Immigrant Acts: On Asian-American Cultural Politics* (Durham: Duke University Press, 1996), p. 5.

79. bell hooks, *Feminist Theory: From Margin to Center* (Boston: South End Press, 1984), pp. 1–6.

80. Houston A. Baker Jr., *Turning South Again: Re-Thinking Modernism/Re-Reading Booker T.* (Durham: Duke University Press, 2001), p. 89.

81. *Turning South Again*, p. 84.

82. Robin D. G. Kelley and Tiffany Ruby Patterson, "How the West Was One: On the Uses and Limitations of Diaspora," *Black Scholar* 30, nos. 3–4, p. 13.

83. Of course North-South differences were particularly significant for African Americans in both the antebellum and post-Reconstruction periods.

84. Arif Dirlik, "Asians on the Rim: Transnational Capital and Local Community in the Making of Contemporary America" in Evelyn Hu-DeHart, Ed., *Across the Pacific: Asian Americans and Globalization* (Philadelphia: Temple University Press, 1999), pp. 47–48.

85. Paul Lyons, "Reading the Literatures of Hawai'i Under an "Americanist" Rubric" in Deborah L. Madsen, Ed., *Beyond the Borders: American Literature and Post-Colonial Theory* (London: Pluto Press, 2003), p. 141.

86. Ranajit Guha, "Dominance without Hegemony and Its Historiography," p. 228, and Dipesh Chakrabarty, *Provincializing Europe* cited in note 9. Guha's theorization of conditions of dominance and subordination working through elements of persuasion-coercion and collaboration-resistance, respectively, in different combinations of strength, specific to the societies where they occur also offers a located way of thinking about power and inequalities.

87. Etienne Balibar, "Ambiguous Universality," *differences* 7 i (1995), p. 69. Balibar's discussion of universality proceeds from the assumption that "no discussion about universality . . . can usefully proceed with a 'univocal' concept of 'the Universal'" (p. 48).

88. Zillah Eisenstein, *Against Empire: Feminisms, Racism, and the West* (New York: Zed Books, 2004), p. 35.

89. Bart Moore-Gilbert points to Henry Louis Gates's use of Soyinka, Black Nationalists' use of Fanon, and the migration of African intellectuals to the United States as evidence of the "cross-fertilization between African-American and postcolonial cultural perspectives." See Moore-Gilbert, *Postcolonial Theory: Contexts, Practices, Politics* (New York: Verso, 1997), p. 9.

90. See Houston A. Baker Jr., "Caliban's Triple Play," in Henry Louis Gates, Jr., Ed., *"Race," Writing and Difference* (Chicago: University of Chicago Press, 1986), pp. 381–396. For Baker, analyses of Otherness, difference, and race in the analytical terms of social scientific and expressive cultural models of academic thinking belie the vernacular model that Gates himself proposes as a means of questioning the Enlightenment dualism between reasoning-human-Westerners and Others.

91. Howard Winant, *The World Is a Ghetto: Race and Democracy Since World War II* (New York: Basic Books, 2001), p. xiv.

92. Winant, p. xiv.

93. The title of chapter four of Winant's book, "The Empire Strikes Back: Resistance to Racial Rule," exemplifies his attempt to link the global politics of race and postcoloniality.

94. Nikhil Pal Singh, *Black Is a Country* (Cambridge: Harvard University Press, 2004).

95. See Joanna Brooks, "Colonization, Black Freemasonry, and the Rehabilitation of Africa," in Malini Johar Schueller and Edward Watts, Eds., *Messy Beginnings: Postcoloniality and Early American Studies* (Brunswick: Rutgers University Press, 2003), pp. 237–250.

96. W. E. B. DuBois, *Black Reconstruction: An Essay Toward a History of the Past which Black Folk Played in the Attempt to Reconstruct Democracy in America, 1860—1880* (New York: Atheneum, 1977; orig pub. 1935), p. 15.

97. My use of fragments and nation echoes Partha Chatterjee's title *The Nation and Its Fragments: Colonial and Postcolonial Histories* (Princeton: Princeton University Press, 1993); Chatterjee also distinguishes between Western nationalism and anticolonial nationalism (p. 5).

98. Rodolfo "Corky" Gonzalez, *Message to Aztlan* (Houston: Arte Publico, 2001), p. 86. In a speech on July 4, 1976, Gonzalez said, "In Angloa, the sons of African slaves from Cuba are going back to liberate Africa, the land of their birth, the land of their origin. Let us look to that. . . . The sons of Mexicanos and the sons of Latinos are standing up against the oppression all across Latin America, Mexico, and Aztlan. We're looking at each other. . . . We are one familia, we are one family, we are related across this country and across these two continents."

99. Huey Newton, *To Die For the People: The Writings of Huey P. Newton*. Intro. Franz Schurmann (New York: Random House, 1972), p. 18.

100. *To Die for the People*, p. 40.

101. See "Reply to Roy Wilkins re: Vietmam: September 26, 1970," in *To Die for the People*, p. 186.

102. Armando Navarro, *La Raza Unida Party: A Chicano Challenge to the U.S. Two-Party Dictatorship* (Temple: University of Philadelphia Press, 2000), p. 259.

103. *To Die for the People*, p. 31.

104. Subcomandante Marcos, "The fourth world war has begun," Le Monde Diplomatique, September 1977, p. 10. http://mondediplo.com/1997/marcos. Neil Lazarus also insists on the importance of maintaining distinctions between bourgeois nationalisms and a liberationist, anti-imperialist nationalism. See Neil Lazarus, *Nationalism and Cultural Practice in the Postcolonial World* (New York: Cambridge University Press, 1999), p. 79.

105. Frantz Fanon, *The Wretched of the Earth*. Trans. Constance Farrington (New York: Grove Press, 1963; orig. pub. 1961), pp. 41, 40.

106. Fanon, *Wretched of the Earth*, p. 216.

107. Fanon, *Wretched of the Earth*, pp. 247–248.

108. Edward Said, *Culture and Imperialism* (New York: Knopf, 1993), p. 214.

109. Gary Okihiro's argument in *Margins and Mainstreams* about marginalized groups such as Asian Americans as central in contributing to mainstream national ideas is pertinent here.

110. See, for instance, Anzaldua's description of the borderlands as a place for "the squint-eyed, the perverse, the queer, the troublesome, the mongrel, the mulatto, the half-breed, the half dead; in short, those who cross over, pass over, or go through the confines of the 'normal'," *Borderlands: The New Mestiza* (San Francisco: Aunt Lute, 1987), p. 3.

111. Amritjit Singh and Peter Schmidt, *Postcolonial Theory and the United States*, pp. 6–7.

112. C. Richard King, *Postcolonial America* (Urbana: University of Illinois Press, 2000), p. 7.

113. King, *Postcolonial America*, pp. 8–9.

114. See Anne McClintock, *Imperial Leather: Race, Gender and Sexuality in the Colonial Context* (New York: Routledge, 1990).

115. I am not, of course, arguing that all minority writing is subversive. Indeed, as I demonstrate in chapter four, this writing can well buy into the narratives of universalization and globalization.

116. John Brown Childs, *Transcommunality: From the Politics of Conversion to the Ethics of Respect* (Philadelphia: Temple University Press, 2003), pp. 8, 10.

117. Mignolo, *Local Histories/Global Designs*, p. 22.

118. Barbara Brinson Curiel, David Kazanjian, Katherine Kinney, Steven Mailloux, Jay Mechling, John Carlos Rowe, George Sanchez, Shelley Streeby, and Henry Yu," "Introduction," *Post-Nationalist American Studies*, Ed. John Carlos Rowe (Berkeley: University of California Press, 2000), p. 2. See also *The Futures of American Studies*, Eds. Donald E. Pease Jr. and Robyn Wiegman (Durham: Duke University Press, 2002).

119. *Post-Nationalist American Studies*, pp. 1, 8.

120. Shelley Fisher Fishkin, "Crossroads of Cultures: The Transnational Turn in American Studies—Presidential Address to the American Studies Association, November 12, 2004" *American Quarterly*, 57 i (March 2005), p. 43.

121. Carolyn Porter, *Remapping American Literary Studies*, p. 468; John Carlos Rowe, *The New American Studies* (Minneapolis: University of Minnesota Press, 2002), p. xvi.

122. Rowe, *The New American Studies*, xvi.

123. Edward W. Said, *Culture and Imperialism* (New York: Alfred A. Knopf, 1993), pp. 45, 47.

124. See Michael Berube, "American Studies without Exceptions," *PMLA* 118 i (2003), p. 109.

125. See, for instance, Ed White, *The Backcountry and the City: Colonization and Conflict in Early America* (Minneapolis: University of Minnesota Press, 2005).

CHAPTER TWO

1. Jenny Sharpe critiques the idea of a homogenized diaspora by pointing out the differences among South Asian diasporic experiences in Canada, the United States, and Britain. See Jenny Sharpe, "Is the United States Postcolonial? Transnationalism, Immigration, and Race," *diaspora* 4 ii (Fall 1995), p. 190. In a manner similar to his work on the black Atlantic, Paul Gilroy also suggests that the idea of diaspora, because outer-national and relational, provides better ways of thinking about identity than particularity, which is static. However, it is significant that Gilroy focuses mainly on the African diaspora and tangentially on the Jewish diaspora and links them through the particular experiences of pain. See Paul Gilroy, *Against Race: Imagining Political Culture beyond the Color Line* (Cambridge: Harvard, Belknap, 2000), pp. 123, 13.

2. David Leiwei Li points out the problems of the diaspora model disregarding race as a category. See Li's *Imagining the Nation: Asian American Literature and Cultural Consent* (Stanford: Stanford University Press, 1998), p. 202.

3. See Carole Boyce Davies, *Black Women, Writing and Identity: Migrations of the Subject* (New York: Routledge, 1994), p. 85.

4. See Nikhil Pal Singh, "Culture/Wars: Recoding Empire in an Age of Democracy," *American Quarterly* 50 iii (1998), pp. 471–522.

5. See John Liu, "Towards an Understanding of the Internal Colonial Model," *Counterpoint: Perspectives on Asian America*, Ed. Emma Gee (Los Angeles: Asian American Studies Center, UCLA, 1976), pp. 160–168.

6. For an explanation of the different politics of race and ethnicity see Michael Omi and Howard Winant, *Racial Formation in the United States* (New York: Routledge, 1986) p. 12. Deepika Bahri and Mary Vasudeva argue that the growth of postcolonial studies and the "context of Anglo-American identity politics indicates the convergence of discourses of postcolonialism, identity and ethnicity." See Bahri and Vasudeva, Eds., *Between the Lines; South Asians and Postcoloniality* (Philadelphia: Temple University Press, 1996), p. 12. My inquiry suggests, on the other hand, the need to interrogate this supposed convergence and to differentiate between different kinds of identity politics and discourses of ethnicity.

7. See Arif Dirlik, "The Postcolonial Aura: Third World Criticism in the Age of Global Capitalism," in Anne McClintock, Aamir Mufti, and Ella Shohat, Eds., *Dangerous Liaisons: Gender, Nation, and Postcolonial Perspectives* (Minneapolis: University of Minnesota Press, 1997), p. 503; See also Aijaz Ahmad, *In Theory: Classes, Nations, Literatures* (London: Verso, 1992), pp. 68–69.

8. Homi K. Bhabha, *The Location of Culture* (New York: Routledge, 1994), p. 11. Hereafter cited parenthetically in text.

9. *Beloved* has often been read in relation to ideas of community, trauma, and history. More recently, postcolonial frameworks have proved useful in reading *Beloved.* See Mary Jane Suero Elliott, "Postcolonial Experience in a Domestic Context: Commodified Subjectivity in Toni Morrison's Beloved," *MELUS* 25 iii–iv (Fall/Winter 2000), pp. 181–202, and Satya P. Mohanty, "The Epistemic Status of Cultural Identity: on *Beloved* and the Postcolonial Condition," *Cultural Critique* 24 (1993), pp. 41–80.

10. See Gauri Viswanathan, *Masks of Conquest: Literary Studies and British Rule in India* (New York: Columbia University Press, 1989), pp. 116, 149, and Gayatri Chakravorty Spivak, *A Critique of Postcolonial Reason: Toward a History of the Vanishing Present* (Cambridge: Harvard University Press, 1999), p. 102.

11. Kumkum Sangari, "The Politics of the Possible," *Cultural Critique* 7 (1987), p. 184.

12. See Stuart Hall, "The Local and the Global," in *Dangerous Liaisons*, pp. 173–187. Hall's celebration of the global and his insistence that the local no longer exists are questionable. To Hall's rhetorical question, "Are there still traditional musics that have never been influenced by modern music?" I would venture to say, "yes." (p. 186).

13. Paul Gilroy, *The Black Atlantic: Modernity and Double Consciousness* (Cambridge: Harvard University Press, 1993), p. 220.

14. Although Deleuze and Guattari criticize binarisms such as the West and the Orient, many of their ideas derive from a sense of West-Other difference. The idea of the rhizome comes from the Oriental despot (19); the idea of plateau comes from the different libidinal economy of the Balinese (xiv). Deleuze, Giles, and Felix Guattari, *A Thousand Plateaus: Capitalism and Schizophrenia*. Trans. Brian Massumi (Minneapolis: University of Minnesota Press, 1987).

15. Rob Wilson, "From the Sublime to the Devious: Writing the Experimental/Local Pacific," *boundary* 2 28 i (2001), pp. 122–123.

16. See Ella Shohat, "Notes on the Post-Colonial," *Social Text* 31/32 (1992), pp. 99–113, Benita Parry, "Problems in Current Theories of Colonial Discourse," *Oxford Literary Review* 9 i–ii (1987), pp. 27–58, Robert Young, *Colonial Desire: Hybridity in Theory, Culture and Race* (New York: Routledge, 1995), pp. 4–8; Pheng Cheah, "Given Culture: Rethinking Cosmopolitical Freedom in Transnationalism," *boundary* 2 24 ii (1997), pp. 170, 172; and Michael Hardt and Antonio Negri, *Empire* (Cambridge: Harvard University Press, 2000), pp 143–145. Hardt and Negri, however, see all of postcolonial theory as fundamentally incapable of dealing with the contemporary world situation (p. 146).

17. Bart Moore-Gilbert critiques Bhabha for assuming that "structures of psychic identification and affect" apply equally to the Western educated and the female subaltern. See Bart Moore-Gilbert, "Homi Bhabha: 'The Babelian Performance'" in *Postcolonial Theory: Contexts, Practices, Politics* (New York: Verso, 1997), p. 150.

18. Paul Gilroy, *The Black Atlantic*, pp. 101, 102.

19. Edward Said uses the term "traveling theory" to point out the ways in which theory travels from one site to another in order to be put to a different use. See Edward Said, *The World, The Text, and The Critic* (Cambridge: Harvard University Press, 1983), pp. 226–227.

20. Arjun Appadurai, *Modernity at Large: Cultural Dimensions of Globalization* (Minnesota: University of Minneapolis Press, 1996), p. 41.

21. Arjun Appadurai, "The Heart of Whiteness," *Callaloo* 16 iv (1993), pp. 806–807.

22. See *Modernity at Large*, p. 45, where the conflict between the "honor of women" and new demands of work are taken as descriptive of all immigrants.

23. Obviously, forms of racial oppression change. Manning Marable, for instance, rightly points out a major change signaled by the civil rights period. However, his suggestion that contemporary African Americans can be race-insulated is debatable. Manning writes, "It is now possible for a member of the present-day Negro elite to live in the white suburbs, work in a white professional office, attend religious services in all all-white church or synagogue, belong to a white country club, and never come into contact with the most oppressed segments of the black community." See Marable, *Beyond Black and White: Transforming African-American Politics* (London: Verso, 1995), p. 102.

24. Arjun Appadurai, "The Heart of Whiteness," p. 803.

25. Werner Sollors, *Beyond Ethnicity* (New York: Oxford University Press, 1986), pp. 4–5.

26. Mexican workers crossing the border do not think of the United States as abroad but rather, as Gloria Anzaldua has powerfully suggested, as borderlands.

27. Arjun Appadurai, "The Heart of Whiteness," p. 803.

28. David B. Wilkins, "Introduction: The Context of Race," in *Color Conscious: The Political Morality of Race* by K. Anthony Appiah and Amy Gutmann (Princeton: Princeton University Press, 1996), p. 23.

29. Arjun Appadurai, "The Heart of Whiteness," p. 804.

30. Arjun Appadurai, "The Heart of Whiteness," p. 804.

31. J. Laplanche and J. B. Pontalis, *The Language of Psycho-Analysis*, Trans. Donald Nicholson-Smith (New York: Norton, 1974), p. 166.

32. Arjun Appadurai, "The Heart of Whiteness," p. 802.

33. See Dipesh Chakrabarty, *Provincializing Europe: Postcolonial Thought and Historical Difference* (Princeton: Princeton University Press, 2000).

34. Gayatri Chakravorty Spivak, *The Post-Colonial Critic: Interviews, Strategies, Dialogues.* Ed. Sarah Harasym (New York: Routledge, 1990), p. 64.

35. DuBois writes in *The Souls of Black Folk*, "It is a peculiar sensation, this double-consciousness, this sense of always looking at one's self through the eyes of others. . . . One ever feels his twoness,—an American, a Negro; two souls, two thoughts, two unreconciled strivings; two warring ideals in one dark body, whose dogged strength alone keeps it from being torn asunder." See *The Souls of Black Folk* (New York: New American Library, 1982; orig pub. 1903), p. 45.

36. Gayatri Chakravorty Spivak, *The Post-Colonial Critic*, p. 126.

37. Immanuel Wallerstein, *The Capitalist World-Economy* (New York: Cambridge University Press, 1979), p. 180.

38. Gayatri Chakravorty Spivak, "Race before Racism: The Disappearance of the American," *boundary 2* 25ii (Summer 1998), p. 51.

39. *The Post-Colonial Critic*, p. 62. In a later interview, Spivak makes a similar connection between South Asians and African Americans; "the only postcolonial society in terms of internal colonization in the United States, for all of us, the new immigrants, is the African American and not ourselves" (Bahri and Vasudeva, p. 71).

40. See Frank Chin and Jeffrey Paul Chan, "Racist Love," in *Seeing Through Shuck*. Ed. Richard Kostelanetz (New York: Ballantine, 1972), p. 75.

41. Gayatri Chakravorty Spivak, "The Political Economy of Women as Seen by a Literary Critic," in *Coming to Terms, Feminism, Theory, Politics* ed. Elizabeth Weed (New York: Routledge, 1989), p. 226. Spivak draws on the distinction Partha Chatterjee makes between the elaborate constitution of the subject through educational and legal apparatuses in the colonial era to the lack of any such constitution or training in the age of electronic capitalism where the subjects are reentering a feudal mode of power characterized by sheer dominance (p. 224). Spivak talks about the necessity of distinguishing between the subjects of postmodern neocolonialism and immigrants in the United States, but her argument only makes sense if we substitute raced subjects or ethnics for the term immigrants. Native Americans, African Americans and many Chicanas, for instance, are not immigrants and the argument would not hold for white immigrants.

42. Spivak's recent essay on Harlem does not exhibit the scrupulous historicity of much of her other writing. The essay proceeds largely through the spatial logic of pastiche, juxtaposing Harlem with other

spaces and interspersing her unanswered questions about Harlem with Alice Attie's photographs. See Gayatri Chakravorty Spivak, "Harlem," *Social Text* 22 iv (2004), pp. 113–139.

43. No mention of critical race theorists appear in the works of these theorists or in Paul Gilroy's *Against Race*. The only exception is Spivak's short critique of Carole Pateman's silencing of Patricia Williams, an instance of the woman from the North silencing a woman from the South, in *A Critique of Post-Colonial Reason*, p. 389.

44. Michael Omi and Howard Winant, *Racial Formation in the United States* (New York: Routledge, 1986), p. 68.

45. Omi and Winant, *Racial Formation in the United States*, p. 62.

46. Noel Ignatiev, *How the Irish Became White* (New York: Routledge, 1995), p. 183.

47. Ignatiev, *How the Irish Became White*, p. 184.

48. David Roediger, *The Wages of Whiteness: Race and the Makings of the American Working Class* (London: Verso, 1991), p. 13.

49. Patricia Williams, *The Alchemy of Race and Rights* (Cambridge: Harvard University Press, 1991), p. 8.

50. Williams, *The Alchemy of Race and Rights*, p. 1.

51. Williams, *The Alchemy of Race and Rights*, pp. 9–10.

52. Richard Delgado, "Introduction," *Critical Race Theory: The Cutting Edge* (Philadelphia: Temple University Press, 1995), p. xv.

53. Toni Morrison, *Playing in the Dark*, p. 96.

54. Frank Chin and Jeffrey Paul Chan, "Racist Love," in *Seeing Through Shuck*, Ed. Richard Kostelanetz (New York: Ballantine, 1972), p. 75.

55. Arun Mukherji makes an excellent argument about the importance of race and its dismissal in postcolonial theory, particularly the Australian versions espoused by Bill Ashcroft, Gareth Griffin, and Helen Tiffin. See Arun P. Mukherjee, "Whose Post-Colonialism and Whose Postmodernism," *World Literature Written in English* 30 ii (1990), pp. 1–9.

56. See Kenneth Mostern, "Postcolonialism After W.E.B. DuBois," in *Postcolonial Theory and the United States: Race, Ethnicity, Literature* (Jackson: University of Mississippi Press, 2000), pp. 258–276. Many scholars of African American studies have found reading anticolonial resistance as a useful paradigm for their work. Much of Henry Louis Gates's work since *The Signifying Monkey* can be seen as an attempt to articulate an indigenous, "anticolonial" voice. Wahneema Lubiano refers to her reading of "Elbow Room" as an explication of it as an anticolonial text. See Lubiano's "Shuckin' Off the African-American Native Other" in *Dangerous Liaisons: Gender, Nation, and Postcolonial Perspectives*, Ed. Anne McClintock et al. (Minneapolis: University of Minnesota Press, 1997), p. 222.

CHAPTER THREE

1. Inderpal Grewal and Caren Kaplan, Eds., *Scattered Hegemonies: Postmodernity and Transnational Feminist Practices* (Minneapolis: University of Minnesota Press, 1994), p. 17.

2. Adrienne Rich, *Blood, Bread, and Poetry: Selected Prose, 1979–1985* (New York: Norton, 1986), p. 219.

3. Caren Kaplan, "The Politics of Location as Transnational Feminist Critical Practice" in *Scattered Hegemonies*, p. 144.

4. Elizabeth Spelman, "Theories of Race and Gender: The Erasure of Black Women," *Quest* 5 iv (1982), p. 43.

5. Gyan Prakash argues that "the concept of multiple selves, incorporating a variety of social identities and thus popular with contemporary liberal multiculturalists, cannot be adequate for conceiving colonial difference. Instead we have to think of the specificity of colonial difference as class overwriting race and gender, of nation overinscribing class, ethnicity, and religion, and so forth—an imbalanced process, but nevertheless a process that can be rearticulated differently." See Gyan Prakash, "Postcolonial Criticism and Indian Historiography" in Anne Mc Clintock et al., *Dangerous Liaisons: Gender, Nation, and Postcolonial Perspectives* (Minneapolis: University of Minnesota Press, 1997), p. 497.

6. Donna Haraway, "A Cyborg Manifesto: Science, Technology, and Socialist-Feminism in the Late Twentieth Century" in her *Simians, Cybrogs, and Women; The Reinvention of Nature* (London: Free Association Books, 1991), p. 149. Hereafter cited parenthetically in the text.

7. Ernesto Laclau and Chantal Mouffe, *Hegemony and Socialist Strategy: Towards a Radical Democratic Politics* (London: Verso, 1985), pp. 167–171, 192.

8. Gilles Deleuze and Felix Guattari, *Anti-Oedipus: Capitalism and Schizophrenia*. Trans. Robert Hurley et al. (Minneapolis: University of Minnesota Press, 1983), p. 76.

9. Homi K. Bhabha, *The Location of Culture* (New York: Routledge, 1994), pp. 11, 207.

10. Donna Haraway, "Situated Knowledges: The Science Question in Feminism and the Privilege of Partial Perspective," *Feminist Studies* 14 (Spring 1988), pp. 584, 579.

11. Chandra Talpade Mohanty, "Under Western Eyes: Feminist Scholarship and Colonial Discourses" in Ann Russo Mohanty and Lourdes Torres, Eds., *Third World Women and the Politics of Feminism* (Bloomington: Indiana University Press, 1991), p. 51.

12. Frederic Jameson, "Third World Literature in the Era of Multinational Capital," *Social Text* (Fall 1986), pp. 65–88.

13. Aijaz Ahmed, "Jameson's Rhetoric of Otherness and the 'National Allegory,'" in *In Theory: Classes, Nations, Literatures* (London: Verso, 1992); orig. pub., 1987.

14. Gilles Deleuze and Felix Guattari, *A Thousand Plateaus: Capitalism and Schizophrenia*. Trans. Brian Massumi (Minneapolis: University of Minnesota Press, 1987), pp. 18–19, xiv, 22.

15. See Luce Irigaray, *Between East and West; From Singularity to Community*. Trans. Stephen Pluhacek (New York: Columbia University Press, 2001) and Julia Kristeva, *About Chinese Women*. Trans. Anita Barrows (New York: Urizen, 1977), pp. 81–84.

16. Joan W. Scott sees a similar problem in Haraway's use of women of color in relation to traditional socialist feminism. Scott writes, "What is the difference between Haraway's looking to these groups for the politics of the future and (the association such a gesture has for me) the romantic attribution by white liberal or socialist women to minority or working-class women of the appropriate (if not authentic) socialist or feminist politics?" See Joan W. Scott, "Commentary: Cyborgian Socialists?" in Elizabeth Weed, Ed., *Coming to Terms: Feminism, Theory, Politics* (New York: Routledge, 1989), pp. 216–217.

17. Gayatri Chakravorty Spivak, "The Political Economy of Women as Seen by a Literary Critic" in *Coming to Terms*, p. 226.

18. Abby Wilkerson, "Ending at the Skin: Sexuality and Race in Feminist Theorizing," *Hypatia* 12 iii (Summer 1997), p. 170.

19. Wilkerson, pp. 170–171.

20. Judith Butler, *Gender Trouble: Feminism and the Subversion of Identity* (New York: Routledge, 1990), p. 139.

21. *Gender Trouble*, p. 143.

22. *Gender Trouble*, p. 143.

23. Judith Butler, *Bodies That Matter: On the Discursive Limits of "Sex"* (New York: Routledge, 1993), p. 11.

24. *Bodies That Matter*, p. 17.

25. *Bodies That Matter*, p. 18.

26. *Bodies That Matter*, p. 18.

27. *Bodies That Matter*, p. 130.

28. *Bodies That Matter*, p. 136. Interestingly, in the context of the Rodney King beating, Butler does see the visual field as racial formation. See Butler's "Engangered/Endangering: Schematic Racism and White Paranoia" in *Reading Rodney King: Reading Urban Uprising*, Ed. Robert Gooding-Williams (New York: Routledge, 1993), pp. 15–22.

29. *Bodies That Matter*, p. 131.

30. In a study focusing on antiblack writing from 1852 to 1915, Mason Stokes cautions against always seeing queerness as a subversive

way out of whiteness. He suggests that the anxiety attendant on white "reproduction makes heterosexuality (via miscegenation) a threat to whiteness unless heterosexuality facilitates white homosociality. See *The Color of Sex Whiteness, Heterosexuality, and the Fictions of White Supremacy* (Durham: Duke University Press, 2001), pp. 183, 18.

31. Judith Butler, *Bodies That Matter*, p. 133.

32. Richard Dyer, "White" *Screen* 9 iv (1988), pp. 45–46.

33. Judith Butler, *Antigone's Claim: Kinship Between Life and Death* (New York: Columbia University Press, 2000), pp. 22–23; 69. Butler mentions African American kinship systems, but critiques the fact that these don't question, but simply replace patriarchy. Her argument that African American theorists have not critiqued the patriarchy inherent in the theory of the denial of male privilege for African American men ignores the very same critiques made by Michelle Wallace and bell hooks. See Michelle Wallace, *Black Macho and the Myth of the Superwoman* (London: Verso, 1978), pp. 22–23, and bell hooks, *Yearning: Race, Gender, and Cultural Politics* (Boston: South End Press, 1990), pp. 58–59.

34. Judith Butler, *Precarious Life: The Powers of Mourning and Violence* (London: Verso, 2004), p. 48.

35. Chela Sandoval, *Methodology of the Oppressed* (Minneapolis: University of Minnesota Press, 2000), p. 171.

36. For an analysis of the hegemonic problems of celebrating mestizaje see Tace Hedrick's *Mestizo Modernism: Race, Nation and Identity in Latin American Culture, 1900–1949* (Brunswick: Rutgers University Press, 2003).

37. Patricia Hill Collins, *Black Feminist Thought: Knowledge, Consciousness, and the Politics of Empowerment* (New York: Routledge, 1990), p. 224.

38. Anne McClintock, *Imperial Leather: Race, Gender and Sexuality in the Colonial Context* (New York: Routledge, 1995), p. 5.

39. Anne McClintock, *Imperial Leather*, p. 184.

40. Siobhan B. Somerville, *Queering the Color Line: Race and the Invention of Homosexuality in American Culture* (Durham: Duke University Press, 2000), p. 4. However, Somerville often uses strategies very similar to Butler in seeing the primacy of the sexual. See, for instance, the analysis of Toomer based on the term "queer" (p. 136) and the insistence that compulsory heterosexuality is "integral" to the logic of racial segregation (p. 137).

41. Zillah Eisenstein, *Against Empire: Feminisms, Racism, and the West* (London: Zed Books, 2004), p. 29.

42. Zillah Eisenstein, *Against Empire,* p. 29.

43. Donna J. Haraway, *Modest_Witness@Second_Millenium. FemaleMan_Meets_OncoMouse: Feminism and Technoscience* (New York: Routlege, 1997), p. 213.

44. *Modest Witness*, p. 249.
45. *Modest Witness*, p. 214.
46. *Modest Witness*, p. 215.
47. *Modest Witness*, p. 264.
48. *Modest Witness*, p. 265.

CHAPTER FOUR

1. See Chidanand Rajghatta, *The Horse That Flew: How India's Silicon Gurus Spread Their Wings* (New Delhi: HarperCollins, 2001).

2. Inderpal Grewal proposes connectivity as a metaphor for transnational cultural relations after the end of the twentieth century because the metaphor includes unevenness, failure, and exclusion. See Inderpal Grewal, *Transnational America: Feminisms, Diasporas, Neoliberalisms* (Durham: Duke University Press, 2005), pp. 24–25.

3. Arjun Appadurai, *Modernity at Large: Cultural Dimensions of Globalization* (Minneapolis: University of Minnesota Press, 1996), p. 29.

4. *Modernity at Large* p. 29.

5. Sanjay Austo, "Pico Iyer: Chronicler of Modern Times," the-south-asian.com May/June 2003.

6. Austo, "Pico Iyer."

7. Pico Iyer, *Video Night in Kathmandu: And Other Reports from the Not-So-Far-East* (New York: Random House, Vintage, 1988), p. 24.

8. Caren Kaplan, *Questions of Travel: Postmodern Discourses of Displacement* (Durham: Duke University Press, 1996), pp. 2–5.

9. Pico Iyer, *The Global Soul* (Random House: Vintage, 2000), p. 18.

10. "Nowhereian," a term borrowed from the Caribbean islanders, is Iyer's appelation for himself in *The Global Soul*, p. 23.

11. This quote, in turn, was the epigraph to the academic bestseller of postcolonial studies, *The Empire Writes Back* (1989).

12. I have discussed this question in my book *U.S. Orientalisms: Race, Nation, and Gender in Literature 1790–1890* (Ann Arbor: University of Michigan Press, 1998).

13. Michael Hardt and Antonio Negri, *Empire*, pp. 145–146.

14. Caren Kaplan, *Questions of Travel*, p. 22.

15. Rey Chow warns against the fashionable fetishizing of exile and migration that unproblematically accepts the idea of ethnics being "aliens from elsewhere." See her *The Protestant Ethic and the Spirit of Capitalism* (New York: Columbia University Press, 2002), p. 34.

16. Mary Louise Pratt, *Imperial Eyes: Travel Writing and Transculturation* (New York: Routledge, 1992), pp. 5, 216–217. Pratt specifically

talks about the continuity of the "monarch-of-all-I-survey" scene in writers like Paul Theroux.

17. Edward Said, *Orientalism* (New York: Vintage, 1979), pp. 207–208.

18. There have been numerous readings of the Rambo films, especially *Rambo II*, as recuperations of masculinity and U.S. imperialism. The best one is Susan Jeffords' chapter, "'Do We Get to Win This Time?'": Reviving the Masculine" in her book *The Remasculinization of America: Gender and the Vietnam War* (Bloomington: Indiana University Press, 1989), pp. 116–143.

19. Anne McClintock, *Imperial Leather: Race, Gender and Sexuality in the Colonial Context* (New York; Routledge, 1995), p. 22.

20. Pico Iyer, *The Lady and the Monk: Four Seasons in Kyoto* (New York: Alfred A. Knopf, 1991), p. 79.

21. See Karen Kelsky, *Women on the Verge: Japanese Women, Western Dreams* (Durham: Duke University Press, 2001).

22. See Partha Chatterjee, *Nationalist Thought in the Colonial World: A Derivative Discourse?* (Minneapolis: University of Minnesota Press, 1986), p. 38.

23. Here I am using Partha Chatterjee's helpful distinction between the problematic and thematic in relation to Orientalism and nationalism. See *Nationalist Thought*, p. 38.

24. Nick Browne, "Race: The Political Unconscious of American Film," *East-West Journal* 6 no. 1 (1992):9. Cited in George Lipsitz "Frantic to Join . . . the Japanese Army" in Lisa Lowe and David Lloyd, Eds., *The Politics of Culture in the Shadow of Capital* (Durham: Duke University Press, 1997).

25. Although it has been criticized by many, Catharine Mackinnon's "Toward a Feminist Theory of the State" still remains an important analysis of the sexualization of hierarchy and the saturation of sexuality with dominance. See "Toward a Feminist Theory of the State" in Sandra Kemp and Judith Squires, Eds., *Feminisms* (New York: Oxford University Press, 1997), p. 354.

26. Ann Laura Stoler, *Carnal Knowledge and Imperial Power: Race and the Intimate in Colonial Rule* (Durham: Duke University Press, 2002), pp. 42, 45.

27. I am referring here to Edward Said's distinction between an unchanging Orientalism as a vector of Western power that Said argues exists in most Orientalist texts and a manifest Orientalism indexed by changes in personal style. See *Orientalism*, p. 206.

28. *Orientalism*, p. 206.

29. Iyer writes about being able to choose selves: "The tradition denoted by my face was something I could erase (mostly) with my voice, or pick up whenever the conversation turned to the Maharishi or patchouli oil" (21).

30. This would include attributing qualities of blackness to whites considered undesirable. I am also not arguing that the West is, in fact, unified. Rather, like Radhakrishnan, I believe that "the West as a global political effect on the non-West has indeed been the result of colonialist-imperialist orchestration, that is, it has spoken with one voice." See *Diasporic Mediations: Between Home and Location* (Minneapolis: University of Minnesota Press, 1996), p. 178.

31. Traise Yamamoto "As Natural as the Partnership of Sun and Moon": The Logic of Sexualized Metonymy in *Pictures from the Water Trade* and *The Lady and the Monk*," *Positions* 4 ii (Fall 1996), 329 (321–341). Yamamoto also sees Iyer in *The Lady and the Monk* as participating in the body of writing in which a Western male protagonist seeks to understand Japan through a sexual relationship with a Japanese woman (323).

32. See Richard Dyer, "White," *Screen* 29 (1988), p. 44.

33. Lavina Dhingra Shankar writes that Alexander "consciously resists and subverts linear and single migration models of Asian American subjectivity and identity," "Postcolonial Diasporics 'Writing in Search of a Homeland': Meena Alexander's *Manhattan Music, Fault Lines, and the Shock of Arrival*," *LIT* 12 (2001), 286.

34. Meena Alexander, *Fault Lines: A Memoir* (New York: The Feminist Press, 1993), p. 3.

35. For an analysis of the ambivalence of continuity within modernity see Ashis Nandy, *The Intimate Enemy: Loss and Recovery of Self Under Colonialism* (New Delhi: Oxford University Press, 1983), p. 61.

36. *Modernity at Large*, p. 30.

37. Homi K. Bhabha, *The Location of Culture*, pp. 250, 254.

38. For an analysis of the ability of the past as myth to function open-endedly to remake the present, see Ashis Nandy, *The Intimate Enemy*, p. 59.

39. Such a narrative might well be unwitting but I am not dealing with intentionality here. I am only analyzing effects.

40. Partha Chatterjee, "The Nation and Its Women" in *The Nation and Its Fragments* (Princeton: Princeton University Press, 1993), pp. 16–35.

41. Johannes Fabian, *Time and the Other: How Anthropology Makes Its Object* (New York: Columbia University Press, 1983), p. 31.

42. Judith Butler, *Gender Trouble: Feminism and the Subversion of Identity* (New York: Routledge, 1990), p. 141.

43. R. Radhakrishnan, "Adjudicating Hybridity, Co-ordinating Betweenness," *Jouvert* 5: 1 (2000). Http://social.chass.ncsu.edu/jouvert/v5il/radha.htm.

44. Meena Alexander, *Manhattan Music* (San Francisco: Mercury House, 1997), p. 47.

45. Early in the novel, the character Draupadi identifies herself (in contrast to the aristocratic Sandhya) as both heir to serfdom and her ability to fashion herself through consumer goods: "Born in America, I must have seemed the epitome of newness, all she might one day be—leather jacket, Benetton sweater, short black hair, subtle eyeshadow, the lot" (*Manhattan Music*, 3).

46. See Frank Chin and Jeffrey Chan, "Racist Love," *Seeing Through Shuck*, Ed. Richard Kostelanetz (New York: Ballantine, 1972), pp. 65–79.

47. Vijay Prashad, *The Karma of Brown Folk* (Minneapolis: University of Minnesota Press, 2000), xi, ix.

48. G. W. F. Hegel, *Phenomenology of Sprit*. Trans. A. V. Miller (New York: Oxford University Press, 1977; orig. pub., 1807), pp. 111, 113.

49. *Black Skin, White Masks*, p. 109. Although Hegel does proceed to theorize on the process of unequal recognition in which, paradoxically, the lord cannot gain recognition from the bondsman whom he has reduced to a thing, and the bondsman can attain selfhood in the sphere of work, Fanon focuses on the unavailability of recognition that Hegel's concept of self implies.

50. Pheng Cheah, "Introduction Part II: The Cosmopolitical—Today" in Pheng Cheah and Bruce Robbins, Eds., *Cosmopolitics: Thinking and Feeling Beyond the Nation* (Minnesota: University of Minneapolis Press, 1998), p. 21.

51. For an elaboration of this argument see Malini Johar Schueller, *U.S. Orientalisms*.

52. Some critics argue that *Jasmine* is a record of the provisionality of identity and of Jasmine causing changes in the new landscape. I am not convinced, however, that Jasmine's cooking of Indian food for her employers or singing to Duff in the rhythm of Indian folk tales constitute a major intervention. See Carmen Wickramagamage, "Relocation as Positive Act: The Immigrant Experience in Bharati Mukherjee's Novels," *Diaspora* 2:2 (1992), 190. On the other hand, Gurleen Grewal, while critical of Mukherjee's attempt to write agency for Jasmine, sees in Jas-

mine's changes a pattern of colonialist dispossession, the turning of the subaltern into colonial subject through education. See Gurleen Grewal, "Born Again American: the Immigrant Consciousness in Jasmine" in Emmanuel S. Nelson, Ed., *Bharati Mukherjee: Critical Perspectives* (New York: Garland, 1993), p. 194.

53. Debjani Banerjee sees Mukherjee's representation of Sikhs as reductive and a trivializing of the complexities of the postcolonial condition (171; quoted in Patricia Chu, *Assimilating Asians: Gendered Strategies of Authorship in Asian America* (Durham: Duke University Press, 2000), p. 129.

54. Bharati Mukherjee, *Jasmine* (New York: Grove Press, 1989), p. 200.

55. Anthony C. Alessandrini suggests that in *Jasmine* Mukherjee produces a literary form that is explicitly transnational and for which common Anglophone forms are inadequate. See "Reading Bharati Mukherjee, Reading Globalization" in *World Bank Literature*, Ed. Amitava Kumar (Minneapolis: University of Minnesota Press, 2002), pp. 265–279.

56. Geraldine Stoneham also points out that Mukherjee demonstrates how Middle America, the location of the old myths of the frontier and homogeneous America, is cracking. I would simply differ with Stoneham in imagining the frontier as homogenous. See "'It's a Free Country': Visions of Hybridity in the Metropolis" in *Comparing Postcolonial Literatures: Dislocations*, Eds. Ashok Bery and Patricia Murray (New York: St. Martin's 2000), p. 87.

57. Debjani Banerjee, 171. Quoted in Chu, *Assimilating Asians*, p. 129.

58. See Bruce Robbins, *Feeling Global: Internationalism in Distress* (New York: New York University Press, 1999), pp. 107–110; Patricia Chu, *Assimilating Asians*, p. 128.

59. See Anindyo Roy, "The Aesthetics of the (Un)willing Immigrant: Bharati Mukherjee's *Days and Nights in Calcutta* and *Jasmine*" in Nelson, *Bharati Mukerjee: Critical Perspectives*, pp. 127–142; Inderpal Grewal, *Transnational America,* pp. 66–68. On the other hand, Sharmani Patricia Gabriel sees Mukherjee participating in a dynamics of diasporic "fluidity and contingency" through the idea of immigrant identity as transformation. See "'Between Mosaic and Melting Pot': Negotiating Multiculturalism and Cultural Citizenship in Bharati Mukherjee's Narratives of Diaspora," *Postcolonial Text* 1 ii (2005). Http://postcolonial.org/index.php/pct/article/viewArticle/420/147. Accessed October 9, 2007.

60. See Bharati Mukherjee, "American Dreamer," *Mother Jones* (January/February 1997). www.motherjones.com/commentary/columns 1997/01/mukherjee-2.html. Accessed October 9, 2007.

61. For an analysis of the denaturalization of whiteness in *Jasmine*, see Ruth Maxley, "'Who wants pale, thin, pink flesh?,'" *Textual Practice* 20 iii (2006), pp. 529, 547.

62. Given the different racial classifications and social systems in different parts of the Caribbean, the term "black" cannot be seen to have the same associations as in the United States.

63. Noel Ignatiev, *How the Irish Became White* (New York: Routledge, 1995).

64. For Arundhati Roy's scathing criticism of this practice, see *Power Politics* (Cambridge: South End Press, 2001), pp. 83–84.

65. See, for instance, "Job's Comforters," Editorial *Times of India*, June 16, 2003, p. 14, and Chidanand Rajghatta, "Don't worry, US assures Jaitley on outsourcing," *Times of India*, June 14, 2003, p. 6.

66. Mike McPhate, "Outsourcing Outrage: Indian Call-Center Workers Suffer Abuse," *San Francisco Chronicle*, November 17, 2005.

67. See Rey Chow, "Between Colonizers: Hong Kong's Postcolonial Self-Writing in the 1990s," *Diaspora* 2:2 (1992), p. 157.

CHAPTER FIVE

1. Eds. Frank Chin, Jeffrey Paul Chan, Lawson Fusao Inada, Shawn Hsu Wong, *Aiiieeeee!: An Anthology of Asian American Writers* (New York: Penguin, 1974), pp. xi–xii.

2. Arif Dirlik, "Asians on the Rim: Transnational Capital and Local Community in the Making of Contemporary America" in Evelyn Hu-DeHart, Ed., *Across the Pacific: Asian Americans and Globalization* (Philadelphia: Temple University Press, 1999), pp. 47–48.

3. Viet Thanh Nguyen and Tina Chen, "Editor's Introduction," *Jouvert* 4 i (2000), p. 2.

4. Susan Koshy, "The Fiction of Asian American Literature," *The Yale Journal of Criticism* 9 ii (1996), p. 336.

5. See Homi Bhabha's postulation of the disruptive power of contramodernity in *The Location of Culture* (New York: Routledge, 1994), p. 6, and Lisa Lowe's concept of disidentification in *Immigrant Acts: On Asian American Cultural Politics* (Durham: Duke University Press, 1996), pp. 103–104.

6. Immanuel Wallerstein, *The Capitalist World Economy* (New York: Cambridge University Press, 1979), p. 60.

7. Jenny Sharpe, "Is the United States Postcolonial? Transnationalism, Immigration, and Race," *Diaspora* 4 ii (Fall 1995), p. 190.

8. R. Radhakrishnan, *Diasporic Mediations: Between Home and Location* (Minneapolis: University of Minnesota Press, 1996), p. 159.

9. See Michael Omi and Howard Winant, *Racial Formation in the United States*, 2nd ed. (New York: Routledge, 1994), pp. 20–21.

10. Viet Thanh Nguyen and Tina Chen, p. 2.

11. Sau-ling C. Wong, "Denationalization Reconsidered: Asian American Cultural Criticism at a Theoretical Crossroads," *Amerasia Journal* 21 1&2 (1995), p. 13.

12. Frank Chin, Jeffery Paul Chan, et al., Eds., *Aiiieeeee!: An Anthology of Asian American Writers* (New York: Mentor, 1991; orig pub. 1974), p. 75.

13. William Wei, *The Asian American Movement* (Philadelphia: Temple University Press, 1993), pp. 206–207.

14. William Wei, p. 210.

15. Cited in William Wei, p. 212.

16. Kim, pp. 23–24; Takaki, *Strangers*, pp. 99–104; Sucheng Chan, pp. 45–61.

17. On globalization theory's use of hybridity and difference via postcolonialism, see Simon Gikandi, "Globalization and the Claims of Postcoloniality," *South Atlantic Quarterly* 3 (Summer 2001), p. 631.

18. I refer to Tseng Kwong Chi as Tseng because that was his last name. He began putting it before his first name in accordance with Chinese custom.

19. Tseng also did commerical photographs for magazines such as *Vanity Fair*, *GQ*, and *Vogue*.

20. Apparently Tseng Kwong Chi's sister, Muna Tseng, later discovered that what Tseng thought was a Mao suit was actually a Nationalist army uniform from the 1930s. See C. Carr, "Just Visiting This Planet," *The Village Voice*, March 9, 1999, p. 67. Cited in Dan Bacalzo, "Portraits of Self and Other: SlutForArt and the Photographs of Tseng Kwong Chi," *Theatre Journal* 53 i (2002), p. 82.

21. Grady T. Turner, "The Accidental Ambassador," *Art in America*, 85 (1997), pp. 81, 83.

22. Peggy Phelan, *Unmarked* (New York: Routledge, 1993), p. 35.

23. Judith Butler, "Imitation and Gender Insubordination," in Ed. Diana Fuss, *Inside/Out: Lesbian Theories, Gay Theories* (New York: Routledge, 1991), pp. 13–31. The first section of *Inside/Out* is titled "Decking Out: Performing Identities." Butler's idea of the performative had earlier appeared in *Gender Trouble: Feminism and the Subversion of Identity* (New York: Routledge, 1990). Biddy Martin has recently pointed out the significance of Butler's performative theory of gender in *Femininity Played Straight* (New York: Routledge, 1996).

24. Turner, p. 85.

25. Margo Machida sees Tseng as turning Orientalism inside out by subjecting the West to an Occidentalist gaze. See Machida's "Out of Asia: Negotiating Asian Identities in America" in *Asia/America Asia/America: Identities in Contemporary Asian American Art* by Margo Machida, Vishakha Desai, and John Tchen (New York: New Perspectives, 1994), p. 96.

26. Turner, p. 82.

27. I am indebted to Marsha Bryant for pointing this out.

28. Homi Bhabha, *The Location of Culture* (New York: Routledge, 1994), pp. 4, 8.

29. Ronald Takaki, *A Different Mirror: A History of Multicultural America* (Boston: Little, Brown, 1993), p. 1.

30. See chapter two of Henry Giroux, *Disturbing Pleasures* (New York: Routledge, 1994).

31. Press release, Tseng Kwong Chi Retrospective, PrideFest America 2002, www.pridefestamerica.com/press-tsengkwongchi.shtml.

32. Although Frank Chin, Jeffrey Chan, et al. use the term "yellow male sexuality" in their preface to the Mentor edition of Aiiieeeee!, sexuality clearly means masculinity and not gay identity (xl).

33. Barbara Maria Stafford, *Visual Analogy: Consciousness as the Art of Connecting* (Cambridge: MIT Press, 1999), p. 41.

34. Richard Martin, "The Expeditionary Photographs of Tseng Kwong Chi," *Arts Magazine* 61 (September 1986), p. 95.

35. Dan Bacalzo, "Portraits of Self and Other: SlutForArt and the Photographs of Tseng Kwong Chi," *Theatre Journal* 53 i (2001), p. 76.

36. Cathy Davidson, "Photographs of the Dead: Sherman, Daguerre, Hawthorne," *SAQ* 89 iv (Fall 1990), p. 669.

37. W. E. B. DuBois, *The Souls of Black Folk* (New York: Signet, 1969), p. 45; Fanon, Frantz, *Black Skin White Masks*. Trans. Charles Lam Markmann (New York: Grove, 1967; orig. pub., 1952), p. 109.

38. I am differentiating here between what I call postmodern elegy and the features Jahan Ramazani sees as characteristic of modern elegy. See *Poetry of Mourning: The Modern Elegy from Hardy to Heaney* (Chicago: University of Chicago Press, 1994), pp. ix–xi.

39. Lucy R. Lippard, "Outside (But Not Necessarily Beyond) the Landscape," *Aperture* 150 (Winter '98), p. 60.

40. Albert Boime uses the term "magisterial gaze" to refer to American landscape painting, but the term applies well to Adams's photographs. See Boime, "Patriarchy Fixed in Stone: Gutzon Borglum's 'Mount Rushmore,'" *American Arts* 51 i&ii (1991), p. 144.

CHAPTER SIX

1. Subcomandante Marcos, "Why We Are Fighting: The Fourth World War Has Begun," *Le Monde Diplomatique*, September 1997; http://mondediplo.com/1997/09/marcos.

2. Angela Davis, "The Prison Industrial Complex," recorded at Colorado College, Colorado Springs, May 5, 1997.

3. Gramsci explains that every social group "creates together with itself, organically, one or more strata of intellectuals which give it homogeneity, and an awareness of its own function not only in the economic but also in the social and political fields." Antonio Gramsci, *Selections from the Prison Notebooks of Antonio Gramsci*. Ed and trans. Quintin Hoare and Geoffrey Nowell (New York: International Publishers, 1991), p. 5.

4. Arnold Krupat sees the postcolonial perspective as "especially promising for the written literature of some indigenous peoples over the last thirty some years." See *Red Matters: Native American Studies* (Philadelphia: University of Pennsylvania Press, 2002), p. 20. Rob Wilson, in relation to a local Pacific identity, suggests that the imaginings of this kind of identity in resistance to the homogenizing forces of the U.S. culture industry, are postcolonial. See Rob Wilson, "From the Sublime to the Devious: Writing the Experimental/Local Pacific," *boundary* 2 28 i (2001), pp. 122–123.

5. A significant exception to this is Nikhil Pal Singh's *Black Is a Country: Race and the Unfinished Struggle for Democracy* (Cambridge: Harvard University Press, 2004).

6. Nikhi Pal Singh, *Black Is a Country*, pp. 204–205. For an excellent study of black power movements as transnational, see the chapter, "Decolonizing America," pp. 175–211.

7. Huey Newton, *Revolutionary Suicide* (New York: Harcourt Brace, 1973), p. 118.

8. Kathleen Neal Cleaver, "Back to Africa: The Evolution of the International Section of the Black Panther Party (1969–1972)," in Ed. Charles E. Jones, *The Black Panther Party Reconsidered* (Baltimore: Black Classic Press, 1998), p. 230.

9. Roy Wilkins, cited in Huey Newton, "Reply to Roy Wilkins re: Vietnam: September 26, 1970" in *To Die for the People: The Writings of Huey P. Newton* (New York: Random House, 1972), p. 186.

10. Huey Newton, *To Die for the People*, p. 32.

11. See Assata Shakur, *Autobiography*, pp. 218, 222, 223.

12. "U.S. prison population largest in world," *The Post and Courier*, Charleston.Net, June 1, 2003. http://www.charleston.net/stories/060103/

wor_01jailbirds.shtml. N. C. Alzenman, "New High in U.S. Prison Numbers," *Washington Post*, February 29, 2008, p. A1. In 2008, "more than one in 100 adults in the United States is in jail or prison."

13. Statement to the UNCHR" 56th Session UN Commission on Human Rights, http://www.hrw.org/campaigns/geneva/item6.htm.

14. Immanuel Wallerstein, "The Construction of Peoplehood: Racism, Nationalism, Ethnicity" in *Race, Nation, Class: Ambiguous Identities* (New York: Verso, 1991), p. 84.

15. "Coalition Building Among People of Color: A Discussion with Angela Y. Davis and Elizabeth Martinez" in Joy James, Ed., *The Angela Y. Davis Reader* (Malden, MA: Blackwell, 1998). P. 308.

16. Shakur cites Huey Newton's refusal to brook criticism from party members and his title as Supreme Commander as major reasons for leaving the party (Shakur, pp. 226, 229). See also Eldridge Cleaver's delineation of the role of women as that of supporting only revolutionary women as "pussy power" in *Post Prison Writings*, p. 143. I don't focus on the problems of male black nationalism and misogyny because I want to shift attention to the transformative aspects of black liberation movements. Here I am following the lead of Angela Davis who in examining the legacy of Malcolm X wonders why Malcolm's later turn toward feminism has been ignored by critics and argues for the importance of transforming Malcolm's memory from a backward and imprisoning one to a forward-looking one generative of change. See "Meditations on the Legacy of Malcolm X" in *The Angela Y. Davis Reader*, Ed. Joy James (Malden, MA: Blackwell, 1998), pp. 285–286. Wahneema Lubiano also suggests caution in dismissing black nationalism as simply male and heterosexual in "Don't Talk with Your Eyes Closed: Caught in Hollywood Gun Sights" http://www.blackculturalstudies.org/lubiano/deepcover.html.

17. Michel Foucault, *Discipline and Punish: The Birth of the Prison.* Trans. Alan Sheridan (New York: Random House, 1979), pp. 89–90.

18. The most comprehensive discussion of Foucault's lack of attention to race and colonialism and his inability to see that relationship between the sexual discourse of empire and European biopolitics in Ann Laura Stoler, *Race and the Education of Desire: Foucault's History of Sexuality and the Colonial Order of Things* (Durham: Duke University Press, 1995).

19. Partha Chatterjee, *The Nation and Its Fragments: Colonial and Postcolonial Histories* (Princeton: Princeton University Press), 1993, pp. 19–22.

20. Michel Foucault, *Discipline and Punish*, p. 209.

21. Assata Shakur, *An Autobiography* (Chicago: Lawrence Hill Books, 2000; orig. pub., 1987), p. 3, 11.

22. Ralph Ellison, *Invisible Man* (New York: Vintage, 1972; orig pub 1952).

23. See, for instance, Reginald Horsman, *Race and Manifest Destiny: The Origins of Racial Anglo-Saxonism* (Cambridge: Harvard University Press, 1981), pp. 119–120.

24. Sandra Hollin Flowers, *African American Nationalist Literature of the 1960s: Pens of Fire* (New York: Garland, 1996), p. 56.

25. See John Loftus and Mark Aaron, *The Secret War Against the Jews: How Western Espionage Betrayed the Jewish People* (New York: St. Martin's, 1994).

26. Here I am using Henri Lefebvre's important distinctions between perceived, conceived, and lived space. See Lefebvre's *The Production of Space*. Trans. Donald Nicholson-Smith (Cambridge: Blackwell, 1991; orig. pub. 1974), pp. 38–41.

27. H. Bruce Franklin, *Prison Literature in America: The Victim as Criminal and Artist* (Westport, CT: Lawrence Hill & Co, 1982; orig. pub., 1978), pp. 247–248.

28. Ed. Amy Jacques Garvey, *Philosophy and Opinions of Marcus Garvey*, vol. 2 (New York: Universal Publishing House, 1925; rpt New York: Antheneum, 1974). Cited in Ed. William L. Van Deburg, *Modern Black Nationalism: From Marcus Garvey to Louis Farrakhan* (New York: New York University Press, 1997), p. 27.

29. Cyril V. Briggs, "*The African Blood Brotherhood*," cited in *Modern Black Nationalism*, p. 36.

30. Cited in *Modern Black Nationalism*, p. 44.

31. Stokely Carmichael, "Pan-Africanism—Land and Power," *Black Scholar*, November 1969; cited in *Modern Black Nationalism*, p. 205.

32. Margo Perkins, *Autobiography as Activism: Three Black Women of the Sixties* (Jackson: University Press of Mississippi, 2000), pp. 41–43.

33. Walter Benjamin, "Theses on the Philosophy of History" in *Illuminations: Essays and Reflections*, Ed. Hannah Arendt (New York: Schocken, 1968), p. 261.

34. Julia Watson and Sidonie Smith, "De/Colonization and the Politics of Discourse in Women's Autobiographical Practices" in Sidonie Smith and Julia Watson, Eds., *De/Colonizing the Subject: The Politics of Gender in Women's Autobiography* (Minneapolis: University of Minnesota Press, 1992), pp. xvii, xx.

35. Antonio Gramsci, *The Prison Notebooks: Selections*. Trans. and Ed. Quintin Hoare and Geoffrey Nowell Smith (New York: International Publishers, 1971), p. 324.

36. Shakur, *Autobiography*, p. 47.

37. Shakur, *Autobiography*, pp. 62–63.

38. Shakur, *Autobiography*, p. 51.

39. Gayatri Spivak, "Can the Subaltern Speak?" in Cary Nelson and L. Grossberg, Eds., *Marxism and the Interpretation of Culture* (Basingstoke: Macmillan, 1988), pp. 71–72.

40. Dylan Rodriguez suggests that imprisoned intellectuals such as Jackson and Davis "focus their praxis on present conditions for the construction of a radically and socially transformative historical bloc, a people's movement that partly emerges from the prison's inside and irrevocably alters the everyday of the nominal free world." See Rodriguez, *Forced Passages: Imprisoned Radical Intellectuals and the US Prison Regime* (Minneapolis: University of Minnesota Press, 2006), p. 136.

41. Paul Davidson, "Interview with Assata Shakur," November 6, 2000. http://www.fantompowa.net/Flame/assata_interview.htm.

42. Shakur, *Autobiography*, p. 152.

43. Huey Newton, *To Die for the People*, p. 92.

44. See Immanuel Wallerstein, "Eurocentrism and Its Avatars: The Dilemmas of Social Science," *New Left Review* 226 (November/December 1997), 105.

45. Frantz Fanon, *The Wretched of the Earth*. Trans. Constance Farrington (New York; Grove Press, 1963; orig. pub., 1961), p. 40.

46. Lisa Lowe offers a particularly thorough analysis of this contradiction in *Immigrant Acts: On Asian American Cultural Politics* (Durham: Duke University Press, 1996), pp. 25–26.

47. Angela Davis, "Black Nationalism: The Sixties and the Nineties" in *The Angela Y. Davis Reader*, p. 291.

48. Huey P. Newton, *Revolutionary Suicide* (New York: Harcourt Brace, 1973), p. 326.

49. Ernesto Laclau and Chantal Mouffe, *Hegemony and Socialist Strategy: Towards a Radical Democratic Politics* (London: Verso, 1987), p. 152.

50. Howard Winant, *The World Is a Ghetto: Race and Democracy Since World War II* (New York: Basic Books, 2001), p. 3.

51. Gilles Deleuze and Felix Guattari, *A Thousand Plateaus: Capitalism and Schizophrenia* (Minneapolis: University of Minnesota Press, 1987), p. 25.

52. See Werner Sollors, *Beyond Ethnicity: Consent and Descent in American Culture* (New York: Oxford University Press, 1986).

53. Shakur, *Autobiography*, p. 262.

54. Shakur, *Autobiography*, p. 263.

55. Shakur, *Autobiography*, p. 274.

56. John Edgar Wideman, "Introduction," *Live from Death Row* by Mumia Abu-Jamal (New York: Avon, 1995), pp. xxx, xxxi.

57. "Open letter from Assata: March 1998." http://www.afrocubaweb.com/assata2.htm.

58. Ibid, pp. 4, 6.

59. Avery F. Gordon, "Globalism and the Prison Industrial Complex: An Interview with Angela Davis," *Race & Class* 40 2/3 (1998/99), p. 153.

60. I am referring to Davis's *Are Prisons Obsolete?* (New York: Seven Stories Press, 2003) in which she notes the high percentage of people of color in prison and deems prisons racist institutions. However, in her analysis of the prison-industrial complex through a genealogy of modern incarceration, race disappears from the picture. Her own question, "What is the relationship between these historical expressions of racism and the role of the prison system today?" remains unanswered in the book (p. 25).

61. See Howard Winant, *The World Is a Ghetto*, pp. 24–27.

62. Assata Shakur, "Letter from Assata on the Prison Industrial Complex," September 25, 1998. http:/www.afrocubaweb.com/assata2.htm.

63. "Open letter from Assata: March 1998." http://www.afrocubaweb.com/assata2.htm.

64. "Racism Conference Drops Reference to Caste." http://www.ambedkar.org/News/Racconfdrops.htm. The Dalits have long recognized their ideological affinities to black resistance in the United States as evidenced by the formation of the Dalit Panthers in Bombay in 1972.

65. Arif Dirlik, "Asians on the Rim: Transnational Capital and Local Community in the Making of Contemporary Asian America" in Evelyn Du-Hart, Ed., *Across the Pacific: Asian Americans and Globalization* (Philadelphia: Temple University Press, 1999), p. 48.

66. R. Upadhyay, "Politics of Race and Caste," South Asia Analysis Group, paper no. 308, September 5, 2001. Http://www.saag.org/papers4/paper308.html.

CHAPTER SEVEN

1. See Veena Das, "Subaltern as Perspective," in *Subaltern Studies VI: Writings on South Asian History and Society*, Ed. Ranajit Guha (Delhi: Oxford University Press, 1989), pp. 310–324.

2. The appropriateness of postcolonial theory to Native American writing has been debated by scholars. Arnold Krupat sees the postcolonial perspective as "especially promising for the written literature of some indigenous peoples over the last thirty some years." See *Red Matters: Native American Studies* (Philadelphia: University of Pennsylvania Press, 2002), p. 20. Rob Wilson, in relation to a local Pacific identity, suggests that the

imaginings of this kind of identity in resistance to the homogenizing forces of the U.S. culture industry are postcolonial. See Rob Wilson, "From the Sublime to the Devious: Writing the Experimental/Local Pacific," *boundary 2* 28 i (2001), pp. 122–123. For an argument about incorporating "postcolonial" into Native terms, particularly in relation to *Almanac of the Dead*, see Yvonne Reineke, "Overturning the (New World) Order: Of Space, Time, Writing, and Prophecy in Leslie Marmon Silko's *Almanac of the Dead*," *Studies in American Indian Literatures* Series 2, 10 iii (1998), p. 65.

3. There is considerable controversy about viewing Apess as a resistant subaltern because of Apess's English education and his being an ordained minister. Arnold Krupat sees Apess's autobiography as very similar to early nineteenth-century white salvationist discourse, but acknowledges the explicit social criticism of Apess's later works. See *The Voice in the Margin: Native American Literature and the Canon* (Berkeley: University of California Press, 1989), p. 147, 176. Other critics have argued against holding Apess to an unmediated form of Indianness that he himself critiqued. See David Murray, *Forked Tongues: Speech, Writing and Representation in North American Indian Texts* (London: Pinter, 1991), p. 58. Laura Donaldson claims that Apess's writings anticipate postcolonial concerns of the politics of recognition, mimicry, and imagined (postcolonial) communities. See Laura Donaldson, "Son of the Forest, Child of God: William Apess and the Scene of Postcolonial Nativity" in C. Richard King, Ed., *Post-Colonial America* (Chicago: University of Illinois Press, 2000), p. 222. Roumiana Velikova has postulated a conscious subversive agency in Apess's rendition of Metacomet (King Philip) as a Pequot. Roumiana Velikova "'Philip, King of the Pequots': The History of an Error," *Early American Literature* 37 ii (2002), p. 330.

4. Barry O'Connell, "Introduction," *On Our Own Ground: The Complete Writings of William Apess, a Pequot*, Ed. Barry O'Connell (Amherst: University of Massachusetts Press, 1992). p. xlvi.

5. Leslie Marmon Silko, *Almanac of the Dead* (New York: Simon and Schuster, 1991), p. 513. Hereafter cited parenthetically in the text.

6. On the difference between people and multitude comprised of singularities, see Michael Hardt and Antonio Negri, *Multitude: War and Democracy in the Age of Empire* (New York: Penguin, 2004), p. 99.

7. John Muthyala points out the differences in the ways Sonoran and Arizona Yacqis referred to themselves to suggest ways in which the border crossings of Yaquis impacted senses of identity and language. See John Muthyala, "*Almanac of the Dead*: The Dream of the Fifth World in the Borderlands," *Literature, Interpretation, Theory* 14 (2003), p. 372.

8. Eva Cherniavsky, "Tribalim, Globalism, and Eskimo Television in Leslie Marmon Silko's *Almanac of the Dead*," *Angelaki* 6 i (2001), p. 111.

9. Michael Omi and Howard Winant, *Racial Formation in the United States* (New York: Routledge, 1994; orig pub 1986), p. 55.

10. Vine DeLoria Jr., "Foreword," *Black Elk Speaks* by Nicholas Black Elk (Lincoln: University of Nebraska Press, 2000; orig pub, 1932), p. xv.

11. Gabrielle Vail, "The Maya Codices," *Annual Review of Anthropology* 35 (2006), pp. 497–519.

12. Leslie Marmon Silko, "Notes on *Almanac of the Dead*," *Yellow Woman and a Beauty of the Spirit*, pp. 135–145. Although Silko believes that only three codices survived, the authenticity of the fourth codex has been accepted by Mayan scholars, at least since the publication of Michael Coe's *Breaking the Maya Code* (New York: Thames and Hudson, 1992).

13. Mayan scholars doubt the existence of a singular priest as author. *Chilam* or *chilan* means priest and *balam* means jaguar. Chilam Balam is therefore a generic title. The prediction of the arrival of the Spanish is also seen as a post-conquest idea. See Ruth Gubler and David Bolles, Eds., *The Book of Chilam Balam of Na.* Facsimile, Translation, and Edited Text (Lancaster, CA: Labyrinthos, 2000), p. 1. Charles Gibson and John B. Glass argue that the books of Chilam Balam contain numerous versions and materials from different periods, many dating to the eighteenth and nineteenth centuries. See "Prose Sources in the Native Historical Tradition. A Census of Middle American Prose Manuscripts in the Native Historical Tradition" in *Handbook of Middle American Indians*, Ed. Robert Wauchope, Volume 15, *Guide to Ethnohistorical Sources*, Part 4, Howard F. Cline, Volume Editor, pp. 322–400 (Austin: University of Texas Press, 1975), pp. 379–380. Silko scholars, however, seem not to have paid much attention to Mayan scholarship. Daria Donnelly, for instance, accepts the idea of a prophet Chilam Balam as well as the idea that the arrival of the Spanish was prophesied. See Daria Donnelly, "Old and New Notebooks: *Almanac of the Dead* as Revolutionary Entertainment" in *Leslie Marmon Silko: A Collection of Critical Essays*, Eds. Louise K. Barnett and James L. Thorson (Albuquerque: University of New Mexico Press, 1999), p. 247.

14. Donnelly, "Old and New Notebooks," p. 246.

15. Caren Irr, "The Timeliness of *Almanac of the Dead*, or a Postmodern Rewriting of Radical Fiction," in *Leslie Marmon Silko: A Collection of Critical Essays*, p. 227. See also Cherniavsky's critique of Irr's contrast between Silko's concept of time and European calendrical time, p. 124.

16. Janet St. Clair, "Cannibal Queers: The Problematics of Metaphor in *Almanac of the Dead*" in *Leslie Marmon Silko: A Collection of Critical Essays*, pp. 207, 220.

17. Annette Van Dyke, "From Big Green Fly to Stone Serpent: Following the Dark Vision in Silko's Almanac of the Dead," *Studies in American Indian Literatures* 10 ii (1998), p. 37. See also Leslie A. Wooten's reading of *Almanac* as "unequivocally reinforcing Indian values and ideas," giving us strong female protagonists who are empowered by their Indian heritage and who "are willing to kill and to die so the great Mother of us all—Mother Earth—can live" in "'We Want Our Mother the Land': Female Power in Leslie Marmon Silko's *Almanac of the Dead*," *North Dakota Quarterly* 64 iv (1997), p. 66.

18. Frantz Fanon, *Black Skin, White Masks*. Trans. Charles Lam Markmann (New York: Grove Press, 1967; orig. pub.1952), p. 109.

19. Annette Van Dyke, "From Big Green Fly to Stone Serpent: Following the Dark Vision in Silko's *Almanac of the Dead*," *Studies in American Indian Literature* Series 2, 10 iii (1998), p. 41.

20. *The Book of Chilam Balam of Chumayel*. Trans Ralph L. Roys (Washington, D.C.: Carnegie Institution, 1933), p. 134. http://www.sacred-texts.com/nam/maya/cbc/cbc23.html.

21. *The Book of Chilam Balam*, p. 138.

22. Walter Benjamin, "Theses on the Philosophy of History," in *Illuminations*, Ed. Hannah Arendt (New York: Schocken Books, 1968), pp. 257, 255.

23. Benjamin, *Illuminations*, p. 255.

24. Rebecca Tillett sees *Almanac* emphasizing the presence of the indigenous dead in order to actively unsettle the Euro-American reader. See Tillett's "'The Indian wars have never ended in the Americas': The politics of memory and history in Leslie Marmon Silko's *Almanac of the Dead*," *Feminist Review* 85 (2007), pp. 21–39.

25. Elizabeth Cook-Lynn, *Why I Can't Read Wallace Stegner and Other Essays: A Tribal Voice* (Madison: University of Wisconsin Press, 1996), p. 93.

26. Cook-Lynn, *Why I Can't Read Wallace Stegner*, p. 88.

27. Ellen Arnold, "Listening to the Spirits: An Interview with Leslie Marmon Silko," *Studies in American Indian Literatures* Series 2 10 iii (1998), p. 12.

28. Mary Crow Dog and Richard Erdoes, *Lakota Woman* (New York: Harper, 1990), p. 105.

29. Mary Crow Dog, *Lakota Woman*, p. 140.

30. Mary Crow Dog, *Lakota Woman*, p. 153.

31. Rose suggests that a pan-tribal identity "is intended to protect those tribal identities, not to replace them." Churchill, like Silko, argues for a global indigenism. See Wendy Rose, Ed., *Winged Words: American Indian Writers Speak* (Lincoln: University of Nebraska Press, 1990), p. 4, and Ward Churchill, *From a Native Son* (Boston: South End, 1996), p. 509.

32. Elizabeth Archuleta sees Zeta as the pan-Indian voice for the indigenous peoples of the Southwest. See Archuleta's "Securing Our Nation's Roads and Border or Re-circling the Wagons? Leslie Marmon Silko's Destablization of 'Borders," *Wicazo Sa Review* 20i (2005), p. 121.

33. See Debora Horvitz, "Freud, Marx and Chiapas in Leslie Marmon's Silko's *Almanac of the Dead*," *Studies in American Indian Literatures* Series 2, 10iii (1998), p. 47.

34. Silko, *Yellow Woman and a Beauty of the Spirit*, p. 153.

35. See John Brown Childs, *Transcommunality: From the Politics of Conversion to the Ethics of Respect* (Philadelphia: Temple University Press, 2003), p. 37.

36. Hardt and Negri do recognize the significance of locatedness to the EZLN but tend to see the specific, local history of the movement as less important than their global agenda. They write: "the EZLN in the Lacadon jungle of Chiapas mixes elements of national history, such as the figure of Zapata and the legacy of peasant revolts, with local indigenous Tzeltal mythology and forges them together with network relationships and democratic practices to create a new life in the common that defines the movement." See *Multitude*, p. 213.

37. Romero Channette, "Envisioning a 'Network of Tribal Coalitions': Leslie Marmon Silko's *Almanac of the Dead*," *American Indian Quarterly* 0095812X (September 1, 2002) 26, no. 4. Online.

38. Channette, ibid.

39. For a history of these alliances in the southern regions of North America and for an examination of the interracial mixtures between Native Americans and African survivors, see Jack D. Forbes, *Black Africans and Native Americans: Color, Race and Caste in the Evolution of Red-Black Peoples* (New York: Blackwell, 1988).

40. *The Book of Chilam Balam of Chumayel*, p. 133.

41. John Brown Childs, *Transcommunity*, p. 25.

42. Daria Donnelly sees the ending of the novel as a deliberate "writerly resistance to closure. . . . She does not resolve the action: the Laguna, for example, ignore Sterling when he returns. She does not resolve the fate of any of her characters. . . . She does not resolve the timing of the repossession of the Americas." See Donnelly, "Old and New Notebooks," p. 254. John Muthyala sees Silko endorsing some kind of return,

but not an affirmation of a true Laguna spirituality. See Muthyala, "*Almanac of the Dead*," p. 379; Caren Irr suggests that while Sterling's search is not complete, he is "on the verge of restoring himself to his community." See Irr, "The Timeliness of *Almanac of the Dead*," p. 231.

43. Leslie Marmon Silko, *Yellow Woman and a Beauty of the Spirit: Essays on Native American Life Today* (New York: Simon & Schuster), p. 93.

CONCLUSION

1. Tony Bennett, Larry Grossberg, and Meaghan Morris, "Originals, Remakes, Assemblages: A Retrospect on New Keywords," *Criticism* 47 iv (2007), p. 567.

2. Michael Denning, *Culture in the Age of Three Worlds* (London: Verso, 2004), p. 11.

3. Susan Hegeman points out the local omissions in her "Williams in a New Key," *Criticism* 47 iv (2007), p. 562.

4. "U.S. prison population largest in world," *The Post and Courier* Charleston.Net, June 1, 2003. http://www.charleston.net/stories/060103/wor_01jailbirds.shtml.

5. Fox Butterfield, "Mistreatment of Prisoners Is Called Routine in U.S.," *New York Times International*, May 8, 2004.

6. Ray Luc Levasseur, "Armed and Dangerous." http://home.earthlink.net/~neoludd/armed.htm.

7. For the idea of contemporary resistances as those against global environmental commons, see David Harvey, *The New Imperialism* (New York: Oxford University Press, 2003), pp. 168–169, 162.

8. Andite Mngxitama, "WSF: The Colonisation of Resistance," *We Write*, 2 i (January 2005), p. 4. www.wewrite.org.

9. Radha D'Souza, "The WSF Revisited: Back to Basics?," *We Write* 2 i (January 2005), p. 5. www.wewrite.org.

10. Randall Robinson, *The Debt: What America Owes to Blacks* (New York: Dutton, 2000), p. 231.

11. Robinson, *The Debt*, p. 145.

12. Reparations: Our Case for an Intercommunal Reparations Campaign: A Political Strategy to Redress the Kidnapping, Murder and Theft of the Land and Labor or Africans, African-Americans and Indigenous People. Http://www.globalpanther.com/rep.shtml.

13. Reparations, ibid.

14. Cited in Manning Marable, "Reparations and our Rendezvous with History" in "Along the Color Line," 2001. www.manningmarable.net.

15. David Horowitz, "The Latest Civil Rights Disaster," May 30, 2000.http://dir.salon.com/news/col/horo/2000/05/30/reparations/index.htm.

16. For an examination of the tensions and problems embodied in the idea of Aztlan, see Rafael Perez-Torres, "Refiguring Aztlan," in Amritjit Singh and Peter Schmidt, Eds., *Postcolonial Theory and the United States* (Jackson: University Press of Mississippi, 2000), pp. 103–121.

17. http://www.pnlru.org/platform.html.

18. http://www.nationalchicanosummit.org/Sept0304comminique.htm.

19. http://www.nationalchicanosummit.org/LRUPsummit.htm.

20. Aziz Choudry, "Bringing It All Back Home: Anti-globalization Activism Cannot Ignore Colonial Realities," *We Write* 2 i (January 2005), p. 2.

21. Aziz Choudry, ibid., p. 2.

22. http://www.nationalchicanosummit.org/TowardsNational Liberation.htm.

23. Ibid.

24. Leti Volpp, "The Citizen and the Terrorist," in Mary L. Dudziak, Ed., *September 11 in History: A Watershed Moment* (Durham: Duke University Press, 2000), p. 147.

25. Noam Chomsky, Invited talk by the Civic Media Center, Gainesville, Florida, October 21, 2003.

26. Samuel P. Huntington, "The Clash of Civilizations?," *Foreign Affairs* Summer 1993, pp. 22–49. See also Edward Said's critique of the book by the same name by Huntington, "The Clash of Ignorance," *The Nation*, October 22, 2001.

27. "Local Protestor dies in Gaza," *Seattle Post-Intelligencer*, March 17, 2003. http://seattlepi.nwsource.com/local/112840_protestor17.shtml.

28. "Rachel's War," *The Guardian*, March 18, 2003. Http://www.guardian.co.uk/print/0,3858,4627222-103552,00.html.

29. Daniel Lautman, "Rachel Corrie does not deserve to be labeled an 'American hero,'" *The Diamondback*, April 8, 2003. http://www.inform.umd.edu/News/Diamondback/archives/2003/04/08/commentary2.html.

30. Joshua Hammer, "The Death of Rachel Corrie," *Mother Jones* (September/October 2003), p. 3. http://www.motherjones/com/news/feature/2003/09/ma_497_01.html.

31. See Naomi Klein, "On rescuing Private Lynch and forgetting Rachel Corrie," *The Guardian*, May 22, 2003. http:/www.guardian.co.uk/print/0,3858,4674374-103552,00.html.

32. Corrie's e-mails talk about her identification with the family who has "adopted" her and whose members worry about her well-being.

Grandmother, for instance, combines Arabic with gesticulation to lecture Corrie about her smoking. "Rachel's War," *The Guardian*, March 18, 2003.

33. Susan Saulny, "In New York and New Jersey, Hundreds Join in as Antiwar Protests Continue," *New York Times* (late edition), March 30, 2003, p. B14.

34. Amitava Kumar, "A Victory for Ms. Kaur," *Ghadar* 5 i (February 21, 2002). http://www.proxsa.org/resources/ ghadar/v5n1/kaur.htm.

35. Immanuel Wallerstein, "The Construction of Peoplehood," in Etienne Balibar and Immanuel Wallerstein, *Race, Nation, Class: Ambiguous Identities*. Trans. Chris Turner (New York: Verso, 1991), p. 84.

36. E. San Juan Jr., *Beyond Postcolonial Theory* (New York: St. Martin's 1998), p. 5.

37. http://www.workersawaaz.org/press2.htm.

38. http://www.imdiversity.com/Villages/Asian/civil_human_equal_rights/Workers_Awaaz_SAsian_Women.asp Accessed November 11, 2007.

39. See http://stopfundinghate.org/faculty/index.htm.

Selected Bibliography

Ahmad, Aijaz. *In Theory: Classes, Nations, Literatures*. New York: Verso, 1992.

Alessandrini, Anthony C. "Reading Bharati Mukherjee, Reading Globalization," in *World Bank Literature*. Edited by Amitava Kumar. Minneapolis: University of Minnesota Press, 2002, 265–79.

Alexander, Meena. *Fault Lines: A Memoir*. New York: Feminist, 1993.

———. *Manhattan Music*. San Francisco: Mercury House, 1997.

Amin, Samir. *Accumulation on a World Scale: A Critique of the Theory of Underdevelopment*, 2 vols. Translated by Brian Pearce. New York: Monthly Review Press, 1974.

———. *The Liberal Virus: Permanent War and the Americanization of the World*. Translated by James H. Membrez. New York: Monthly Review Press, 2004.

Anzaldua, Gloria. Borderlands: *The New Mestiza*. San Francisco: Aunt Lute, 1987.

Apess, William. *On Our Own Ground: The Complete Writings of William Apess, a Peqout (Native Americans of the Northeast)*. Edited by Barry O'Connell. Amherst: University of Massachusetts Press, 1992.

Appadurai, Arjun. *Fear of Small Numbers: An Essay on the Geography of Anger*. Durham: Duke University Press, 2006.

———. "The Heart of Whiteness," *Callaloo* 16, 4 (1993): 796–807.

———. *Modernity at Large: Cultural Dimensions of Globalization*. Minneapolis: University of Minnesota Press, 1996.

Appiah, Anthony K., and Amy Gutman. *Color Conscious: The Political Morality of Race*. Princeton: Princeton University Press, 1996.

Appiah, Kwame Anthony. *Cosmopolitanism: Ethics in a World of Strangers*. New York: Norton, 2006.

———. "Cosmopolitan Patriots," in *Cosmopolitics: Thinking and Feeling beyond the Nation*. Edited by Pheng Cheah and Bruce Robbins. Minneapolis: University of Minnesota Press, 1998, 91–114.

Archuleta, Elizabeth. "Securing Our Nation's Roads and Border or Recircling the Wagons?" *Wicazo Sa Review* 20, 1 (2005): 113–37.

Arnold, Ellen. "Listening to the Spirits: An Interview with Leslie Marmon Silko," *Studies in American Indian Literature,* Series 2, 10, 3 (1998): 1–33.

Austo, Sanjay. "Pico Iyer: Chronicler of Modern Times." the_south_asian.com May/June 2003.

Bacalzo, Dan. "Portraits of Self and Other: SlutForArt and the Photographs of Tseng Kwong Chi," *Theatre Journal* 53, 1 (2001): 73–94.

Bahri, Deepika, and Vasudeva Mary, eds. *Between the Lines: South Asians and Postcoloniality*. Philadelphia: Temple University Press, 1996.

Baker, Houston A., Jr. "Caliban's Triple Play," in *"Race," Writing, and Difference*. Edited by Henry Louis Gates, Jr. Chicago: University of Chicago Press, 1986, 381–96.

———. *Turning South Again: Re-Thinking Modernism/Re-reading Booker T.* Durham: Duke University Press, 2001.

Balibar, Etienne. *We, the People of Europe? Reflections on Transnational Citizenship*. Princeton: Princeton University Press, 2004.

———, and Immanuel Wallerstein. *Race, Nation, Class: Ambiguous Identities*. Translated by Chris Turner. New York, Verso, 1991.

Benjamin, Walter. *Illuminations*. Edited by Hannah Arendt. New York: Schocken, 1968.

Bennett, Tony, Larry Grossberg, and Meaghan Morris. "Originals, Remakes, Assemblages: A Retrospect on New Keywords," *Criticism* 47, 4 (2007): 567–71.

Berube, Michael. "American Studies without Exceptions," *PMLA* 118, 1 (2003): 103–13.

Bhabha, Homi. *The Location of Culture*. New York: Routledge, 1994.

Black Elk, Nicholas. *Black Elk Speaks*. Edited by Vine DeLoria, Jr. Lincoln: University of Nebraska Press, 2000 (originally published, 1932).

Blassingame, John W. *The Slave Community: Plantation Life in the Antebellum South*. New York: Oxford University Press, 1972.

Boime, Albert. "Patriarchy Fixed in Stone: Gutzon Borglum's 'Mount Rushmore,'" *American Arts* 51, 1/2 (1991): 142–67.

Book of Chilam Balam of Chumayel, The. Translated by Ralph L. Roys. Washington, DC: Carnegie, 1933, 134. http://www.sacred_texts.com/nam/maya/cbc/cbc23.html.

Bosniak, Linda. "Universal Citizenship and the Problem of Alienage," *Northwestern University Law Review* 94, 3 (2000): 963–82.

Bruce, Robbins. *Feeling Global: Internationalism in Distress*. New York: New York University Press, 1999.

Butler, Judith. *Antigone's Claim: Kinship between Life and Death*. New York: Columbia University Press, 2000.

———. *Bodies That Matter: On the Discursive Limits of "Sex."* New York: Routledge, 1993.

———. "Endangered/Endangering: Schematic Racism and White Paranoia," in *Reading Rodney King: Reading Urban Uprising*. Edited by Robert Gooding Williams. New York: Routledge, 1993, 15–22.

———. *Gender Trouble: Feminism and the Subversion of Identity*. New York: Routledge, 1990.

———. *Precarious Life: The Powers of Mourning and Violence*. London: Verso, 2004.

Butterfield, Fox. "Mistreatment of Prisoners Is Called Routine in U.S." *New York Times International*, May 8, 2004. http://query.nytimes.com/gst/fullpage.html?res=9D04E6DA143CF93BA35756C0A9629C8B63.

Castells, Manuel. *The Information Age: Economy, Society and Culture*. Vol 2, *The Power of Identity*. Malden, MA: Blackwell, 1997.

Chakrabarty, Dipesh. *Provincializing Europe: Postcolonial Thought and Historical Difference*. Princeton: Princeton University Press, 2000.

Chambers, Iain. *Migrancy, Culture, Identity*. New York: Routledge, 1994.

Channette, Romero, "Envisioning a 'Network of Tribal Coalitions': Leslie Marmon Silko's *Almanac of the Dead*," *American Indian Quarterly* 26, 4 (September 1, 2002): Online.

Chatterjee, Partha. *The Nation and Its Fragments: Colonial and Postcolonial Histories*. Princeton: Princeton University Press, 1993.

———. *Nationalist Thought in the Colonial World: A Derivative Discourse?* Minneapolis: University of Minnesota Press, 1986.

Cheah, Pheng. "Given Culture: Rethinking Cosmopolitical Freedom in Transnationalism," *boundary 2* 24, 2 (Summer 1997): 157–97.

———, and Bruce Robbins, eds. *Cosmopolitics: Thinking and Feeling beyond the Nation*. Minneapolis: University of Minnesota Press, 1998.

Cherniavsky, Eva. "Tribalim, Globalism, and Eskimo Television in Leslie Marmon Silko's *Almanac of the Dead*," *Angelaki* 6, 1 (2001): 111–26.

Childs, John Brown. *Transcommunality: From the Politics of Conversion to the Ethics of Respect*. Philadelphia: Temple University Press, 2003.

Chin, Frank, and Jeffrey Paul Chan. "Racist Love," in *Seeing Through Shuck*. Edited by Richard Kostelanetz. New York: Ballantine, 1972, 65–79.

———, eds. *Aiiieeeee! An Anthology of Asian American Writers*. New York: Mentor, 1991 (originally published, 1974).

Chomsky, Noam. *Hegemony or Survival?* New York: Metropolitan, 2003.

Choudry, Aziz. "Bringing It All Back Home: Anti-globalization Activism Cannot Ignore Colonial Realities," *We Write* 2, 1 (January 2005). http://www.wewrite.org/Articles/Aziz.pdf.

Chow, Rey. "Between Colonizers: Hong Kong's Postcolonial Self-Writing in the 1990s," *Diaspora* 2, 2 (1992): 151–70.

———. *The Protestant Ethnic and the Spirit of Capitalism*. New York: Columbia University Press, 2002.

Chu, Patricia. *Assimilating Asians: Gendered Strategies of Authorship in Asian America*. Durham: Duke University Press, 2000.

Churchill, Ward. *From a Native Son*. Boston: South End, 1996.

Cleaver, Eldridge. *Post-Prison Writings and Speeches*. Edited by Robert Scheer. New York: Random House, 1969.

Coe, Michael. *Breaking the Maya Code*. London: Thames and Hudson, 1992.

Collins, Patricia Hill. *Black Feminist Thought: Knowledge, Consciousness, and the Politics of Empowerment*. New York: Routledge, 1990.

Cook-Lynn, Elizabeth. *Why I Can't Read Wallace Stegner and Other Essays: A Tribal Voice*. Madison: University of Wisconsin Press, 1996.

D'Souza, Radha. "The WSF Revisited: Back to Basics?" *We Write* 2, 1 (January 2005): 5. www.wewrite.org.

Dancy, Jonathan. "The Particularist's Progress," in *Moral Particularism*. Edited by Brad Hooker and Margaret Olivia Little. Oxford: Oxford University Press, 2000, 130–55.

Daniel Lautman, "Rachel Corrie Does Not Deserve To Be Labeled an 'American Hero,'" *The Diamondback* (April 8, 2003). http://www.inform.umd.edu/News/Diamondback/archives/2003/04/08/commentary2.html.

Das, Veena. "Subaltern as Perspective," in *Subaltern Studies 6: Writings on South Asian History and Society*. Edited by Ranajit Guha. Delhi: Oxford University Press, 1989, 310–24.

Davidson, Cathy. "Photographs of the Dead: Sherman, Daguerre, Hawthorne," *SAQ* 89, 4 (Fall 1990): 667–701.

Davidson, Paul. "Interview with Assata Shakur," November 6, 2000. http://www.fantompowa.net/Flame/assata_interview.htm.

Davies, Carole Boyce. *Black Women, Writing and Identity: Migrations of the Subject*. New York: Routledge, 1994.

Davis, Angela. *The Angela Y. Davis Reader*. Edited by Joy James. Malden, MA: Blackwell, 1998.

———. *An Autobiography*. New York: International Publishers, 1988 (originally published, 1974).

———. *Are Prisons Obsolete?* New York: Seven Stories, 2003.

———. "The Prison Industrial Complex," recorded Colorado College, Colorado Springs, May 5, 1997.

Deleuze, Gilles, and Felix Guattari. *Anti-Oedipus: Capitalism and Schizophrenia*. Translated by Robert Hurley et al. Minneapolis: University of Minnesota Press, 1983.

———. *A Thousand Plateaus: Capitalism and Schizophrenia*. Translated by Brian Massumi. Minneapolis: University of Minnesota Press, 1987.

Delgado, Richard. *Critical Race Theory: The Cutting Edge*. Philadelphia: Temple University Press, 1995.

Denning, Michael. *Culture in the Age of Three Worlds*. London: Verso, 2004.

Dirlik, Arif. "Asians on the Rim: Transnational Capital and Local Community in the Making of Contemporary America," in *Across the Pacific: Asian Americans and Globalization*. Edited by Evelyn Hu-DeHart. Philadelphia: Temple University Press, 1999, 29–60.

———. "The Postcolonial Aura: Third World Criticism in the Age of Global Capitalism," in Anne McClintock et al., eds., *Dangerous Liaisons*, 501–28.

Dobson, Lynn. *Supranational Citizenship*. Manchester: Manchester University Press, 2006.

Dog, Mary Crow, and Richard Erdoes. *Lakota Woman*. New York: Harper, 1990.

Donaldson, Laura. "Son of the Forest, Child of God: William Apess and the Scene of Postcolonial Nativity," in *Postcolonial America*. Edited by C. Richard King. Chicago: University of Chicago Press, 2000, 201–22.

Donnelly, Daria. "Old and New Notebooks: *Almanac of the Dead* as Revolutionary Entertainment," in *Leslie Marmon Silko: A Collection of Critical Essays*. Edited by Louise K. Barnett and James L. Thorson. Albuquerque: University of New Mexico Press, 1999, 245–59.

Drinnon, Richard. *Facing West: The Metaphysics of Indian Hating and Empire Building*. New York: American Library, 1980.

D'Souza, Radha. "The WSF Revisited: Back to Basics?" *We Write* 2, 1 (January 2005): 5. www.wewrite.org.

DuBois, W. E. B. *Black Reconstruction: An Essay Toward a History of the Past which Black Folk Played in the Attempt to Reconstruct Democracy in America, 1860–1880.* New York: Atheneum, 1977 (originally published, 1935).

———. *The Souls of Black Folk.* New York: New American Library, 1982 (originally published, 1903).

Ducille, Ann, "Postcolonialism and Afrocentricity: Discourse and Dat Course," in *The Black Columbiad.* Edited by Werner Sollors and Maria Diedrich. Cambridge: Harvard University Press, 1994.

Dyer, Richard. "White," *Screen* 9, 4 (1988): 44–64.

Dyson, Mike Eric. *Race Rules: Navigating the Color Line.* Reading, MA: Addison-Wesley, 1996.

Eisenstein, Zillah. *Against Empire: Feminisms, Racism, and the West.* London: Zed, 2004.

Elliott, Mary Jane Suero. "Postcolonial Experience in a Domestic Context: Commodified Subjectivity in Toni Morrison's Beloved," *MELUS* 25, 3/4 (Fall/Winter 2000): 181–202.

Ellison, Ralph. *Invisible Man.* New York: Vintage, 1972 (originally published, 1952).

Fabian, Johannes. *Time and the Other: How Anthropology Makes Its Object.* New York: Columbia University Press, 1983.

Falk, Richard. "Revisioning Cosmopolitanism," in *For Love of Country.* Edited by Martha C. Nussbaum. Boston: Beacon, 1996, 53–60.

Fanon, Frantz. *Black Skin, White Masks.* Translated by Charles Lam Markmann. New York: Grove, 1967 (originally published, 1952).

———. *The Wretched of the Earth.* Translated by Constance Farrington. New York: Grove, 1963 (originally published, 1961).

Farag, Fatemah. "Empire of Chaos Challenged," *Al-Ahram* 609 (October 2002): 24–30.

Fishkin, Shelley Fisher. "Crossroads of Cultures: The Transnational Turn in American Studies. Presidential Address to the American Studies Association, November 12, 2004," *American Quarterly* 57, 1 (March 2005): 17–57.

Flowers, Sandra Hollin. *African American Nationalist Literature of the 1960s: Pens of Fire.* New York: Garland, 1996.

Forbes, Jack D. *Black Africans and Native Americans: Color, Race, and Caste in the Evolution of Red-Black Peoples.* New York: Blackwell, 1988.

Foucault, Michel. *Discipline and Punish: The Birth of the Prison.* Translated by Alan Sheridan. New York: Vintage, Random House, 1979.

Franklin, H. Bruce. *Prison Literature in America: The Victim as Criminal and Artist*. Westport, CT: Hill, 1982 (originally published, 1978).

Gabriel, Sharmani Patricia. "'Between Mosaic and Melting Pot': Negotiating Multiculturalism and Cultural Citizenship in Bharati Mukherjee's Narratives of Diaspora," *Postcolonial Text* 1, 2 (2005). Http://postcolonial.org/index.php/pct/article/viewArticle/420/147. Accessed October 9, 2007.

Garvey, Amy Jacques. *Philosophy and Opinions of Marcus Garvey*, vol. 2. New York: Universal, 1925 (reprint New York: Antheneum, 1974).

Gibson, Charles, and John B. Glass. "Prose Sources in the Native Historical Tradition: A Census of Middle American Prose Manuscripts in the Native Historical Tradition," in *Handbook of Middle American Indians*. Edited by Robert Wauchope. Volume 15, *Guide to Ethnohistorical Sources,* Part 4, Howard F. Cline, volume editor, 322–400 (Austin: University of Texas Press, 1975), 379–80.

Giddens, Anthony. *The Consequences of Modernity*. Stanford: Stanford University Press, 1990.

Gikandi, Simon. "Globalization and the Claims of Postcoloniality," *South Atlantic Quarterly* 3 (Summer 2001): 627–58.

Gilroy, Paul. *Against Race: Imagining Political Culture beyond the Color Line*. Cambridge, MA: Harvard, Belknap, 2000.

———. *The Black Atlantic: Modernity and Double Consciousness*. Cambridge, MA: Harvard University Press, 1993.

Giroux, Henry. *Disturbing Pleasures*. New York: Routledge, 1994.

Gonzalez, Rodolfo "Corky." *Message to Aztlan*. Houston: Arte Publico, 2001.

Gordon, Avery F. "Globalism and the Prison Industrial Complex: An Interview with Angela Davis," *Race and Class* 40, 2/3 (1998/99): 145–57.

Gramsci, Antonio. *Selections from the Prison Notebooks of Antonio Gramsci*. Edited and translated by Quintin Hoare and Geoffrey Nowell. New York: International, 1991.

Grewal, Gurleen. "Born Again American: The Immigrant Consciousness in Jasmine," in *Bharati Mukherjee: Critical Perspectives*. Edited by Emmanuel S. Nelson. New York: Garland, 1993, 181–96.

Grewal, Inderpal. *Transnational America: Feminisms, Diasporas, Neoliberalisms*. Durham: Duke University Press, 2005.

———, and Caren Kaplan, eds. *Scattered Hegemonies: Postmodernity and Transnational Feminist Practices*. Minneapolis: University of Minnesota Press, 1994.

Gubler, Ruth, and David Bolles, eds. *The Book of Chilam Balam of Na*. Facsimile, translation, and edited text. Lancaster, CA: Labyrinthos, 2000.

Guha, Ranajit. "Dominance without Hegemony and Its Historiography," in *Subaltern Studies 6: Writings on South Asian History and Society*. Edited by Ranajit Guha. New Delhi: Oxford University Press, 1989, 210–309.

Hall, Stuart. "The Local and the Global: Globalization and Ethnicity," in Anne McClintock et al., eds., *Dangerous Liaisons*, 173–87.

Hammer, Joshua. "The Death of Rachel Corrie," *Mother Jones* (September/October 2003): 3. http://www.motherjones/com/news/feature/2003/09/ma_497_01.html.

Haraway, Donna. "A Cyborg Manifesto: Science, Technology, and Socialist_Feminism in the Late Twentieth Century," in her *Simians, Cyborgs, and Women: The Reinvention of Nature*. London: Free Association Books, 1991, 149–81.

———. *Modest_Witness@Second_Millenium. FemaleMan_Meets_Onco Mouse: Feminism and Technoscience*. New York: Routledge, 1997.

———. "Situated Knowledges: The Science Question in Feminism and the Privilege of Partial Perspective," *Feminist Studies* 14 (Spring 1988): 575–99.

Hardt, Michael, and Antonio Negri. *Empire*. Cambridge, MA: Harvard University Press, 2000.

———. *Multitude: War and Democracy in the Age of Empire*. New York: Penguin, 2004.

Harvey, David. *The New Imperialism*. New York: Oxford University Press, 2003.

———. *Spaces of Hope*. Berkeley: University of California Press, 2000.

Hedrick, Tace. *Mestizo Modernism: Race, Nation, and Identity in Latin American Culture, 1900–1949*. New Jersey: Rutgers University Press, 2003.

Hegel, G. W. F. *Phenomenology of Spirit*. Translated by A. V. Miller. New York: Oxford University Press, 1977 (originally published, 1807).

Hegeman, Susan. "Williams in a New Key," *Criticism* 47, 4 (2007), 561–66.

Henwood, Doug. "What Is Globalization Anyway?" in *World Bank Literature*. Minneapolis: University of Minnesota Press, 2002, 59–63.

hooks, bell. *Feminist Theory: From Margin to Center*. Boston: South End, 1984.

———. *Yearning: Race, Gender, and Cultural Politics*. Boston: South End, 1990.

Horowitz, David . "The Latest Civil Rights Disaster," May 30, 2000. http://dir.salon.com/news/col/horo/2000/05/30/reparations/index.htm.

Horsman, Reginald. *Race and Manifest Destiny: The Origins of Racial Anglo-Saxonism*. Cambridge: Harvard University Press, 1981.

Horvitz, Debora. "Freud, Marx, and Chiapas in Leslie Marmon's Silko's *Almanac of the Dead*," *Studies in American Indian Literature*, Series 2, 10, 3 (1998): 47–64.

Huntington, Samuel P. "The Clash of Civilizations?" *Foreign Affairs* (Summer 1993): 22–49.

Ignatiev, Noel. *How the Irish Became White*. New York: Routledge, 1995.

Irigaray, Luce. *Between East and West: From Singularity to Community*. Translated by Stephen Pluhacek. New York: Columbia University Press, 2001.

Irr, Caren. "The Timeliness of *Almanac of the Dead*, or a Postmodern Rewriting of Radical Fiction," in *Leslie Marmon Silko: A Collection of Critical Essays*. Edited by Louise K. Barnett and James L. Thorson. Albuquerque: University of New Mexico Press, 1999, 223–44.

Iyer, Pico. *The Lady and the Monk: Four Seasons in Kyoto*. New York: Knopf, 1991.

———. *The Global Soul*. New York: Random House/Vintage, 2000.

———. *Video Night in Kathmandu and Other Reports from the Not-So-Far-East*. New York: Random House/Vintage, 1988.

Jameson, Frederic. "Third World Literature in the Era of Multinational Capital," *Social Text* (Fall 1986): 65–88.

Jeffords, Susan. "'Do We Get To Win This Time?' Reviving the Masculine," in *The Remasculinization of America: Gender and the Vietnam War*. Bloomington: Indiana University Press, 1989, 116–43.

"Job's Comforters," Editorial *Times of India*, Monday, June 16, 2003, p. 14.

Jones, Charles E. *The Black Panther Party Reconsidered*. Baltimore: Black Classic, 1998.

Juan, E. San, Jr. *Beyond Postcolonial Theory*. New York: St. Martin's, 1998.

Kaplan, Caren. *Questions of Travel: Postmodern Discourses of Displacement*. Durham: Duke University Press, 1996.

Kelley, Robin D. G, and Tiffany Ruby Patterson. "How the West Was One: On the Uses and Limitations of Diaspora," *Black Scholar* 30, 3/4: 31–35.

Kelsky, Karen. *Women on the Verge: Japanese Women, Western Dreams*. Durham: Duke University Press, 2001.

Klein, Naomi. "On Rescuing Private Lynch and Forgetting Rachel Corrie," *The Guardian*, Thursday May 22, 2003. http:/www.guardian.co.uk/print/0,3858,4674374_103552,00.html.

———. *No Logo*. New York: Picador, 2000.

King, C. Richard. *Postcolonial America*. Urbana: University of Illinois Press, 2000.

Koshy, Susan. "The Fiction of Asian American Literature," *The Yale Journal of Criticism* 9, 2 (1996): 315–46.

Kristeva, Julia. *About Chinese Women.* Translated by Anita Barrows. New York: Urizen, 1977.

Krupat, Arnold. *Red Matters: Native American Studies.* Philadelphia: University of Pennsylvania Press, 2002.

———. *The Voice in the Margin: Native American Literature and the Canon.* Berkeley: University of California Press, 1989.

Kumar, Amitava. "A Victory for Ms. Kaur," *Ghadar*, vol. 5, 1 (February 21, 2002). http://www.proxsa.org/resources/ ghadar/v5n1/kaur.htm.

Laclau, Ernesto, and Chantal Mouffe. *Hegemony and Socialist Strategy: Towards a Radical Democratic Politics.* London: Verso, 1987.

Laplanche J., and J. B. Pontalis. *The Language of Psycho-Analysis.* Translated by Donald Nicholson-Smith. New York: Norton, 1974.

Lazarus, Neil. *Nationalism and Cultural Practice in the Postcolonial World.* New York: Cambridge University Press, 1999.

Lefebvre, Henri. *The Production of Space.* Translated by Donald Nicholson-Smith. Cambridge, MA: Blackwell, 1991 (originally published 1974).

Lenin, V. I. *Imperialism: The Highest Stage of Capitalism.* New York: International, 1939 (originally published 1916).

Levasseur, Ray Luc. "Armed and Dangerous." http://home.earthlink.net/~neoludd/armed.htm.

Li, David Leiwei. *Imagining the Nation: Asian American Literature and Cultural Consent.* Stanford: Stanford University Press, 1998.

Lippard, Lucy R. "Outside (But Not Necessarily Beyond) the Landscape," *Aperture* 150 (Winter 1998): 60–73.

Lipsitz, George. "Frantic to Join . . . the Japanese Army": The Asia Pacific War in the Lives of African American Soldiers and Civilians," in *The Politics of Culture in the Shadow of Capital.* Edited by Lisa Lowe and David Lloyd. Durham: Duke University Press, 1997, 324–53.

Liu, John. "Towards an Understanding of the Internal Colonial Model." *Counterpoint: Perspectives on Asian America.* Edited by Emma Gee. Los Angeles: Asian American Studies Center, UCLA, 1976, 160–68.

"Local Protestor Dies in Gaza," *Seattle Post-Intelligencer*, March 17, 2003. http://seattlepi.nwsource.com/local/112840_protestor17.shtml.

Loftus, John, and Mark Aaron. *The Secret War against the Jews: How Western Espionage Betrayed the Jewish People.* New York: St. Martin's, 1994.

Lowe, Lisa. *Immigrant Acts: On Asian American Cultural Politics.* Durham: Duke University Press, 1996.

———, and David Lloyd. *The Politics of Culture in the Shadow of Capital.* Durham: Duke University Press, 1997.

Lubiano, Wahneema. "Don't Talk with Your Eyes Closed: Caught in Hollywood Gun Sights." http://www.blackculturalstudies.org/lubiano/deepcover.html.

———. "Shuckin' Off the African American Native Other," in Anne McClintock et al., eds., *Dangerous Liaisons*, 204–29.

Lyons, Paul. "Reading the Literatures of Hawai'i under an 'Americanist' Rubric," in *Beyond the Borders: American Literature and Postcolonial Theory*. Edited by Deborah L. Madsen. London: Pluto, 2003.

Lyotard, Jean Francois. *The Postmodern Condition: A Report on Knowledge*. Translated by Geoff Bennington and Brian Massumi. Minneapolis: University of Minnesota Press, 1984.

Machida, Margo. "Out of Asia: Negotiating Asian Identities in America," in *Asia/America: Identities in Contemporary Asian American Art*. Edited by Margo Machida, Vishakha Desai, and John Tchen. New York: New Perspectives, 1994, 65–109.

Mackinnon, Catharine. "Toward a Feminist Theory of the State," in *Feminisms*. Edited by Sandra Kemp and Judith Squires. New York: Oxford University Press, 1997, 351–57.

———. "Reparations and Our Rendezvous with History," in "Along the Color Line," 2001. www.manningmarable.net.

Marable, Manning. *Beyond Black and White: Transforming African American Politics*. London: Verso, 1995.

Marcos, Subcommandant. "The Fourth World War Has Begun," *Le Monde Diplomatique*, September 1977, 10. http://mondediplo.com/1997/marcos.

———. "Why We Are Fighting: The Fourth World War Has Begun," *Le Monde Diplomatique*, September 1997. http://mondediplo.com/1997/09/marcos.

Martin, Biddy. *Femininity Played Straight*. New York: Routledge, 1996.

Martin, Richard. "The Expeditionary Photographs of Tseng Kwong Chi," *Arts Magazine* 61 (September 1986): 94–97.

Marx, Karl. "Supplementary Texts," in Karl Marx and Frederick Engels, *The German Ideology.* Edited by C. J. Arthur. New York: International, 1995, 121.

Maxley, Ruth. "Who Wants Pale, Thin, Pink Flesh?" *Textual Practice* 20, 3 (2006): 529–47.

McClintock, Anne et al., eds. *Dangerous Liaisons: Gender, Race, and Postcolonial Perspectives*. Minneapolis: University of Minnesota Press, 1997.

———. *Imperial Leather: Race, Gender, and Sexuality in the Colonial Context.* New York: Routledge, 1995.

McPhate, Mike. "Outsourcing Outrage: Indian Call-center Workers Suffer Abuse," *San Francisco Chronicle*, Thursday, November 17, 2005.

Metzger, Sean. "Charles Parsloe's Chinese Fetish: An Example of Yellowface Performance in Nineteenth-century American Melodrama," *Theater Journal* 56, 4 (2004): 627–51.

Mignolo, Walter D. *Local Histories/Global Designs: Coloniality, Subaltern Knowledges, and Border Thinking*. Princeton: Princeton University Press, 2000.

Miller, Toby. "Introducing . . . Cultural Citizenship," *Social Text* 19, 4 (2001): 1–5.

Mishra, Vijay, and Bob Hodge. "What Is Postcolonialism?" in *Colonial Discourse and Postcolonial Theory: A Reader*. Edited by Patrick Williams and Laura Chrisman. New York: Columbia University Press, 1994.

Mngxitama, Andite. "WSF: The Colonisation of Resistance." *We Write* 2, 1 (January 2005), 4. www.wewrite.org.

Mohanty, Satya P. "The Epistemic Status of Cultural Identity: On the Beloved and the Postcolonial Condition," *Cultural Critique* 24 (1993): 41–80.

Mohanty, Chandra Talpade. "Under Western Eyes: Feminist Scholarship and Colonial Discourses," in *Third World Women and the Politics of Feminism.* Edited by Ann Russo Mohanty and Lourdes Torres. Bloomington: Indiana University Press, 1991, 51–50.

Moore-Gilbert, Bart. "Homi Bhabha: 'The Babelian Performance,'" in *Postcolonial Theory: Contexts, Practices, Politics*. New York: Verso, 1997, 114–51.

Morrison, Toni. *Playing in the Dark: Whiteness and the Literary Imagination*. New York: Random House, 1993.

Mostern, Kenneth. "Postcolonialism after W.E.B. DuBois," in *Postcolonial Theory and the United States: Race, Ethnicity, and Literature*. Edited by Amritjit Singh and Peter Schmidt. Jackson: University of Mississippi Press, 2000, 258–76.

Mukherjee, Arun P. "Whose Postcolonialism and Whose Postmodernism," *World Literature Written in English* 30, 3 (1990): 1–9.

Mukherjee, Bharati. "American Dreamer," *Mother Jones* (January/February 1997). www.motherjones.com/commentary/columns/1997/01/mukherjee_2.html. Accessed October 9, 2007.

———. *Jasmine*. New York: Grove, 1989.

Murray, David. *Forked Tongues: Speech, Writing, and Representation in North American Indian Texts*. London: Pinter, 1991.

Muthyala, John. "*Almanac of the Dead*: The Dream of the Fifth World in the Borderlands," *Literature, Interpretation, Theory* 14 (2003): 357–85.

Nandy, Ashis. *The Intimate Enemy: Loss and Recovery of Self under Colonialism*. New Delhi: Oxford University Press, 1983.

Navarro, Armando. *La Raza Unida Party: A Chicano Challenge to the U.S. Two-party Dictatorship*. Philadelphia: Temple University Press, 2000.

Newton, Huey. *To Die for the People: The Writings of Huey P. Newton*. Introduced by Franz Schurmann. New York: Random House, 1972.

———. *Revolutionary Suicide*. New York: Harcourt Brace, 1973.

Nguyen, Viet Thanh, and Tina Chen. "Editor's Introduction," *Jouvert* 4, 1 (2000). http://social.chass.ncsu.edu/Jouvert/v4i3/ed43.htm.

Omi, Michael, and Howard Winant. *Racial Formation in the United States*. New York: Routledge, 1994 (originally published, 1986).

Parry, Benita. "Problems in Current Theories of Colonial Discourse," *Oxford Literary Review* 9, 1–2 (1987): 27–58.

———. "The Postcolonial: Conceptual Category or Chimera?" *Yearbook of English Studies* 27 (1997): 3–21.

Parry, Robert. *Colonial Desire: Hybridity in Theory, Culture, and Race*. New York: Routledge, 1995.

Pease, Donald E., and Robyn Wiegman, eds. *The Futures of American Studies*. Durham: Duke University Press, 2002.

Perez-Torres, Rafael. "Refiguring Aztlan," in *Postcolonial Theory and the United States: Race, Ethnicity, and Literature*. Edited by Amritjit Singh and Peter Schmidt. Jackson: University Press of Mississippi, 2000, 103–21.

Perkins, Margo. *Autobiography as Activism: Three Black Women of the Sixties*. Jackson: University Press of Mississippi, 2000.

Phelan, Peggy. *Unmarked*. New York: Routledge, 1993.

Porter, Carolyn. "What We Know That We Don't Know: Remapping American Literary Studies," *American Literary History* 3 (1994): 467–526.

Prakash, Gyan. "Postcolonial Criticism and Indian Historiography," in Anne McClintock et al., eds., *Dangerous Liaisons*, 491–500.

Prashad, Vijay. *The Karma of Brown Folk*. Minneapolis: University of Minnesota Press, 2000.

Pratt, Mary Louise. *Imperial Eyes: Travel Writing and Transculturation*. New York: Routledge, 1992.

"Rachel's War," *The Guardian,* Tuesday, March 18, 2003. Http://www.guardian.co.uk/print/0,3858,4627222_103552,00.html.

Radhakrishnan, R. "Adjudicating Hybridity, Coordinating Betweenness," *Jouvert* 5, 1 (2000). Http://social.chass.ncsu.edu/jouvert/v5il/radha.htm.

———. *Diasporic Mediations: Between Home and Location.* Minneapolis: University of Minnesota Press, 1996.

———. *Theory in an Uneven World.* New York: Blackwell, 2003.

Rajghatta, Chidanand. *The Horse That Flew: How India's Silicon Gurus Spread Their Wings.* New Delhi: Harper Collins, 2001.

Ramazani, Jahan. *Poetry of Mourning: The Modern Elegy from Hardy to Heaney.* Chicago: University of Chicago Press, 1994.

Reineke, Yvonne. "Overturning the (New World) Order: Of Space, Time, Writing, and Prophecy in Leslie Marmon Silko's *Almanac of the Dead, Studies in American Indian Literature,* Series 2, 10, 3 (1998): 65–84.

Reparations: Our Case for an Intercommunal Reparations Campaign: A Political Strategy to Redress the Kidnapping, Murder, and Theft of the Land and Labor or Africans, African Americans and Indigenous People. Http://www.globalpanther.com/rep.shtml.

Rich, Adrienne. *Blood, Bread, and Poetry: Selected Prose, 1979–1985.* New York: Norton, 1986.

Robbins, Anindyo. "The Aesthetics of the (Un)willing Immigrant: Bharati Mukherjee's Days and Nights in Calcutta and Jasmine," in *Bharati Mukerjee: Critical Perspectives.* Edited by Emmanuel S. Nelson. New York: Garland, 1993, 127–42.

Robbins, Bruce. *Feeling Global: Internationalism in Distress.* New York: New York University Press, 1999.

Robinson, Randall. *The Debt: What America Owes to Blacks.* New York: Dutton, 2000.

Rodriguez, Dylan. *Forced Passages: Imprisoned Radical Intellectuals and the U.S. Prison Regime.* Minneapolis: University of Minnesota Press, 2006.

Roediger, David. *The Wages of Whiteness: Race and the Makings of the American Working Class.* London: Verso, 1991.

Rose, Wendy, ed. *Winged Words: American Indian Writers Speak.* Lincoln: University of Nebraska Press, 1990.

Rowe, John Carlos. *The New American Studies.* Minneapolis: University of Minnesota Press, 2002.

———. *Literary Culture and U.S. Imperialism.* Durham: Duke University Presss, 2000.

———, ed. *Postnationalist American Studies*. Berkeley: University of California Press, 2000.

Roy, Arundhati. *Power Politics*. Cambridge, MA: South End, 2001.

Roy, Chidanand. "Don't Worry, U.S. Assures Jaitley on Outsourcing," *Times of India*, Saturday, June 14, 2003, p. 6.

Said, Edward. *Culture and Imperialism*. New York: Knopf, 1993.

———. *Orientalism*. New York: Vintage, 1978.

———. "The Clash of Ignorance," *The Nation,* October 22, 2001. http://www.thenation.com/doc.mhtml?i=20011022&s=said.

———. "Globalizing Literary Study," *PMLA* 116, 1 (January 2001): 64–68.

———. *The World, the Text, and the Critic*. Cambridge, MA: Harvard University Press, 1983.

San Juan, E., Jr. *Beyond Postcolonial Theory*. New York: St. Martin's, 1998.

Sandoval, Chela. *Methodology of the Oppressed*. Minneapolis: University of Minnesota Press, 2000.

Sangari, Kumkum. "The Politics of the Possible," *Cultural Critique* 7 (1987): 157–86.

Saran, Rohit. "How We Live," *India Today International*, July 28, 2003.

Saul, John Ralston. "The Collapse of Globalism and the Rebirth of Nationalism," *Harper's Magazine* (March 2004): 33–43.

Saulny, Susan. "In New York and New Jersey, Hundreds Join in as Antiwar Protests Continue," *The New York Times* (late edition), March 30, 2003, B14.

Schueller, Malini Johar, and Edward Watts. *Messy Beginnings: Postcoloniality and Early American Studies*. New Jersey: Rutgers University Press, 2003.

———. *U.S. Orientalisms: Race, Nation, and Gender in Literature 1790–1890*. Ann Arbor: University of Michigan Press, 1998.

Scott, Joan W. "Commentary: Cyborgian Socialists?" in *Coming to Terms: Feminism, Theory, Politics*. Edited by Elizabeth Weed. New York: Routledge, 1989, 215–17.

Shakur, Assata. *An Autobiography*. Chicago: Hill, 2000 (originally published, 1987).

———. "Open Letter from Assata: March 1998." http://www.afrocubaweb.com/assata2.htm.

———. "Letter from Assata on the Prison Industrial Complex," September 25, 1998. http:/www.afrocubaweb.com/assata2.htm.

Shankar, Lavina Dhingra. "Postcolonial Diasporics 'Writing in Search of a Homeland': Meena Alexander's *Manhattan Music, Fault Lines*, and 'The Shock of Arrival,'" *LIT* 12 (2001): 285–312.

Sharpe, Jenny. "Is the United States Postcolonial? Transnationalism, Immigration, and Race" *Diaspora* 4, 2 (Fall 1995): 181–99.

Shohat, Ella. "Notes on the Postcolonial," *Social Text* 31/32 (1992): 99–113.

Silko, Leslie Marmon. *Almanac of the Dead*. New York: Simon and Schuster, 1991.

———. *Yellow Woman and a Beauty of the Spirit: Essays on Native American Life Today*. New York: Simon and Schuster, 1996.

Singh, Nikhil Pal. *Black Is a Country: Race and the Unfinished Struggle for Democracy*. Cambridge, MA: Harvard University Press, 2004.

———. "Culture/Wars: Recoding Empire in an Age of Democracy," *American Quarterly* 50, 3 (1998): 471–522.

Sollors, Werner. *Beyond Ethnicity: Consent and Descent in American Culture*. New York: Oxford University Press, 1986.

Somerville, Siobhan B. *Queering the Color Line: Race and the Invention of Homosexuality in American Culture*. Durham: Duke University Press, 2000.

Spelman, Elizabeth. "Theories of Race and Gender: The Erasure of Black Women" *Quest: A Feminist Quarterly* 5 (1982): 36–62.

Spivak, Gayatri Chakravorty. "Can the Subaltern Speak?" in Cary Nelson and L. Grossberg, Eds., *Marxism and the Interpretation of Culture*. Macmillan: Basingstoke, 1988, 271–313.

———. *A Critique of Postcolonial Reason: Toward a History of the Vanishing Present*. Cambridge, MA: Harvard University Press, 1999.

———. "Harlem," *Social Text* 22, 4 (2004): 113–39.

———. "The Political Economy of Women as Seen by a Literary Critic," in *Coming to Terms, Feminism, Theory, Politics*. Edited by Elizabeth Weed. New York: Routledge, 1989, 218–29.

———. *The Post-Colonial Critic: Interviews, Strategies, Dialogues*. Edited by Sarah Harasym. New York: Routledge, 1990.

———. "Race before Racism: The Disappearance of the American," *boundary 2* 25, 2 (Summer 1998): 35–53.

St. Clair, Janet. "Cannibal Queers: The Problematics of Metaphor in *Almanac of the Dead*," in *Leslie Marmon Silko: A Collection of Critical Essays*. Edited by Louise K. Barnett and James L. Thorson. Albuquerque: University of New Mexico Press, 1999, 207–21.

Stafford, Barbara Maria. *Visual Analogy: Consciousness as the Art of Connecting*. Cambridge, MA: MIT Press, 1999.

Stecopoulos, Harilos. *Reconstructing the World: Race, Region, and Empire in the American Century, 1898–1976*. Ithaca: Cornell University Press, 2008.

Stokes, Mason. *The Color of Sex: Whiteness, Heterosexuality, and the Fictions of White Supremacy*. Durham: Duke University Press, 2001.

Stoler, Ann Laura. *Carnal Knowledge and Imperial Power: Race and the Intimate in Colonial Rule*. Durham: Duke University Press, 2002.

———. *Race and the Education of Desire: Foucault's History of Sexuality and the Colonial Order of Things*. Durham: Duke University Press, 1995.

Stoneham, Geraldine. "'It's a Free Country': Visions of Hybridity in the Metropolis," in *Comparing Postcolonial Literatures: Dislocations*. Edited by Ashok Bery and Patricia Murray. New York: St. Martin's, 2000, 81–92.

Suleri, Sara. "Woman Skin Deep: Feminism and the Postcolonial Condition," in *Colonial Discourse and Postcolonial Theory: A Reader*. Edited by Patrick Williams and Laura Chrisman. New York: Columbia University Press, 1994, 244–56.

Takaki, Ronald. *A Different Mirror: A History of Multicultural America*. Boston: Little, Brown, 1993.

Tillett, Rebecca. "'The Indian Wars Have Never Ended in the Americas': The Politics of Memory and History in Leslie Marmon Silko's *Almanac of the Dead*," *Feminist Review* 85 (2007): 21–39.

Turner, Grady T. "The Accidental Ambassador," *Art in America* 85 (1997): 81, 83.

"U.S. Prison Population Largest in World," *The Post and Courier*, Charleston.Net, June 1, 2003. http://www.charleston.net/stories/060103/wor_01jailbirds.shtml.

Upadhyay, R. "Politics of Race and Caste," *South Asia Analysis Group*, paper no. 308, Sept. 5, 2001. Http://www.saag.org/papers4/paper308.html.

Vail, Gabrielle, "The Maya Codices," *Annual Review of Anthropology* 35 (2006).

Van Dyke, Annette. "From Big Green Fly to Stone Serpent: Following the Dark Vision in Silko's *Almanac of the Dead*," *Studies in American Indian Literature*, Series 2, 10, 3 (1998): 34–46.

Velikova, Roumiana. "'Philip, King of the Pequots': The History of an Error," *Early American Literature* 37, 2 (2002): 311–34.

Viswanathan, Gauri. *Masks of Conquest: Literary Studies and British Rule in India*. New York: Columbia University Press, 1989.

Volpp, Leti. "The Citizen and the Terrorist," in *September 11 in History: A Watershed Moment*. Edited by Mary L. Dudziak. Durham: Duke University Press, 2000.

Wallace, Michelle. *Black Macho and the Myth of the Superwoman*. London: Verso, 1978.

Wallerstein, Immanuel. *The Capitalist World Economy*. New York: Cambridge University Press, 1979.

———. "Eurocentrism and Its Avatars: The Dilemmas of Social Science," *New Left Review* 226 (November/December 1997): 93–107.

———. *The Decline of American Power: The U.S. in a Chaotic World*. New York: New Press, 2003.

Watson, Julia, and Sidonie Smith. "De/Colonization and the Politics of Discourse in Women's Autobiographical Practices," in *De/Colonizing the Subject: The Politics of Gender in Women's Autobiography*. Edited by Sidonie Smith and Julia Watson. Minneapolis: University of Minnesota Press, 1992.

Wei, William. *The Asian American Movement*. Philadelphia: Temple University Press, 1993.

West, Cornel. *Race Matters*. New York: Random House, 1994.

White, Ed. *The Backcountry and the City: Colonization and Conflict in Early America*. Minneapolis: University of Minnesota Press, 2005.

Wickramagamage, Carmen. "Relocation as Positive Act: The Immigrant Experience in Bharati Mukherjee's Novels," *Diaspora* 2, 2 (1992): 171–200.

Wideman, John Edgar. "Introduction," *Live from Death Row*. Edited by Mumia Abu-Jamal. New York: Avon, 1995.

Wilkerson, Abby. "Ending at the Skin: Sexuality and Race in Feminist Theorizing," *Hypatia* 12, 3 (Summer 1997): 164–173.

Williams, Patricia. *The Alchemy of Race and Rights*. Cambridge, MA: Harvard University Press, 1991.

Wilson, Rob. "From the Sublime to the Devious: Writing the Experimental/Local Pacific," *boundary* 2 28, 1 (2001): 121–151.

———. *Reimagining the American Pacific: From South Pacific to Bamboo Ridge and Beyond*. Durham: Duke University Press, 2000.

Winant, Howard. *The World Is a Ghetto: Race and Democracy since World War II*. New York: Basic, 2001.

Wong, Sau-ling C. "Denationalization Reconsidered: Asian American Cultural Criticism at a Theoretical Crossroads," *Amerasia Journal* 21, 1/2 (1995): 1–28.

Wooten, Leslie A. "'We Want Our Mother the Land': Female Power in Leslie Marmon Silko's *Almanac of the Dead*," *North Dakota Quarterly* 64, 4 (1997): 57–69.

World Development Report 1995, *Workers in an Integrating World*. Washington, DC: World Bank.

Yamamoto, Traise. "As Natural as the Partnership of Sun and Moon: The Logic of Sexualized Metonymy in *Pictures from the Water Trade* and *The Lady and the Monk*," *Positions* 4, 2 (Fall 1996): 321–41.

Young, Iris Marion. "Polity and Group Difference: A Critique of the Ideal of Universal Citizenship," *Ethics* 99 (1989): 250–74.

Young, Robert. *Postcolonialism: An Historical Introduction*. New York: Blackwell, 2001.

Index